BUTTERFLIES
AND MOTHS

scholastic 💡 nonfiction
an imprint of
📖 SCHOLASTIC

This silkworm moth has a wingspan of about five inches.

Copyright © 2009 by Nic Bishop.
All rights reserved. Published by Scholastic Inc.
SCHOLASTIC, SCHOLASTIC NONFICTION, and associated logos
are trademarks and/or registered trademarks of Scholastic Inc.

LIBRARY OF CONGRESS CATALOGING-IN-PUBLICATION DATA
Bishop, Nic, 1955– • Nic Bishop butterflies and moths / Nic Bishop.
p. cm. • 1. Butterflies—Juvenile literature. 2. Moths—Juvenile literature.
I. Title. • QL544.2.B48 2009 • 595.78'9—dc22 • 2008015290

ISBN-13: 978-0-439-87757-2 • ISBN-10: 0-439-87757-1
10 9 8 7 6 5 4 3 2 1   09 10 11 12 13

Printed in Singapore 46 • First printing, March 2009
Book design by Nancy Sabato

The magnification of animals shown at actual size or larger
is indicated in parentheses.

Hummingbird moth
(shown at 1.5 times actual size)

*The butterfly on
the title page is a zebra
longwing butterfly.*
(shown at 2 times actual size)

Mourning cloak butterfly
(shown at 1.5 times actual size)

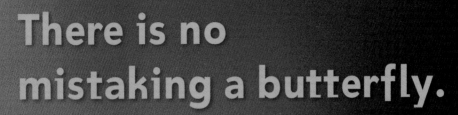

There is no mistaking a butterfly.

Its colorful wings skip in the air like petals blown by the wind. Blues, reds, and yellows dance in the sunlight. Some shimmer like tinsel.

A creature so beautiful should belong in a fairy tale. But butterflies are real. They dance through the woods and glide over fields. You can see them in parks and backyards. And they always catch your attention.

The tiger swallowtail is one of the most beautiful butterflies seen flying in gardens, forests, and meadows.
(shown at 2 times actual size)

Moths are more secretive. Most fly at night while you are in bed. If you are lucky, you might find one in the morning, sleeping by a porch light that has been left on. And if you take a look, you will see how moths differ from butterflies.

Moths are less colorful than butterflies, and many rest with their wings open, not closed. **Moths also often have fatter bodies, covered with furry hairs.** But it is not always easy to tell the two apart. A few moths are as brightly hued as butterflies and fly in the daytime, while some butterflies are as dull as moths. Yet both lead similar lives, changing from eggs to caterpillars to adults.

You can tell a moth from a butterfly by the antennae on its head. A male moth, like this luna moth, often has feathery antennae, while a female moth has thinner antennae with pointed tips. Butterfly antennae look different because they are thin with distinct knobs at the tips.
(shown at 5 times actual size)

Scientists have discovered more than 170,000 different types of butterflies and moths. They live everywhere there are plants for their caterpillars to eat, from high mountains to dry deserts.

Most live in the rain forest, where there are thousands of different food plants. That is where you will find the world's largest butterfly, the Queen Alexandra's birdwing of New Guinea. It is also where the biggest moth lives, the Atlas moth of Southeast Asia. Both have a *wingspan* of almost a foot.

Other moths are so tiny that you need a hand lens to see them. And there are weird moths, too. One feeds on the tears of sleeping animals. Another drinks blood. But perhaps the most amazing thing about butterflies and moths is the way they grow up.

There are 10 times as many types of moths as butterflies, and their caterpillars are often beautiful. But you had better not touch this silkworm moth caterpillar from Costa Rica. Those spines will sting.
(shown at 2 times actual size)

**The life of a butterfly or moth begins
with an egg, no bigger than a grain of sand.**
This egg may look like a ball, a barrel, or a saucer. It may have

been laid alone or with a group of eggs. Some butterflies lay

their eggs on top of each other, like stacks of tiny teacups.

About a week after it is laid, each egg will have a tiny dot

inside, and the dot will be moving. With a hand lens, you will

see that the dot is the head of a caterpillar, chewing a hole to

wriggle its way out.

As soon as a monarch butterfly caterpillar hatches, it eats its old eggshell.

(shown at 45 times actual size)

When the caterpillar crawls out, it is barely bigger than a comma, and all it wants to do is eat. First it may eat its old eggshell. Then it starts on the main course, which is usually right under its feet. That is because most caterpillar mothers lay their eggs on the favorite food plant of their young. So after a baby hatches, it just eats everything in sight. And a caterpillar is very good at that. It has strong jaws to chew up chunks of leaf.

A caterpillar's body is simple. It has a large stomach and a mouth with sensors, like taste buds, to help it recognize food. There are twelve or so tiny eyes that can tell dark from light, but cannot recognize objects. **There are also small hairs on a caterpillar's body, which sense touch and warn it about enemies.**

One neat thing caterpillars do is spin silk from glands near their mouths. Often they stick this to leaves, like webbing, so they can move around without falling off their precious food. And to keep an extra-tight hold, they also have six legs and usually ten claspers, called *prolegs*, which have hooks like Velcro.

This caterpillar close-up shows three prolegs. The small hairs on the caterpillar's body sense touch, and the long spines are stingers. The three orange football-shaped dots are breathing holes, called spiracles, which let air into the caterpillar's body.
(shown at 8 times actual size)

As the hungry caterpillar eats and grows, it becomes too big for its skin.

So it *molts*. The old skin splits open and the caterpillar wriggles out in a brand-new skin. Then it often eats the old skin before going back to its favorite job of munching leaves.

Eventually a caterpillar may eat all of its food plant. Then it has a big problem. Most caterpillars only eat one or two types of plants, so they must quickly find the right one. Other caterpillars are not as fussy about their food. A few will even eat your old clothes! But most caterpillars just starve unless they find exactly the right food.

This cecropia moth caterpillar will grow to four inches long and eventually turn into North America's largest moth, with a wingspan of about six inches.
(shown at 8 times actual size)

By the time it is a week old, the wriggling creature the size of a comma will have grown into a plump caterpillar. Now it must watch for birds, wasps, lizards, squirrels, and many other *predators* that want to eat it.

But a caterpillar is not always easy to catch.

Many are green or brown, so they are hard to spot. Some use their silk to sew leaves into little shelters to hide in. Others leap away on silk threads like bungee jumpers when they are scared. They climb back when the danger has passed.

When scared, this rain forest caterpillar twists its body around and puffs up its front end to look like a poisonous snake. It even waves its body like a snake. But look closely and you will see that its snake eyes are not real. They are black-and-white markings normally hidden underneath the caterpillar.

(shown at 3 times actual size)

A few caterpillars seem too disgusting to eat. They look just like bird poop, or they will vomit green juice if they are attacked. Then there are the tricksters. Some of the most beautiful and furry-looking caterpillars have stinging hairs. One touch can hurt for days. Pretty yellow-and-black monarch caterpillars have poisons in their bodies. Any bird that eats one gets sick and will never want to try another.

Other caterpillars have bodyguards. They ooze a sweet drink that ants like, and in return, the ants attack anything that comes near. Some of these caterpillars can even call to their ant helpers with scraping, singing sounds.

A caterpillar of the black swallowtail butterfly defends itself by sticking out a smelly orange organ called an osmeterium. It will try to wipe the stinky osmeterium on its attacker.
(shown at 5 times actual size)

One day, after it has molted several times, the caterpillar will finally stop eating. By now it may be more than 3,000 times heavier than when it hatched, and it is ready for the next stage of its life.

The caterpillar wanders away to find a safe place to turn into a *pupa*.

A moth caterpillar may first spin itself a silk shelter, called a *cocoon*. But a butterfly caterpillar simply finds a quiet spot to spin a silk pad and perhaps a safety harness to hang from. Then it wriggles out of its caterpillar skin.

Underneath, the pupa is enclosed in a case, which turns hard. It barely moves day after day. But inside, there is a miracle happening, called *metamorphosis*. Much of the caterpillar's body is breaking down into a soup. Other parts, like growing buds, are turning into wings, legs, and other bits of the adult body. Many of these changes had started while the pupa was still a caterpillar, but they were small and hidden. Now they happen quickly.

A monarch butterfly caterpillar hangs upside down from a silk pad and squeezes out of its old skin to turn into a beautiful green pupa (left). After a week or two, you can see the body of the butterfly ready to emerge (right).
(shown at 2 times actual size)

The pupa will stay motionless for about two weeks, or sometimes longer. **Then one day, it splits open and the adult crawls out.** A moth might need to cut its way out of its silk cocoon. But a butterfly can just hang from its old pupa case and rest.

At first it looks crumpled, which you might expect after being crushed inside a pupa. Then, bit by bit, the body expands and straightens. Its soft, limp wings fill with blood and open like beautiful sails, then dry hard.

A monarch butterfly often emerges from its pupa in the early morning so its wings can expand and dry in the warming sun.
(shown at 4 times actual size)

These wings are one of the most amazing creations of nature. They are lighter than feathers, yet strong enough to carry a butterfly or moth for hundreds of miles of flying. **Look closely and you will see that they are covered in tiny scales.** Each has a single color, like a piece of glass in a cathedral window. Together they create the wonderful patterns and colors of a moth or butterfly wing.

These wing scales come off easily, which is useful if a butterfly or moth flies into its worst enemy: the spiderweb. When this happens, the butterfly or moth can pull its wings away and escape. All that is left behind are a few scales stuck to the web. And a hungry spider!

Thousands of colored scales are arranged in neat rows on this butterfly wing. The long straight tubes, called veins, help to make the wing stiff and strong.
(shown at 20 times actual size)

About an hour after the butterfly has emerged from its pupa, it will stretch its new legs and gently move its new wings. It seems to test them, as if it is realizing it has a completely new body.

Instead of the twelve or so tiny eyes it had as a caterpillar, the butterfly now has thousands of light sensors. These are grouped together to make two very big eyes, called *compound eyes*. For the first time, it can see the simple shapes and colors of leaves and other butterflies. It also has two long *antennae* on its head, which are covered with organs that sense touch and even smell. It is suddenly aware of the perfumes of flowers and can feel the wind tug at its new wings. Soon, the young butterfly becomes curious. It takes off.

This glasswing butterfly from the Amazon rain forest has transparent wings. You can see that the butterfly body has three main parts: the head, with eyes and antennae; the thorax, with wings and legs; and the abdomen, which contains the heart.
(shown at 5 times actual size)

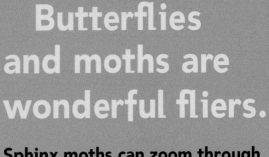

Butterflies and moths are wonderful fliers.

Sphinx moths can zoom through the air at thirty miles an hour. Hummingbird moths can hover and even fly backward as they zip from flower to flower. Some butterflies fly hundreds of miles when they migrate from place to place. The most amazing are monarch butterflies. During the fall, they can fly 2,000 miles from Canada to Mexico, where they spend the winter.

A butterfly takes off by opening both wings very quickly. This pushes down hard on the air and flips the butterfly into the sky. Every time the butterfly's wings flap, they create little swirls of air that push and tug it along.

(shown at 2 times actual size)

As it flies, a butterfly is on the lookout for the bright colors of flowers. When it lands, it checks for food with its feet. Butterfly feet can taste sugar, just like your tongue, except they are about 200 times more sensitive.

Next, the butterfly uncurls a long feeding tube, called a *proboscis*, and pokes it into the flower to sip nectar. Nectar is a sweet energy drink made by flowers. It is the liquid fuel that a butterfly uses to keep flying. The butterfly will visit dozens of flowers each day, filling up like a car that needs to stop at every gas station.

A hairstreak butterfly from Australia perches on a flower to sip nectar through its proboscis. Each flower only makes a little nectar at a time, so it will not be long before the butterfly needs to stop again.
(shown at 20 times actual size)

In time, a butterfly will learn to recognize its favorite flowers and visit them more often. But some butterflies prefer other foods. Woodland butterflies often feed on tree sap. The blue morpho butterfly likes to sip juice from fruit rotting on the rain forest floor.

The males of many butterflies sip salts from wet soil and even animal dung to get the nutrients they need for mating. And some males are very picky about which type of dung. In Africa, they prefer the dung of meat eaters, like lions and other big cats. Leopard dung is a favorite.

The blue morpho butterfly shines and shimmers in the rain forests of South and Central America. It is often seen flying along streams and in sunny clearings, looking for a mate.
(shown at actual size)

Perhaps the strangest thing is that some moths eat nothing at all. **The luna moth, for example, does not even have a mouth.** It relies on food stored in its body from when it was a caterpillar.

A luna moth will live for about one week, while many other butterflies and moths live for two or three weeks. A few butterflies, such as question marks and mourning cloaks, can live for six to ten months. When winter comes, they find a safe place to sleep. Then they wake when it warms in spring.

The luna moth, which has a wingspan of four inches, is one of the most beautiful moths in North America. Its name comes from the Latin word for the moon.
(shown at 2 times actual size)

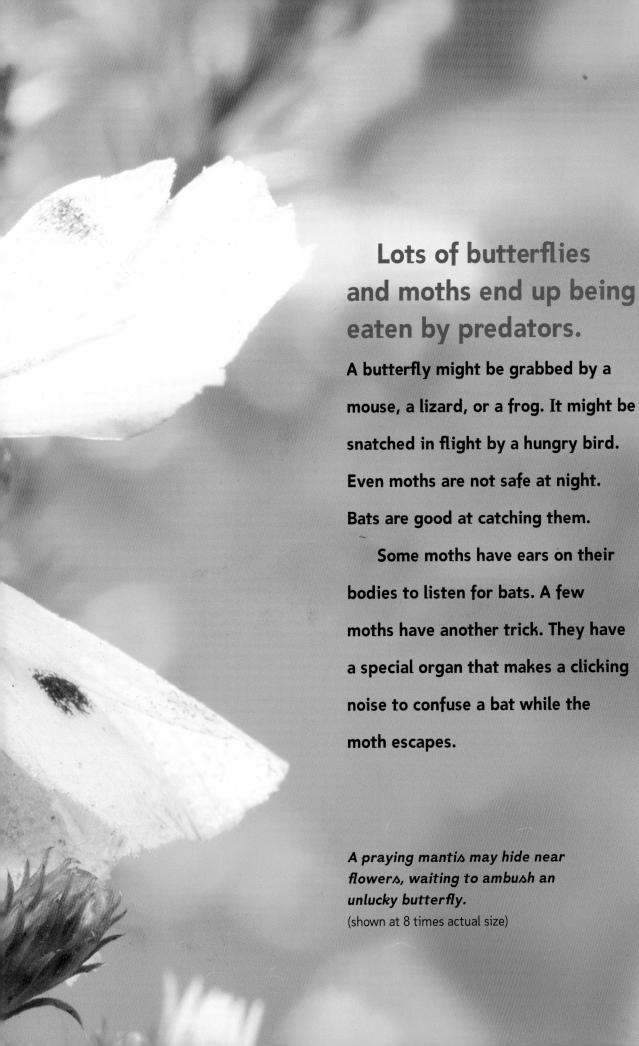

Lots of butterflies and moths end up being eaten by predators.

A butterfly might be grabbed by a mouse, a lizard, or a frog. It might be snatched in flight by a hungry bird. Even moths are not safe at night. Bats are good at catching them.

Some moths have ears on their bodies to listen for bats. A few moths have another trick. They have a special organ that makes a clicking noise to confuse a bat while the moth escapes.

A praying mantis may hide near flowers, waiting to ambush an unlucky butterfly.
(shown at 8 times actual size)

39

Butterflies outfox birds with their helter-skelter flight. It's hard to catch something that bobs and skips through the air. **Butterflies may also have large spots on their wings that look like eyes.** These *eyespots* confuse birds, which cannot decide which end is the butterfly's head. And if that doesn't work, a butterfly still has another trick. It can suddenly fold its wings and drop to the ground like a dead leaf. The brown underside of its wings helps the butterfly vanish into its surroundings.

Of course, it's hard to escape a hungry bird every time. But even if the bird grabs a wing, the butterfly may still tear loose. Many butterflies have bits missing from their wings. Yet they still fly.

A blue morpho butterfly blends perfectly with dead leaves on the rain forest floor when it closes its wings. The round circles on its wings are eyespots, which help confuse predators. (shown at 2 times actual size)

These swallowtail butterflies are mating.
The female, which is the butterfly at the
top, will soon be ready to lay her eggs.
(shown at 1.5 times actual size)

When a male moth is not looking for food, he will search for a mate. He finds her in the dark by following a perfume she releases into the air. He smells it with his large antennae and follows the scent trail, even from a few miles away.

A male butterfly may look for female mates near flowers where they feed. Or he may search along rivers and sunny trails, swooping on anything that looks like a female. It might just be a falling leaf, or even a bumblebee. It doesn't take much to confuse the male. But if it is a female, he will court her. Often he dips and climbs in front of her, and sprinkles her with perfume from his body.

If she is impressed, she will land so he can continue. He may shiver his wings, tap her antennae with his, or dust her with more perfume. Then she will let him mate. The two butterflies clasp each other, end to end, so he can fertilize her eggs.

Next, the female will look for a plant to lay her eggs on.

But it will not be just any plant. Her young may eat only one type of plant, so it must be the right one.

Even then, she is particular. She wants the healthiest plant with the best leaves for her caterpillars. It will have to be growing where it is not too hot or cold, or too wet. So she flies, searching here and there.

When she lands on a plant, she kicks it. Special sensors on her feet tell her what she wants to know. Does it taste right? Is it healthy? She may check for other eggs or caterpillars. If she sees or senses some, she will fly on. Otherwise there might not be enough food left for her young when they hatch.

She tests dozens of plants until she finds just the right one. Perfect! She lays some of her eggs and fastens them with special glue. Then she searches for another similar plant. Soon, there will be more wriggling caterpillars.

When a cabbage white butterfly is ready to lay her eggs, she homes in on a mustard-smelling chemical found in cabbage leaves. This is the same chemical that gives cabbages the bitter taste that some people love and others can't stand.
(shown at 3 times actual size)

Butterflies are the most beautiful of insects. The thrill of seeing one never fades.

While working on this book, I was amazed by the vivid blue of morpho butterflies flying along rain forest trails. Another time, I hung from ropes high in the canopy while butterflies danced all around me. I was envious of their freedom to sail through the treetops. And I was astonished, too, because every one was a type I had never seen before.

Some occasions were amusing. While taking a break in the rain forest, I was baffled to see a line of leaf-cutter ants running to their nest carrying white circles of fabric. It looked so bizarre, but then I remembered that I'd just put my butterfly net on the ground. They had snipped holes into it in minutes.

Photographing butterflies took patience. I waited for days or even weeks to take pictures of eggs as they hatched, or butterflies as they emerged from pupae. Taking photographs of butterflies in flight required lots of special equipment, including sensitive lasers and high-speed flash guns, which took days to set up.

But photographing the snakelike caterpillar on pages 16–17 took the longest time of all. I first learned of it while helping a scientist study caterpillars in the rain forest of Costa Rica. Its scary snake act had amazed him when he first saw one, about ten years earlier. But he had never been able to find another. We searched for them on the caterpillar's food plant, but I eventually had to return home. I thought I would never get to see one.

So when I met the scientist a year later, I was in for a surprise. He told me how he had found a second caterpillar, just hours after I had left! I was so upset that I begged him to e-mail me if he ever found another. A couple more years passed and then I got the e-mail. He had another one! "But you'd better come quickly," the e-mail said. "It is full grown and will turn into a pupa at any minute."

I bought tickets and flew to Costa Rica the next day. I jumped into a taxi at the airport for a sixty-mile ride at breakneck speed through the mountains and down to the rain forest. Then I stumbled along the trail to camp well after dark, kicking myself for having forgotten my flashlight in the rush, and hoping not to tread on a poisonous snake.

I was up at sunrise the next morning, and you can imagine how relieved I was to discover that the caterpillar had not turned into a pupa. After waiting for years, all that remained was for me to take my photographs. I was so happy!

Index
Entries in **bold** indicate photographs.

Glossary

Antennae A pair of moveable sense organs found on the heads of insects.

Metamorphosis The process of changing form dramatically, which some animals undergo to become adults.

Molt To periodically shed an outer layer, such as skin, shell, hair, feathers, or horns.

Predator An animal that lives by hunting other animals for food.

Pupa The stage of life of some insects during which metamorphosis happens.

Wingspan The distance from the tip of one wing to the tip of the other.

ITALY

ANYWHERE

VIKING

75 years

LIVING AN ITALIAN

CULINARY LIFE

WHEREVER YOU CALL HOME

LORI DE MORI

*With Jean-Louis De Mori
and Antonio Tommasi*

VIKING

ITALY

ANYWHERE

VIKING

Published by the Penguin Group

Penguin Putnam Inc., 375 Hudson Street, New York, New York, 10014, U.S.A.

Penguin Books Ltd, 27 Wrights Lane, London W8 5TZ, England

Penguin Books Australia Ltd, Ringwood, Victoria, Australia

Penguin Books Canada Ltd, 10 Alcorn Avenue, Toronto, Ontario, Canada M4V 3B2

Penguin Books (N.Z.) Ltd, 182–190 Wairau Road, Aukland 10, New Zealand

Penguin Books Ltd, Registered Offices:
Hammondsworth, Middlesex, England

First published in 2000 by Viking Penguin,
a member of Penguin Putnam Inc.

1   3   5   7   9   10   8   6   4   2

LIBRARY OF CONGRESS CATALOGING-IN-PUBLICATION DATA

De Mori, Lori

Italy anywhere : living an Italian culinary life wherever you call home / Lori De Mori.

p.   cm.

ISBN 0–670–88539–8

1. Cookery, Italian.   I. Title

TX723.D334 2000

641.5945—dc21   00–028104

Interior illustrations © Heather McReynolds

This book is printed on acid-free paper. ∞

Printed in the United States of America
Set in Bulmer with Sackers Italian Script and Wood Type Ornaments
Designed by Betty Lew

Sarah,

Tony,

Julien,

Vanessa,

Michela

and

Diego . . .

this is for you.

Grazie

I still remember so vividly the warm Italian afternoon, several summers ago, when the tiny seed that grew into this book was planted. It was no more than a thought: "I will write a book about the way Italians eat—not so much *what* they eat, but the larger picture of their culinary lives."

These thanks are for everyone who helped this little seed along. It might seem odd to thank my coauthors, as the merits of this book are equally attributable to their own efforts and talents, but since the pen is in my hand, I will begin with them: *Grazie* Jean-Louis, for selflessly giving me the time and space to write this book and for not giving up on me, even when on our second date I ignored every word you told me about the wonders of Tuscan olive oil and insisted you ask the waiter for butter anyway. You have been my best teacher. Antonio, *amico mio,* thank you for so generously sharing your extraordinary culinary wisdom and for making all the hard work feel like so much fun.

I had imagined the world of agents, editors, and publishers to be a sort of dark, venomous lions' pit from which one could only hope to emerge alive. The truth is, I haven't experienced such nurturing, support, and encouragement since those first scary days of kindergarten. Our agents, now friends, Maureen and Eric Lasher, brought tremendous energy and expertise to this project, along with an abundance of warmth and kindness that I can only believe they bring to everything they do. We could not have been in better hands. Our experience at Viking Books was exhilarating. To walk into an editor's office and have her look you in the eye and tell you "I love your proposal" is every writer's dream. To my editor, Carole De Santi, thank you for believing in this project and giving it the best possible home; for always asking my opinion and not getting annoyed with me that I always had one; and for never force feeding me editorial changes (that I ended up making anyway, because in the end, of course, you were right). Amy Mintzer, my editor in the trenches—for all those times your sheer humor and wit gave me the energy to go through the manuscript yet another time, thank you. Little Rosie—*thank you* for your patience every time your mom's "quick" phone call to me ended up lasting two hours. *Tantissimi grazie* to Alexandra Babanskyj at Viking for her unfailing good spirits no matter what crisis or deadline we were facing. Beth Greenfeld, our copy editor, *grazie* for all your good work and for sharing some of your own Italian tales with me. We are especially grateful to Chika Azuma for taking Heather McReynold's beautiful artwork and designing a book jacket that is at once joyful, inviting, and in perfect harmony with the spirit of *Italy Anywhere.*

A handful of women, who among other things are also wonderful cooks, painstakingly tested many of these recipes in their home kitchens and provided us with invaluable comments and queries. Chris Bruscagli in Florence (*you* should be writing a cookbook); Gina Burrell, Laure Stern, Ellen Poyer, Carolyn Diemer, and Les Martinez in Malibu; and my own sweet sister, Valerie, in San Diego—a million heartfelt *grazie* to you all.

Special thanks to my favorite succulent, wild women: Heather McReynolds for making me feel like it was an honor for her to do the artwork for *Italy Anywhere,* even though I felt and still do that the pleasure was all ours. Katharine Johnson for reading and rereading this manuscript and practically every other word I've ever written, and using the utmost humor and tact to suggest that I banish such phrases as "modern-day megalith" from my vocabulary. Peggy Markel for telling me that I didn't need a permission slip to write this book, but that she would write me one anyway if it would make me feel better.

At one point *Italy Anywhere* seemed like the little seed that would never sprout—not because we couldn't find anyone to publish it, but because it took awhile for my enthusiasm for the idea to transform into the discipline necessary to bring it to life. Most of my friends were satisfied with an oblique "fine" when they asked how the project was coming along—not Karen Kaplan. She *really* wanted to know. Karen, I am fairly certain that without your insightful questions and gentle prodding I never would have stopped talking about *Italy Anywhere* long enough to actually write it.

At intervals throughout the writing of this book you could find me lurking in the kitchens of Locanda Veneta or Ca' Brea restaurants, a battle-worn sheaf of recipes in one hand, a pencil or spoon in the other. Mille grazie to Massimo Ormani and Luigi Barducci, Locanda Veneta and Ca' Brea's talented executive chefs, for allowing me to invade their kitchens and their minds, and to our partners Elio De Santo, Gaetano Foiani, Rodolfo Costello, Tom Sweet, Franco Simplicio, and Saverio Posarelli for their friendship and support. To our customers, who have sipped wine and broken bread at our tables with such extraordinary enthusiasm and appreciation, we offer our most heartfelt thanks. Without you we would not have a stage on which to sing.

Finally, but perhaps most important, loving thanks to our parents, each of them, for bestowing upon us their vast and varied gifts, and most of all for their wisdom and boundless love.

Contents

ITALY

ANYWHERE

Italy Anywhere

"In my next life I'm going to be Italian," my father announced the day of his departure back to Los Angeles after a weeklong visit to our house in Italy. He and my mother had been perfect houseguests. No requests for trips to the Prada outlet, no marathon excursions to Florence to wander dizzily through the Uffizi Galleries, Pitti Palace, the Accademia (home of Michelangelo's David), and a thousand shops all in one day. All they wanted to *see,* they claimed, were their two grandchildren, Julien and Michela, my husband, Jean-Louis, and of course me, their eldest child, who for the past couple of years had been spending most of her time in a small, restored farmhouse in the Tuscan countryside. All they wanted to *do* was "whatever it is you usually do in this place you're now calling home."

This meant that most mornings, after we dropped the kids off at school, we'd walk through the woods above the house, and over the pale gravel road that cuts through acres of vineyards and olive groves, until we reached the tiny town of Mercatale Val di Pesa. There we'd set up temporary camp at a sunny table in the square and battle over the crossword puzzle in the *Herald Tribune* while making our way through frothy cappuccini, pots of tea, panini with prosciutto and butter, and cakey brioche filled with apricot jam.

I took them to my favorite farmers' markets, where we'd wander among the crowded tables piled high with fruits and vegetables, choosing whatever appealed to us most. We'd buy pounds of the tiniest clams they had ever seen and cook them with tomatoes, white wine, parsley, and garlic; or thick Chianina steaks and grill them over the hot embers of the kitchen fireplace.

My father helped me hang laundry on the clothesline strung between two acacia trees in the garden. He even took it upon himself to wash our dog Kelly and brush her red-gold fur until he'd removed every last thistle she'd picked up from the wild fields just past the house. My mom was more intrigued by the vegetable patch, venturing through the rough wooden gate with a basket and a pair of shears and snipping lettuce, peas, small bunches of herbs, or whatever else the day's menu seemed to require. Sometimes she'd just lie in the shade in the hammock reading a book. In the late afternoons, when Julien and Michela sat at the kitchen table doing their homework, they'd help us make dinner—or at least watch with great fascination.

Uneventful as it was, they seemed to think this one of the best vacations they could remember, and admitted to being not at all sure they were ready to return to "real life."

"So don't," Jean-Louis told them. "Well, we can't just move here," my mother answered. "I know," said Jean-Louis, "but you can take Italy with you."

My husband has always seemed to think of Italy as being as much a state of mind as a place. Something to carry around with you wherever you go. Maybe because as a child growing up in Paris, he was constantly reminded of his Italian heritage, both by friends who teasingly called him "macaroni" and by his Italian parents, who, still longing for their native Veneto, continued to cook and eat as if they had never left home.

Actually, though, few people have been as skilled at maintaining an Italian approach to a life lived outside Italy than our friend and partner, Antonio Tommasi. He had no choice, really. One fall morning in 1979, he left his home near Venice, Italy, and boarded a plane bound for Los Angeles. The uneventful flight left him so traumatized that it would be ten years before he set foot on another airplane. In the meantime, he remained in Los Angeles, honed his already considerable culinary skills at some of the city's best Italian restaurants, cruised around town in a bright red Ferrari, and had himself a couple of very darling kids, Antonio (Jr.) and Vanessa.

Antonio's dream had been to return to Italy to open a small inn (or "locanda," as they are known in northern Italy) somewhere in the country with a farm out back, a little winery, and a grappa distillery just like his grandfather's. But America seduced him as it did Jean-Louis—by its brashness, its openness to change and new ideas, and its overwhelming enthusiasm for things Italian, food in particular. And so, in the spring of 1988, Jean-Louis and Antonio found themselves a tiny forty-seat restaurant on a busy Los Angeles thoroughfare and opened it with the goal of bringing the very best of Italy—both in food and spirit—to the hungry City of Angels. They named the place "Locanda Veneta"—inspired by the imaginary Italian country inn of their dreams.

Of course, there is nothing that remarkable about two Italians wearing their "Italianness" as if it were some sort of immutable physical attribute, or seeking to bring "their Italy" to America. It's easy to be what we are born to be. But to embrace some ineffable quality of a culture other than your own, simply because it speaks to you, and to weave it into the fabric of your own life—that is a harder thing. And it is what this book is about.

Nowhere is Italian life more seductive than in the kitchen and at the table. Yet, if you think about it, the essence of Italy's appeal has less to do with the extraordinary food that seems to abound wherever you look than with the combination of grace, generosity, and simplicity with which it is offered. This is the Italy that is more concerned with the delectable than the practical, that slows down for meals, for beauty, for friends and family; and that markets, cooks, and invites with passion rather than pretension. This is the Italy that finds the pleasure in a perfect tomato, value in the most humble ingredients, and comfort in working with them. This Italy is available to anyone. And it can exist anywhere—wherever or however you live.

We've filled these pages not only with scores of tried-and-true recipes from our restaurants and our own kitchens, but also with ruminations about a uniquely Italian approach to cooking—one that celebrates the part of culinary life that gives us:

- a daily opportunity for unhampered creativity,
- a sensibility to the colors, textures, and flavors that surround us, and
- the chance to share it all with friends.

Living an Italian culinary life has nothing to do with making three-course meals every night for dinner, or spending the vast majority of your day laboring in the kitchen. It does not require that you live in a farmhouse in the countryside, or in the bell tower of a crumbling medieval town. Actually, the vast majority of Italians are packed into a few severely overcrowded cities. They live with a fraction of the "modern conveniences" we so rely on in America. They work. Their country is eternally plagued with political scandals and upheaval. Yet they have an enormous passion for anything that pleases the senses—and what

pleases the senses more than a group of friends around a table filled with food that is at once both unpretentious and outrageously delicious?

Italy Anywhere is a collaborative effort—the product of a twenty-year-old friendship, which has already produced one marriage, one partnership, six restaurants, and many, many good times. Three distinct voices have contributed to its creation:

Antonio Tommasi: Chef *extraordinaire* and culinary mastermind behind our family of restaurants: Locanda Veneta, Ca' Brea, Il Moro, Ca' Del Sole, Allegria, and I Padri. He was practically born into the kitchen. His father was a chef at Venice's famed Locanda Cipriani—to hear him tell it, while the rest of his friends spent their summers wading in the warm waters of the Adriatic, he was at his father's side peeling potatoes, scrubbing baking sheets, and soaking up a wealth of culinary knowledge.

Jean-Louis De Mori: Consummate host and philosopher of food and the fine art of dining Italian-style. Antonio's longtime friend, partner, and collaborator. Born of northern Italian parents but raised in Paris, his family brought the first French restaurant to Florence, and he, with Antonio, the first northern Italian locanda (more on locandas later) to Los Angeles.

Lori Zimring De Mori: Our trio's designated storyteller. As American as her husband, Jean-Louis, is European, but an impassioned convert to the Italian approach to culinary life. Here's hoping you'll become one, too!

FROM *LOCANDA* TO LOCANDA VENETA

Locanda. An Italian word that means "inn" and refers to the simple country inns scattered throughout Italy's towns and back roads. Northern Italy, particularly the Veneto, is filled with these little jewels. Like inns of old, they offer food, drink, and a simple place to sleep—the emphasis being, as with most things Italian, on the food and drink, with often only a handful of rooms available for weary travelers. The food is honest and unpretentious. It is also among the most delicious in all of Italy.

A locanda is a home away from home, a refuge from the pressures of modern life. It is a place to relax and renew, to eat food that is earthy and genuine, prepared from local ingredients and using age-old recipes handed down through generations. Locanda cooking can be as light and refreshing as it is hearty and substantial. The flavors and ingredients reflect the surrounding geography, climate, and local history—in Venice and in the small towns along the Adriatic, the menu abounds with local seafood and shellfish: risotto with black squid ink, fried whitebait, fish soup, and calamari in every conceivable style. In the countryside, hearty bean soups and stews are savored with local Merlots and Tocais. The dining room is often dominated by a *fogolar,* a four-sided fireplace open at all ends where meats, cheese, polenta, and radicchio are grilled. In the kitchen, gleaming copper pots filled with polenta cook over slow fires.

In 1988, Antonio and Jean-Louis found a tiny, redbrick storefront in Los Angeles that inspired them to open their own little locanda—it wasn't actually an inn at all, but to their enthusiastic eyes, its very size and simplicity conjured up the feeling of the real thing. The two friends invested all of $4,500, spruced up the place as much as their severely limited budget would permit, and set out to bring Los Angeles what they liked best about the locandas of Italy—a place where steaming golden polenta, wild mushrooms, and a glass of red wine among friends would delight the senses as much as the finest caviar and champagne.

In terms of sheer physical reality, Antonio and Jean-Louis's "locanda" is as unlike the real thing as one could imagine—it sits unassumingly across the street from a major hospital, down the road from a trendy shopping mall, smack in the heart (if one could say that Los Angeles has a heart) of what is perhaps the world's most sprawling metropolis. And, yet, despite the restaurant's admittedly un-Italian attributes, Italy's respected *Veronelli*

Guide describes Locanda Veneta as a place where *"si respira un'autentica aria di casa"*— a place that feels like home. Considering the fact that there was a time, not so long ago, when Italians traveled abroad lugging extra-virgin olive oil, boxes of pasta, and wedges of Parmesan cheese wrapped in layers of tin foil and clothing—*Veronelli*'s compliment is not only immensely gratifying, it also validates something we've always known on an intuitive level.

That something is this: that the essence of a place comes from its *spirit*—not from what it looks like, and even less from what it pretentiously tries to be. This simple truth explains a lot of things. For instance, it explains why our friends felt as much in Italy in Jean-Louis's first LA apartment (rent, $270 a month) as they do now in our farmhouse in Tuscany. Despite a pastiche of rented and hand-me-down furniture, and a kitchen the size of a broom closet, something always happened somewhere in between the glass of Campari soda Jean-Louis handed you at the door, and the tiramisù he brought out many hours later, that made you sure you could hear ancient church bells in the distance, or the splash of water lapping up against a gondola. It didn't matter that my father thought Campari soda tasted like mouthwash, or that the sound in the distance was actually a car alarm. The thing that was so Italian about the meal was the simplicity, honesty, and warmth with which it was offered—and, of course, that it was delicious.

Giant commercial complexes have gone up in places like Beverly Hills and Las Vegas that attempt to imitate, sometimes stone by stone, "real" European streets, hotels, or even cities. While these attempts at re-creating France in Florida, or Venice under the glow of neon lights, have their own appeal, they never really succeed in transporting you to the places they depict. Why? Because they are essentially soulless—for all their coy, Old World quaintness, they lack the ephemeral qualities of the real thing, qualities that no amount of corporate investment can reproduce.

The good news is that whether you live in an urban apartment, a house in the country, a commune or a houseboat, the very things that brought us success in our kitchens should bring you happiness in yours. The most "Italian" thing you could do to your home and your kitchen, wherever and however it may be, is to infuse it with food that warms both the belly and the soul.

The "Essential Essentials"

There are many wonderful Italian cookbooks that set forth in enormous detail the essentials of the Italian kitchen—everything from mezzalune and knives for chopping vegetables, to various qualities and characteristics of rice suitable for making risotto. Those distinctions, though useful, are beyond the scope of this book.

Italian cooking is defined by its accessibility. Unlike many other cuisines, it actually requires very little in the way of special ingredients or equipment. With little more than a handful of seasonal fresh vegetables and a box of good Italian pasta, you are well on your way to a delicious meal.

For the most part, discussions of ingredients are where you would most expect them—we'll talk about rice when we talk about risotto, and polenta in the chapter containing polenta recipes.

Nonetheless, a few fundamentals need to be highlighted, so totally do they permeate every aspect of Italian cuisine. These we've termed the "essential essentials," and they deserve a brief mention before we start. . . .

OLIVE OIL

Jean-Louis had to spend a couple of days in an Italian hospital several years ago. The large room he shared with three other men several decades older than himself was furnished with four narrow beds, four small bedside tables, and an equal number of utilitarian-looking chairs. I was there one day at lunchtime when the large cart bearing pasta, roasted chicken, boiled potatoes, yogurt, and fruit was wheeled into the room. As the young, uniformed attendant passed out trays of food, each of Jean-Louis's roommates leaned over and opened the little cupboard beside his own bed, extracting a small, unlabeled bottle of olive oil brought from home.

The conversation at lunch revolved almost entirely around a lively debate as to why each man thought his olive oil best. They knew the hills from which the olives came, the particular characteristics of the climate and soil and how they affected the oil. They described its color, fragrance, and flavor with the skill of grand sommeliers discussing exceptional wines. And they were generous—offering their bottles of oil to Jean-Louis, who hadn't had the good sense to bring some along with the toothbrush and toothpaste he had packed in his bag.

Olive oil is perhaps *the* essential ingredient in any Tuscan kitchen. Our family consumes roughly fifty liters of olive oil a year—almost a liter a week—which is about average for the typical household here. And although olive oil is produced all over central and southern Italy and throughout the Mediterranean, our palates clamor for the ripe fruitiness and rich, green color of Tuscan olive oil. We actually buy most of our oil at one time, usually during the month of November, right after the olives have been pressed. It comes from our neighbor Beatrice's family's wine estate, Capezzana. Many of the best Tuscan olive oils (and this is surely one of the best) come from premier wine producers. This oil is a deep, murky green and when it is "new" (i.e., recently pressed), it has both a rich, fruity flavor and a bite that catches at the back of the throat as it does down. It mellows in both flavor and color after about a month but still maintains its characteristic fruitiness. We buy the oil all at once because by January at the latest the entire year's production has been sold.

Extra-virgin olive oil comes from olives harvested and pressed in much the same way as they have been for centuries. Large tarps are spread beneath one tree at a time and the olives are shaken from the branches or raked off using small handheld combs. Many of the same people who harvested grapes in early fall return to the fields to pick olives. It is much more exacting work than snipping full clusters of grapes from low-growing vines. Nonetheless, it is not uncommon to see a seventy-year-old man perched upon a rickety ladder pulling olives off the high, gnarled limbs of centuries-old trees. Almost everyone who picks olives for someone else will choose to be paid in oil rather than lire. Not because they're getting any bargain on the price (which they don't), but because the oil from the olives they've picked is worth more to them than money.

"Virgin" olive oil comes from olives crushed under granite millstones or in stone mortars so that the oil is extracted without heat. The label "extra-virgin" means that the oil has an acidity level no greater than 1 percent and is considered the finest of all olive oils. That said, flavor can vary wildly among olive oils, even, perhaps especially, with those labeled "extra-virgin olive oil," when the essence of the olive is most pronounced. Every nuance, from the weather to the soil in which the olive trees grow, adds its subtle contribution to the overall flavor of the oil.

At home and in our restaurants, we use a good commercial extra-virgin olive oil for cooking and our favorite (and more costly) estate-bottled extra-virgin olive oil for dressing salads and drizzling over pasta, meat, or whatever dish could benefit from its ripe, fruity flavor. Really wonderful olive oil can cost as much as $30 for one liter, but it will elevate the flavors with which it mingles like no other ingredient in your kitchen. Heating olive oil softens its flavor, which is why there's no need to use your extra-special olive oil for cooking. In your own kitchen, try using a commercial Italian extra-virgin olive oil for cooking—you will find several brands available in most supermarkets—and have a look around your local specialty-foods store for estate-bottled Tuscan olive oils. Try out a couple of half-liter bottles until you find the one that pleases your palate most. There are no absolutes here—and in this sense you must think of olive oil as you would think of wine—the experts will have lots of opinions as to what is best, but nothing can advise you better than your own tastebuds.

PARMESAN

Italy has many great cheeses: pecorino, mozzarella, Gorgonzola, Taleggio, Asiago, and Fontina, just to name a few. But none comes close in complexity of flavor and texture to the king of Italian cheeses, *parmigiano*. True Italian Parmesan cheese is labeled "Parmigiano-

Reggiano" and has been made in much the same way for centuries in the provinces of Parma and Reggio Emilia (from which the cheese gets its name), as well as Bologna, Mantua, and Modena. A whole form of Parmigiano-Reggiano weighs up to seventy pounds, and will have been aged from eighteen months to three years. The words "Parmigiano-Reggiano" will be stenciled on its hard, golden-hued rind.

The cheese itself is a lovely straw color and has a layered, slightly crumbly texture and a mellow, rich flavor. Imported Parmigiano-Reggiano is widely available in America and is well worth its hefty price tag. Other hard Italian grating cheeses are simply labeled "*grana.*" Of these, *grana padana* is the most comparable to Parmigiano-Reggiano.

Though most often you will find Italian Parmesan grated onto pasta, risotto, and soups, or thinly shaved and scattered over carpaccio or salads, it is superb as an eating cheese. There is no better end to a truly fine meal than a full-bodied glass of red wine and a piece of Parmigiano-Reggiano. Nonetheless, despite its wondrous characteristics as both an eating and cooking cheese, *parmigiano* is not used indiscriminately in Italian cooking. It is rarely used with fish (although Antonio will sometimes use a small amount in butter- or cream-based sauces for stuffed seafood pastas). It is always freshly grated just before using and *never, ever* purchased already grated. And although it is expensive, a little bit goes a long way.

WINE
Il Vino

We in America have let ourselves be intimidated by wine. It seems to have insinuated itself along with opera, contemporary art, and poetry as one of those subjects best left to experts, university professors, and the scholarly. We feel apologetic or miserly if we order the third-least-expensive bottle of wine off a long wine list, assuming that everyone's first choice, if they could only afford it, would be a dusty vintage bottled some time when they were still in diapers. We open a wine for guests, apologizing for our ignorance in enological matters. For some reason, those same trusty tastebuds that have served us so well throughout our lives are deemed unfit for deciding whether or not we think a wine actually tastes good.

Italians have a quite different relationship with wine. It is essential to a meal, but at the same time it holds no more importance than the pasta, the parmesan, the olive oil, or anything else that's on the table. The strange aura of sophistication/danger we've attached to wine in America is largely absent. In Italy, even children occasionally ask for half a glass of watered-down wine, and a pregnant woman still allows herself a sip of *vino* with dinner if she feels like it.

There is refreshingly little pomp and snobbery associated with the drinking of wine in Italy—it is as everyday as bread, water, or air—not brought out only at "special occasions" but at almost *every* occasion when there is food to be eaten (except, of course, at breakfast). Wine in Italy is for everyone—from the farmer to the nobleman. A good inexpensive table wine isn't considered an inferior product, but is appreciated for what it is—the perfect companion to a simple meal. Of course, there are extraordinary, as well as astronomically expensive, Italian wines that can compete with the best French reserves, and they are wonderful, but they are only part of the picture.

If you don't know a thing about wine, maybe it's time you made friends with it. Begin by tossing out all feelings of insecurity/ inferiority/ignorance—they do not serve you well. Then engage your senses. Putting your nose to a glass of wine to smell its fragrance is no more snobbish than inhaling the scent of a gorgeous rose. Look at the wine in the glass. Young reds are usually quite clear and colored a bright, lively red. Aged wines are darker and denser-looking. Older wines and wines aged in oak barrels are more complex both in aroma and taste—which, of course, doesn't mean that you have to like them. Californians go mad over Chardonnay, which to my particular palate tastes as if it has been aged in sawdust. You might enjoy wines that are exceptionally dry, or slightly floral, or fruity. You might prefer young wines with straightforward, uncomplicated flavors.

Like what you will. Avoid what you don't. There's plenty of wine for every palate.

SALTING
Il Sale

All over Italy salt is used liberally and generously as a seasoning. The palate seems to adapt over time to the "saltiness" of the environment in which it finds itself. Nevertheless, my first meal in an Italian trattoria after I've been away for some time leaves my lips as wrinkled as if I'd just gone through a large tub of popcorn at the movies. On the other extreme, it takes my tastebuds several meals back in Los Angeles to be able to discern that any salt at all has been added to my food.

Affinity for and tolerance to salt varies among individuals. Since so many people choose to restrict their intake of salt for health or dietary reasons, we have decided that except where the integrity of the recipe relies on a given amount of salt, you the reader and cook should be the arbiter of the saltiness (or saltlessness) of your food.

That said, here are a few guidelines:

- Unless a recipe instructs you otherwise, add salt about three quarters of the way through a dish's cooking time, when the other flavors have had a chance to blend. Allow each of your base ingredients to make whatever statement it will before turning up the volume by salting.
- Take into account the saltiness of your base ingredients. For example, pancetta, olives, capers, and certain cheeses are quite salty in their own right. It will take awhile during cooking for their saltiness to impart itself to the other ingredients. Give them a chance to make their contribution before adding additional salt.
- Antonio especially advises salting meats and vegetables toward the end of their cooking time because to do so before pulls out the food's moisture prematurely. He prefers to coax the moisture out gently by the heat of the flame.
- Keep in mind that saltiness often can vary even with the same ingredient. For example, both Italian Gorgonzola cheese and prosciutto can fluctuate wildly in saltiness. In Italy, milder, less salty versions of certain foods like prosciutto are referred

to as *"dolce,"* meaning "sweet" or "mild." Imported Italian products found in American markets don't always offer the consumer the distinction.

- Remember that it is easier to salt than to unsalt (although it can be done—more on that in a second). Therefore, when you can, salt a little at a time, in two, even three small doses, rather than all at once. It takes a couple of minutes for salt to dissolve—and at least that long for you to taste the contribution it has made to whatever you have simmering on the stove.

- Correcting oversalting: I saw Antonio do this trick once when he found that he had been a bit heavy-handed salting a pasta sauce made with fresh peas. He peeled a medium potato, cut it into large chunks and let it simmer with the sauce for about ten minutes before removing it. The potato had absorbed a fair share of the salt and the sauce was delicious.

Stuzzichini

CULINARY FOREPLAY
Stuzzichini

Foreplay is everything. Well . . . maybe not *everything,* but there are few better or more pleasing ways to set the tone for an evening and tickle the senses before a meal than with a judicious dose of culinary foreplay.

The Italian word for a savory, appetite-awakening morsel of food is wonderfully descriptive and evocative—*stuzzichino*—from the verb *stuzzicare,* which means "to tease, to excite, to whet." A *stuzzichino* warms the senses without sating them, its purpose is to tease rather than appease.

Stuzzichini tend to be foods that can be eaten easily standing up with a glass of wine. Things like sausage-filled olives encased in crisp golden crusts, chunks of smoked mozzarella flavored with herbs and spices, or wafer-thin crisps of flatbread topped with cured meats and slivers of aged Parmesan.

There's an informality about *stuzzichini* that smooths the seams of a dinner party as it sputters to life. This chapter contains an assortment of our favorites. Just take care not to overdo them . . . unless, of course, rather than foreplay, you intend them as the play itself.

Spicy Green Olives
Olive Verdi Marinate

FILLS A 1½-PINT MASON JAR

Make a batch of these little firecrackers to bring to a friend's house in lieu of the ubiquitous bottle of wine. The olives look beautiful in a simple Mason jar—a shade lighter than the fruity oil in which they rest, the bay leaves pressed against the glass, and flashes of red pepper, garlic, and herbs scattered throughout.

3 cups large, unpitted green
    olives, packed in brine
6 very small red chili peppers
3 cloves garlic, peeled
1 teaspoon black peppercorns
1 teaspoon coriander seeds

1 teaspoon dried oregano
1 teaspoon fennel seed
2 bay leaves
2 cups extra-virgin olive oil
    (approximately)

⌒ Drain the olives of their brine and then use a sharp-tipped knife to make three slits along the length of each olive (this will help the herbs and spices penetrate).

⌒ Spoon half of the olives into a Mason jar, then sprinkle half of the seasonings over the top. Cover with the rest of the olives, the remainder of the seasonings, and pour olive oil over the top until all the olives are covered. Leave the jar uncovered for a couple of hours while the olives settle and begin to soak up some of the oil. You may find that you need to add a bit more oil to keep the olives covered.

⌒ Close the jar and allow the olives to marinate at room temperature for 5 days, then store them in the refrigerator. Let them warm to room temperature before serving.

Lemony Black Olives
Olive Nere al Limone
FILLS A 1-PINT MASON JAR

These olives are delicious in their own right, but we especially enjoy them with crusty bread and little wedges of marinated cheese.

2 cups unpitted black olives, packed
   in brine
¾ cup extra-virgin olive oil
3 tablespoons white wine vinegar
¼ lemon, unpeeled and thinly sliced

2 cloves garlic, peeled and quartered
3 peppercorns
1 teaspoon paprika
1 bay leaf

Drain the olives and transfer them to a 1-pint Mason jar.

Whisk together the oil and vinegar, then stir in the remaining ingredients. Pour the herbed oil over the olives.

Let the jar sit uncovered for a couple of hours while the contents settle. Add additional oil to cover if necessary, then close the jar and leave to marinate at room temperature for 3 days before serving. Once they have marinated, store them in the refrigerator, but allow them to warm to room temperature before serving.

THE "REAL" VENICE
La Vera Venezia

There is no getting around the unfortunate fact that Venice is as much a major tourist attraction as a real city. It can be daunting for the independent traveler—that "non-tourist" whose only dream is to tread the unbeaten path and discover the true spirit of a place. On a bad day, *"La Serenissima,"* as the Republic of Venice was once known, is anything *but* serene. The city takes on an eerie resemblance to Disneyland, with hordes of tourists

marching in a straight line from the train station to Piazza San Marco so they can stand in the square feeding pigeons or pay the equivalent of $10 for the privilege of sipping a cappuccino at the famed Florian Café.

Yet there is a Venice that lives alongside the whole tourist circus, and it is full of magic—culinary and otherwise. It can be found in much the same way as children in fairy tales stumble upon magic kingdoms. By wandering. And not following signs. By watching the crowds, and heading in the opposite direction. You can glimpse this Venice in the early morning, when the *calle* are filled with parents walking their children to school and the air shimmers with the echo of church bells. Or in the stillness of night, when the lagoon is an inky black and the only sounds are of water lapping up against sleeping gondolas . . . or of lovers whispering (for there is no denying the extravagantly romantic aura of the place). Venice's hidden world is marked by a labyrinth of passageways opening upon wide, open squares, and by narrow canals festooned with laundry flapping in the breeze. It is seen in the wild, overgrown gardens that flourish behind twisted iron gates, and on the faces of old men fishing from stone benches along the lagoon's less-trafficked edge.

Gastronomically speaking, the "real" Venice is the Rialto fish market at dawn and the humble *bacari* or wine bars scattered along the city's narrow back alleys. These simple, rustic bars offer a variety of good local wines such as Tocai, Merlot, or sparkling Prosecco, and an even greater assortment of bite-size appetizers known as *cicheti*—which can be anything from roasted squid, fried sardines, or tiny boiled octopus called *moscardini,* to more unusual offerings like *spienza* (boiled calf's spleen sliced thinly and dressed in oil and vinegar) and *nervetti conzi,* literally "savory nerves," which are cut up into small pieces and eaten with toothpicks. The truly unadventurous usually can be satisfied by sampling from a selection of cured meats and cheeses, meatballs, and deviled eggs with anchovies and capers.

Theoretically, *cicheti* are meant to be little more than an appetizing snack during the lull before lunch or dinner. In practice, Jean-Louis and I have spent countless afternoons going *"a cicheti,"* weaving our way in and out of our favorite *bacari* until our appetite for food and drink is so thoroughly sated that our next meal becomes the furthest thing from our thoughts—leaving us all the more time to wander.

Breaded Green Olives Stuffed with Sausage
Olive all'Ascolana
SERVES 4

Although this recipe gets its name from Ascoli Piceno, a town in the Marches rarely visited by Americans, it is just the sort of savory tidbit you could expect to find in a Venetian *bacaro.* We often make them for friends to nibble on with a glass of cold white wine before dinner. Beware—they are addictive.

20 (but best make more) very large green pitted olives, packed in brine

10 ounces Italian sausage

2 whole eggs plus 1 egg yolk

2 tablespoons freshly grated Parmesan cheese

Pinch of nutmeg

½ cup white flour

½ cup bread crumbs, fresh or dried

2 cups corn oil

Pastry bag (or make your own by snipping the corner off a medium ziplock plastic bag)

᠆ Soak the olives in a bowl of water for 15 minutes, strain them in a colander, then shake them free of any remaining water and pat dry with paper towels.

᠆ In the meantime, peel off the sausage skins and place the sausage in a food processor together with the egg yolk, Parmesan, and nutmeg. Blend until pastelike, then transfer the mixture into a large nozzled pastry bag. Gently squeeze the bag to fill each olive.

᠆ Beat 2 eggs and set them aside. Roll the olives first in white flour, then in the eggs, then in the bread crumbs. Refrigerate for 2 hours (or overnight if you wish).

᠆ Heat the oil in a small saucepan until it is hot but not smoking. Test the oil's temperature by dropping a crumb of bread into the pan—the oil is hot enough if the crumb sizzles upon contact with the oil. Fry 10 olives at a time, using a mesh or slotted skimmer to gently set them in the hot oil. When the crust turns golden, lift the olives out of the oil onto several layers of paper towels. Blot free of excess oil, then transfer the olives to a small bowl and serve immediately.

Marinated Cheeses
Formaggi Insaporiti
SERVES 4 TO 6

It's hard to muster up much desire to cook during the height of summer, when the air is thick and white with heat, and our appetites demand only fresh, light flavors. Can there be a more perfect repast for the dog days of summer than a simple salad of ripe, juicy tomatoes, a thick slice of country bread, and a plate of soft chunks of cheese bathed in fruity olive oil and scattered with fragrant herbs and spices?

1 pound fresh Italian mozzarella or
   smoked mozzarella (scamorza) or
   semisoft goat or pecorino (sheep's
   milk) cheese

½ cup extra-virgin olive oil
Small handful of fresh basil leaves,
   washed and torn into small pieces
1 teaspoon fresh tarragon leaves

½ teaspoon dried oregano or marjoram
1 small dried red chili pepper, crumbled
A few black peppercorns

Sprinkling of paprika, optional
Freshly ground black pepper, optional

∞ Cut the cheese into bite-sized chunks or ½-inch slices. Lay the pieces in a shallow ceramic or glass dish.

∞ Pour the olive oil into a small mixing bowl. Sprinkle in the herbs and spices (except for the paprika and ground pepper). Pour the herbed oil over the cheese. Cover and refrigerate from 2 hours up to 2 days.

∞ Warm to room temperature before serving. Remove the cheese from the oil and transfer it to a serving plate. Cover with the herbed oil and, if you wish, sprinkle with paprika and freshly ground black pepper.

Shallots in Balsamic Vinegar
Scalogni al Balsamico
FILLS A 1½-QUART MASON JAR

Antonio frequently uses vinegar when he cooks. He likes the contrast of flavors it produces. When first heated, vinegar gives off an acrid vapor that stings the eyes and throat. It has cooked down sufficiently when you still smell the vinegar but the vapors no longer overpower. These tart, crunchy shallots are delicious with cured meats, such as prosciutto, bresaola, or speck, or scattered on a platter of the meat from a beef or chicken broth. Nonetheless, we've put this recipe here with the stuzzichini, since we almost always end up devouring at least half of the shallots straight from the jar. There's no need to splurge on a fancy aged balsamic vinegar to prepare them this way. A young balsamic with a relatively high acidity grade, such as 7½ percent, will serve you best.

5 cups water, salted with 1½ tablespoons salt	1 teaspoon black peppercorns
	3 bay leaves
3 cups red wine vinegar	2 cloves
1 pound shallots, papery skins removed	3 cups balsamic vinegar (approximately)

↝ Bring the salted water and wine vinegar to a boil in a large saucepan. Add the shallots and cook them at a low boil for 10 minutes, then drain them in a colander.

↝ When the shallots have stopped steaming but aren't completely cooled, spoon them into a 1½-quart Mason jar, add the peppercorns, bay leaves, and cloves and cover with balsamic vinegar.

↝ Leave the jar uncovered until the contents have cooled completely, then close the jar and leave it to marinate in a cool, dark spot in the kitchen for 5 days before using. Store in the refrigerator.

BRUSCHETTA

More often than not, dinner at our house includes bruschetta. Not so much because it's delicious, which it is, but because it gives our guests something to *do* while we get on with the mechanics of the rest of the meal. We give them a plate full of freshly peeled garlic cloves, a loaf of the heaviest country bread we can come up with, and send them to the kitchen fireplace to toast the bread and rub it with garlic. When their "work" is done, we reward them by slathering the fragrant, golden bread with anything from translucent green extra-virgin olive oil to something more earthy like sautéed wild mushrooms laced with mint.

Bruschetta is also a wonderful vehicle for leftover sauces and cooked vegetables. The best bread to use is an unsalted country loaf, with a heavy, spongy crumb and a thick, solid crust that will easily serve as a vessel for whatever you decide to use as your topping. But, really, any country bread will work, including salted and whole grain breads.

For convenience, all our bruschetta recipes call for the bread to be toasted in the oven. Of course, you may toast it in a toaster, over a barbecue grill or campfire just as easily.

Bruschetta with Red and Yellow Peppers
Bruschetta ai Peperoni

SERVES 4

This midsummer bruschetta is as flavorful as it is colorful.

1 red pepper, ribs and seeds removed

1 yellow pepper, ribs and seeds removed

3 tablespoons extra-virgin olive oil

1 white onion, halved lengthwise, then thinly sliced

2 plum tomatoes, cut into chunks

Small handful of fresh basil leaves

Salt

Freshly ground black pepper

4 thick slices country bread

2 cloves garlic, peeled

∾ Preheat oven to 375°.

∾ Cut the peppers in half crosswise and then into long, thin strips.

∾ Warm the oil in a pan, then add the onion, peppers, tomatoes, and basil. Stir the ingredients well. Cover and cook over a medium flame until the vegetables are soft and cooked through (about 20 minutes), stirring occasionally. Season to taste with salt and freshly ground black pepper. Allow the peppers to cool slightly.

∾ In the meantime, toast the bread in the oven until it is golden brown. Cut the slices in half and rub with garlic. Spoon the warm vegetable mixture over the bread and serve.

ON MUSHROOMS

Daybreak. The skies are gray and misty, and it has rained intermittently all week. In the woods, the soil is damp and pungent, smelling of pine, decaying leaves, and wildflowers. Tiny yellow crocuses and wild lavender-hued orchids grow beside the web of footpaths that traverses the countryside. On such a day, you can be sure that well off the beaten paths, the search for wild mushrooms has begun.

Mushroom gathering is a cloak-and-dagger affair in Italy, where the seemingly benign pastime is fraught with danger and secrecy. Danger, because each year a handful of reckless mushroom gatherers end up in the hospital—or worse—when a supposedly good mushroom reveals itself to be one of its poisonous cousins. Secrecy, because although a friend or gardener will delight in presenting you with a basket of freshly gathered mushrooms, he will *never* reveal the location of his secret cache—the place where he returns faithfully after each rain, to walk slowly, head bowed, eyes scanning the woods' decaying detritus for signs of the elusive mushroom. True aficionados are known to ramble seemingly aimlessly until they are convinced that no one is on their trail.

Mushroom gathering is also an exercise in restraint. Gatherers make sure to leave a few small or less-than-perfect mushrooms anchored in the damp earth so that their spores will spread to provide another harvest after the next rain. Nonetheless, despite the obvious perils and travails inherent in mushroom gathering, for the ardent mushroom lover, there are few pleasures that match the delight of finding a cluster of porcini mushrooms at the foot of a chestnut tree.

For although the Italian woodlands yield a variety of wild mushrooms—ovoli, chiodini, and geloni, to name just a few—none is as prized as the brown, dome-capped porcino, whose rich earthy flavor and consistency is unmatched. The coveted large heads are grilled and drizzled with olive oil; smaller mushrooms are sliced thin and sautéed with garlic, olive oil, and parsley or wild mint, or incorporated into sauces for pasta, risotto, soup, and polenta.

Fresh porcini are still a rarity in most American markets. But, thankfully, of all Itaiy's wild mushrooms, porcini dry the best and are quite easy to find abroad. When mixed with cultivated white mushrooms, they are quite a reasonable impersonation of the real thing. Moreover, their intense, musky flavor makes them a proper culinary tool in their own right.

NOTE: There is a tendency these days to eat raw, or just barely cooked, vegetables. Although some varieties of mushrooms can be eaten raw (such as the divine ovolo, which is best sliced thinly and covered with shaved Parmesan, olive oil, salt, and pepper), many edible mushrooms should only be eaten cooked. Tolerance to mushrooms varies among individuals—some can eat raw porcini without a problem, others couldn't even consider it.

Wild Mushroom Bruschetta
Bruschetta con Funghi di Bosco
SERVES 4

Any combination of porcini, oyster, stemmed shiitake, and chanterelle mushrooms will work wonderfully for this bruschetta.

¾ pound mixed fresh wild mushrooms

3 tablespoons extra-virgin olive oil, plus oil for drizzling

5 cloves garlic, thinly sliced

½ cup dry white wine

1 tablespoon finely chopped fresh mint, plus a few whole leaves for garnishing

Salt

Freshly ground black pepper

4 thick slices country bread

Trim off and discard the tips of the mushroom stems. Clean the mushrooms with a damp cloth or paper towel. If they are very dirty, run them under cold water in a colander, wipe them clean, and dry. Slice the mushrooms thinly.

Heat the olive oil in a pan over a low flame. Add the garlic and sauté lightly until it is fragrant. Add the mushrooms and sauté for 5 minutes while they release some of their moisture and begin to soften. Increase the heat to high, add the wine and let the alcohol bubble away for a minute, then reduce the heat and simmer until the liquid evaporates almost completely. Add the chopped mint and continue cooking over a low flame for a minute, stirring continuously while the flavors blend. Season to taste with salt and freshly ground pepper.

∽ Preheat oven to 375°. Toast the bread until it is golden brown. Cut the slices in half.

∽ Spoon the mushrooms over the toasted bread and drizzle with extra-virgin olive oil. Garnish with fresh mint leaves.

Bruschetta with Herbed Olive Paste
Bruschetta alle Olive
MAKES ABOUT 1 CUP

This bruschetta works best with olives that carry a trace of bitterness, like Greek kalamata. If you are pressed for time, use 1 cup of unseasoned black olive paste. Cover any unused herbed olive paste with a thin layer of olive oil and store in the refrigerator. Spread it on sandwiches, or add a spoonful to tomato sauce for a flavorful pasta.

4 thin slices country bread	Pinch of dried oregano
2½ cups oil-cured kalamata olives	2 fresh basil leaves
2 tablespoons extra-virgin olive oil	½ clove garlic
1 teaspoon red wine vinegar	

∽ Preheat oven to 350°. Lightly toast the bread in the oven or a toaster. Cut into quarters.

∽ Squeeze the olives gently to free them of their stones. Place the olives in a blender with the olive oil, vinegar, oregano, basil, and garlic. Blend until the mixture forms a coarse paste.

∽ Spread on the thinly sliced toasted bread and serve.

Bruschetta with Tuna
Bruschetta al Tonno
SERVES 4

Somewhere wedged in between the rounds of cheese and jumble of cured meats on display in many of Italy's small food shops there will almost always be an enormous tin of tuna packed in olive oil. If you're lucky, it will be labeled *"ventresca,"* which is the choice underbelly of the fish. The best substitute stateside is a high-quality albacore packed in olive oil from Italy or Spain.

4 slices country bread

6 ounces tuna, packed in olive oil

1 tablespoon capers

Splash of white wine

3 tablespoons mayonnaise

1 teaspoon Dijon mustard

2 tablespoons chopped chives

Preheat oven to 375°. Toast the bread in the oven until golden, then cut the slices in half.

Lightly drain the tuna, then mash it with a fork until smooth. Stir in the capers and white wine, then fold in the mayonnaise and mustard.

Spread over the toasted bread, sprinkle with chopped chives and serve.

ITALIAN-STYLE TAPENADES
Inzuppapane

It might not be considered a great idea from an economic standpoint for a restaurant to make a habit of setting little ramekins of savory vegetable spreads on the table with homemade bread before a meal, but we have always done it and our customers have come to expect a little something to take away the sharp edge of hunger while waiting for their meal.

Our tapenades change depending upon the season and the whims of the kitchen. In warm weather, Antonio favors a blend of summer vegetables seasoned with olive oil, lemon, and basil or a savory potato pesto with pine nuts and basil. The delicate artichoke spread and creamy blend of fresh green spinach are wonderful options during the cooler seasons.

Restraint is the key to serving these delicious spreads.

Blended Vegetable Tapenade
Inzuppapane di Verdure
SERVES 6 TO 8

At the restaurants, we serve this light and flavorful tapenade with slivers of warm focaccia. At home, we set it in the center of a platter of crisp raw vegetables as an alternative to the traditional olive oil, lemon, salt, and pepper *pinzimonio* that is more commonly used in Italy for dipping raw vegetables.

7 plum tomatoes, skins and seeds removed

1 carrot, peeled and cut into chunks

2 small inner stalks celery, coarsely chopped

½ green pepper, ribs and seeds removed, coarsely chopped

¼ cucumber, peeled and seeded

2 spring onions, white tops only

1 clove garlic

Small handful of fresh basil leaves

½ cup extra-virgin olive oil

Juice of ½ lemon

Salt

Freshly ground black pepper or dash of cayenne pepper oil (page 28)

∾ Roughly chop the skinned and seeded tomatoes and set aside.

∾ Place the carrot, celery, pepper, cucumber, onions, and garlic in a food processor and pulse blend until very finely chopped. Add the tomatoes and basil and blend briefly until the mixture forms a creamy base dotted with tiny pieces of chopped vegetables.

∾ In a separate bowl, whisk together the olive oil and lemon juice. Stir in the vegetable puree and season to taste with salt and either freshly ground black pepper or cayenne pepper oil. Chill in the refrigerator.

Cayenne Pepper Oil
Infuso di Peperoncino

There are some dishes, like spicy penne arrabbiata (pasta with tomato and hot chili peppers), that our next-door neighbor André likes so fiery hot he actually breaks out in a sweat at the table. Antonio is another member of the red-hot-chili-pepper fan club. His kids are not. Their still-tender palates exclude them from joining . . . yet. The rest of us fall somewhere between the extremes. What to do? Letting the kids eat their pasta on the bland side while you sprinkle your own with chili pepper flakes or powdered cayenne is one solution, but it can sometimes leave you with tiny pockets of overwhelming spiciness and big, spiceless holes. Antonio opts for this pepper-infused oil instead—the oil (a little bit goes a long way) coats food more evenly than flakes and powders and the deep orange color of the infusion begs at least to be tried. Use it on pasta, in soups, on meat, or make a habit of putting a tiny bowl of it on the table at mealtimes for whoever wants a bit of extra "bite."

⇝ NOTE: Chili peppers will spread their heat on whatever they touch—always wash your hands well after handling them, and take care not to rub your eyes or face while working (as I did once when I decided to string a basket of tiny red peppers into a long necklace to hang in the kitchen . . . *aarrgghhhh!!!*).

½ pound whole fresh cayenne peppers, short stems attached if possible

2 cups red wine vinegar

1 teaspoon salt

2 carrots, finely chopped

1 onion, finely chopped

2 cups extra-virgin olive oil

10 cloves garlic, peeled and halved lengthwise

3 large shavings of lemon zest

2 bay leaves

∽ Wash the peppers in cold water, then drain in a colander.

∽ Heat the vinegar and salt to a boil over a medium flame (you will want to keep your nose away from the strong vapors of the heated vinegar). Add the peppers. When the liquid returns to a boil, cook the peppers covered for 5 minutes, then uncovered for another 5 minutes. Strain the peppers into a colander, and set the vinegar aside.

∽ In the meantime, place the carrots and onion in a saucepan with the olive oil. Gently heat the oil over a low flame, and stir the vegetables regularly until they soften but do not brown. Turn off the flame and add the garlic, lemon zest, and bay leaves. Pour in the reserved vinegar and heat the mixture over a medium flame until it reduces and turns a rusty brown (about 6 minutes). Turn off the heat and allow the mixture to sit for 5 minutes before removing the bay leaves and lemon zest.

∽ Spoon the cooled peppers into a medium Mason jar, then cover with the seasoned oil and vinegar mixture. The contents will settle over the next couple of days as the air pockets in the peppers fill with oil. Add additional fresh olive oil if necessary to keep the peppers submerged.

∽ Leave the peppers to rest in a cool spot in the kitchen for 2 days, then store in the refrigerator. Serve in a small ramekin with a demitasse spoon.

Artichoke Tapenade
Passato di Carciofi
SERVES 4

The flavor of this spread relies almost entirely on the artichokes themselves, which makes it more important than ever that they be very fresh and tender. Try to use the purplish-green baby artichokes, as they have yet to develop furry chokes around their hearts and are plentiful during the height of spring, when artichokes are at their prime. If you are using larger artichokes with fully developed chokes, just trim away the fibrous hairs.

12 baby artichokes or 4 globe artichokes
Juice of 1 lemon
3 tablespoons extra-virgin olive oil
3 cloves garlic, peeled and sliced

2 sprigs Italian parsley, leaves only
¼ cup dry white wine
Salt
Freshly ground black pepper

Remove all but the top inch of each artichoke's stem, then trim away the outer layer of the remaining stem. Peel away the outer leaves until you reach the tender yellow-and-purple-tinged inner leaves. Turn each artichoke on its side and cut off the tough green tops of the leaves until all that remains is the tender edible portion of the leaves. Cut the artichokes lengthwise down the middle, then use a paring knife to cut away any fibrous hairs surrounding the heart. Soak the trimmed artichokes in a large bowl of water with the lemon juice for 30 minutes.

Place the artichokes, oil, garlic, and parsley in a shallow pan and heat over a medium flame. When the skillet is hot, add the wine and stir the contents for a couple of minutes while the alcohol evaporates. Pour in 1 cup of water, sprinkle with salt and freshly ground pepper, then lower the flame and cover the pot until the artichokes are tender and all the liquid has evaporated (about 20 minutes). You may add more water if the liquid has evaporated before the artichokes have finished cooking.

∾ Let the artichokes cool and then puree them in a food processor until they form a paste. Serve in a small bowl surrounded by small, thin slices of toasted bread.

TREASURES IN A PINECONE
Pinoli

During the relentless heat of August, half the local population of Florence seems to disappear (replaced by an equal number of profusely perspiring tourists). A huge number of these *fiorentini* are only about an hour away in Versilia, where Tuscany meets the Mediterranean on wide sandy beaches lined with row upon row of colored umbrellas, wooden cabanas, outdoor restaurants, and, of course, people. You pay dearly for the privilege of securing a spot on the sand among the hordes—upward of a thousand dollars for the whole month of August and more if you want your own private cabana.

Not too far from the madding crowd are the *spiagge libere,* or free beaches, unspoiled stretches of sand offering little in the way of the amenities many Italians have come to expect as part of their beach-going experience. The best of them are accessed only after a short trek through a fragrant woods alive with the steady thrum of cicadas and crickets. In the early morning or at dusk, if you veer far enough from the beaten path and sit silently for a while, anything from a deer to a wild boar might quietly reveal itself, only to disappear just as quickly into a thicket (and leave you wondering whether or not you imagined the whole thing).

The botanical stars of these woods are the pine trees—not the tall Christmas pines of the high Alps, but beautiful umbrella pines, scattered throughout the flat, sprawling woods like giant green mushrooms leaning gracefully into the sea breeze. Trees loved for their beauty, for the canopy of shade found under their outstretched limbs, and for the pale ivory nuts hidden within their cones.

Toward the end of the summer, you will likely come across small groups of people combing the woods, lugging bags or baskets filled with pinecones the wind has blown from the trees. Hand harvesting the tiny nuts from the cones is slow and laborious. Each "petal" of the cone must be pried open to reveal one pale brown pine seed. The shells in turn must be cracked gently so as not to damage the tender, pale nutmeat inside. Quite a lot of work for one little sliver of a nut—which must be why gathering and cracking open pinecones seems to be the sort of labor that appeals equally to the very young and the very old, bypassing almost completely the supermarket-savvy generations in between.

Why go to all the effort? There is distinct pleasure in drinking wine from grapes that you have picked yourself, or eating an omelette from eggs you've collected from the dim interior of a rural henhouse—as if somehow the flavors have been enhanced by your very labor. Too often in our search for efficiency we forget the simple notion of doing something for the sheer pleasure of the experience. What we gain by the ease with which we can plunk down a few dollars in exchange for a hermetically sealed plastic bag of this or that, we lose in flavor . . . and experience. A hand-harvested pine nut tastes of the tree from which it came. A store-bought bag of pine nuts tastes like . . . well . . . a store-bought bag of pine nuts—good, just not *as* good.

Potato Pesto
Inzuppapane al Pesto di Patate
SERVES 4

No herb captures the essence of Italian summer more than fresh basil. A basil plant will continue growing tender fragrant leaves as long as the weather is warm and the tops of the plants are pinched off regularly to keep them from going to seed. A trip to the herb garden for a "pinching" expedition usually ends up generating a basketful of bright green leaves. Our basil bounty led Jean-Louis to come up with this summery dip, which we spoon into ramekins and serve with freshly baked focaccia.

1 cup loosely packed fresh basil leaves

1 clove garlic, peeled

⅓ cup pine nuts

½ cup extra-virgin olive oil

2 medium potatoes, boiled in their skins, then peeled

Salt

~ Blend the basil, garlic, and pine nuts with the olive oil in a food processor.

~ Roughly mash the potatoes with a fork. Add them to the food processor and blend to a rough paste. Season with salt and serve with warm focaccia.

Fresh Spinach Puree
Purè di Spinaci Freschi
SERVES 4 TO 6

This brilliant green puree of fresh spinach seasoned with olive oil, lemon, and garlic takes all of three minutes to make. We serve it at Locanda Veneta during the cooler seasons, when spinach is at its most tender and flavorful.

1 pound fresh baby spinach

½ cup extra-virgin olive oil (approximately)

Juice of ½ lemon

1 clove garlic, peeled and quartered

Salt

Freshly ground black pepper

~ Wash the spinach well in several changes of cold water. Remove the stems and chop the leaves into large pieces.

~ Divide the spinach leaves into 4 bunches and process each bunch in a blender or food processor until very finely chopped. Transfer all of the chopped spinach into the glass pitcher of a stationary blender or, if you are using a hand blender, into a medium mixing bowl. Add ¼ cup of olive oil, the lemon juice, and garlic and blend for a couple of minutes until the mixture forms a bright green paste. Season to taste with salt, pepper, and the remaining olive oil. Serve in small ramekins with fresh warm bread or raw vegetables.

SOMETHING TO ASK YOURSELF

Let's say that three times a week you have to drive to a given destination. There are two possible routes. One is a twenty-minute drive on a somewhat bleak yet efficient modern highway. The other carries you along a meandering country lane, winding past tiny villages and over hills covered with grapevines and ancient olive trees. The price for such beauty is ten more minutes in the car. Which road would you take? Are you ruled by your watch or by your senses? Is the trip as important to you as the destination? Think about it, and consider the possibility that 90 percent of our lives *is* the trip—not a game where the winner is the one who gets the most done in the least amount of time.

If there is one quality that most characterizes the Italian approach to cooking, it is the sensual delight taken in every aspect of the process—from the marketing and preparation of a meal, to the setting of the table and the receiving of friends. Think of Italy as a place where the circuitous road to the table is as important as the dishes ultimately placed upon it.

Take a good look at how you market and cook. Are you a list maker? Do you dutifully and efficiently check off each item as it lands in your shopping cart? Or do you allow yourself the pleasure of ambling around the market with your senses awake and alert, looking, sniffing, touching, waiting to see what inspires or appeals to you? It's not that you shouldn't make lists. No one could get by in the modern world without them. Just do give yourself some space for those wonderful, delicious, or surprising things that may unexpectedly cross your path . . . and which you will only notice if you look up from your list once in a while.

The approach is the same wherever you live and however grand or limited your marketing options. Even if there is not a farmers' market within one hundred miles of your house and you have no choice but to do all your shopping at the same giant, sterile supermarket week in and week out, there is no excuse for turning off your senses. Can you look past the long aisle of packaged breakfast cereals and allow yourself to be inspired by the bundles of asparagus standing like bright green saplings in a shallow pool of water? Would you notice the loaf of crusty bread that just begs to be toasted, rubbed with garlic, and drizzled with olive oil? Would you buy yourself a tiny bunch of fresh herbs just because you liked the way they smelled, and trust you'd figure out how to use them later?

It is actually much less important that you make a perfect risotto than that you *delight in making it*. Approaching cooking with a mixture of enthusiasm, curiosity, and sensuality will do more for the quality of the food you put on your table than even the most slavishly rigorous recipe following. Allow yourself to be bold and brave in the kitchen. You don't really need to follow a cookbook's instructions religiously *every* time. It's a good idea the first or second time you try something, but it's not a way to cook on a regular basis. It's not fun, it's not creative, and it takes your own senses completely out of the loop. Cooking should be more like painting a watercolor out in the garden than building a bookcase. It requires the presence of your senses as well as your mind.

Consider going ever so slightly out of your way solely to please your senses. Make an effort to slow down and enjoy even those things you've always regarded as chores. A trip to the market, the preparation of a meal, laying a table—they are all little destinations in and of themselves. Not distasteful tasks to try to avoid, nor simply a means to an end. Grace them with your attention and not only might you begin to enjoy them more than you could imagine, but also the results of your efforts will be all the more delicious for the spirit and enthusiasm you've put into them.

ITALIAN FLATBREAD
Focaccia

We don't have the kitchen space in all of our restaurants to make focaccia—but if we did, we would. On any given day at Ca' Brea, the kitchen will come up with three or four types of focaccia, which are cut into small wedges and brought warm to the table with little ramekins of herbed olive pâté. At lunch there the other day, Gigi Barducci, Ca' Brea's northern Italian executive chef brought me a basket of his current favorites. There were, of course, a few pieces of focaccia *"semplice"* drizzled with olive oil and sprinkled with crystals of rock salt ("plain" is too drab a word for this simplest of focacce), in addition to a focaccia covered with thin slivers of potato and rosemary, another whose dough had been laced with Italian olives from Gaeta, and finally a beautiful burnished russet focaccia that had been painted with tomato paste before going into the oven.

For those (many) of us who are not serious bread bakers, focaccia is one of the most satisfying breads to make. The dough is not as finicky as that of traditional loaf breads, you don't need to set aside an entire day to make it, and, best of all, it lends itself to endless variation and virtually begs for culinary flights of fancy.

One recipe will make one large round or rectangular focaccia. But you can just as well roll the dough into smaller rounds for individual focaccine, which can be sliced through the middle for sandwiches or eaten whole. We prefer our focaccia soft and spongy and about an inch and a half high. However, the dough can also be rolled out very thin for a crisp, almost crackerlike focaccia. You can flavor focacce by incorporating anything from cured meats, olives, herbs, or vegetables into the dough, or you can scatter herbs or vegetables over the top before baking.

Italian Flatbread

Focaccia

MAKES 1 LARGE FOCACCIA

1 cake compressed fresh yeast or	2 tablespoons extra-virgin olive oil,
1 package active dry yeast	plus oil for brushing
½ cup warm water	½ cup room-temperature water

3½ cups unsifted all-purpose flour, plus	½ teaspoon salt
flour for dusting	⅓ cup cool water
1 teaspoon sugar	Coarse salt

   In a small mixing bowl, dissolve the yeast into the warm water, mixing gently. Let the mixture stand for 10 minutes; as the yeast "wakes up," the liquid will turn opaque and creamy. Stir in the olive oil and ½ cup room-temperature water.

   Combine the flour, sugar, and salt in a large mixing bowl. Make a well in the center and pour in the yeast mixture. With one hand, swirl the liquid in the center, slowly incorporating the dry ingredients from the sides of the well. When roughly half of the flour has been incorporated, add an additional ⅓ cup of cool water. Fold the mixture from the sides of the bowl toward the center, then flatten it down, repeating the motion over and over until the mixture forms a cohesive ball. Wash your hands and lightly flour a flat work surface.

   Knead the dough until it becomes smooth and elastic, about 7 to 10 minutes. The dough should be as moist as possible without sticking to your hands. Dust with additional flour if the dough is too sticky or sprinkle with water if it feels too dry.

   Clean off your work surface, dust it with flour, place the ball of dough on top and cover with a clean mixing bowl. Allow the dough to rise until it doubles, 1 to 1½ hours, keeping in mind that the cooler the outdoor temperature, the longer it will take for the dough to rise. Once the dough has risen, knead it once more for a couple of minutes. It will be very elastic, springing back when you press down on it with a finger.

   Preheat the oven to 400°. Flour your work surface and roll out the dough from the center outward, using a steady, even pressure but without pressing down hard on the rolling pin. Roll the dough into a large circle or rectangle roughly ¾ inch thick. Lightly oil a baking pan large enough to accommodate the unbaked focaccia and transfer the shaped dough to the pan. Cover the pan with a towel and let the dough rise for an additional 30 minutes.

   Use your fingers to "dimple" the dough, covering the surface with craterlike indentations. Brush with olive oil, sprinkle with rock salt, and bake the focaccia until it is golden brown, about 30 to 35 minutes.

   Remove from the oven and drizzle with additional olive oil if you wish. Cool until warm on a wire rack, then serve.

Flavoring the Dough

Olives

   1 cup unpitted Gaeta, kalamata, or niçoise olives, cured in oil

   1 recipe focaccia dough (page 36), before kneading

∾ Use a small paring knife to cut the flesh of the olive away from the stone so that each olive is cut into 2 to 4 pieces.

∾ Follow the master recipe for focaccia, incorporating the olives into the dough three quarters of the way through the first kneading. Rise, shape, and bake according to the master recipe.

Rosemary

This focaccia gets its rich herbal flavor both from the rosemary itself and from the olive oil in which the herb is gently sautéed.

   1 tablespoon coarsely chopped fresh rosemary

   3 tablespoons extra-virgin olive oil

   1 recipe focaccia dough (page 36), unmixed

∾ Over a medium-low flame, gently sauté the rosemary in the olive oil until it is crisp. Strain the oil into a small cup and allow it to cool. Set aside the rosemary.

∾ Make the focaccia according to the master recipe with the following changes:

1. Substitute the oil in which you have sautéed the rosemary for the plain olive oil that is mixed with the yeast and water at the beginning of the recipe.

2. Incorporate the sautéed rosemary into the dough three quarters of the way through the first kneading.

∾ Rise, shape, and bake according to the master recipe.

Toppings

Rather than incorporating flavors into the dough, these focacce are "dressed" only after they've been rolled into their final shapes.

Plum Tomatoes and Oregano

Oregano is the exception to our general preference for using fresh herbs. Dried oregano is richly fragrant and perfumed without the bitter, peppery edge of the fresh herb. We do still grow it in the garden, cutting it into big bunches that we hang out to dry under the pergola outside our kitchen.

4 ripe plum tomatoes, stem ends removed
1 recipe focaccia dough (page 36), kneaded, left to rise, and rolled out into a large circle or rectangle

1 teaspoon dried oregano
Coarse salt
Extra-virgin olive oil for drizzling

∾ Preheat oven to 400°.

∾ Cut the tomatoes into thin slices and lay them along the top of the focaccia. Sprinkle with oregano and rock salt, drizzle with olive oil, and bake for 30 to 35 minutes, until golden on top. Set on a wire rack until cool enough to handle. Cut and serve warm.

Onions

We sauté the onions lightly before baking them with the focaccia so that they remain soft and sweet. Raw onions would dry to a crisp.

1 large onion, halved and thinly sliced
3 tablespoons extra-virgin olive oil
1 recipe focaccia dough (page 36), kneaded, left to rise, and rolled out into a large circle or rectangle
Coarse salt

⌒ Preheat the oven to 400°.

⌒ Sauté the onions in the olive oil over a low flame until they are soft and translucent. Spoon the onions evenly over the top of the focaccia, sprinkle with rock salt and bake for 30 to 35 minutes, until golden. Cool on a wire rack and serve warm or at room temperature.

Tomato Paste

I suppose you might call this a culinary cheap trick since the results are so striking for an effort so small. All you do is lightly brush the raw focaccia dough with olive oil and tomato paste, then bake as usual in the oven. The result is a wonderful sienna-hued bread that carries with it just a hint of tomato.

> 1 recipe focaccia dough (page 36), kneaded, left to rise, and rolled out into a large circle or rectangle
> Extra-virgin olive oil for brushing
> ¼ cup tomato paste

⌒ Preheat the oven to 400°.

⌒ Brush the dough first with the olive oil, then the tomato paste, and bake for 30 to 35 minutes until the surface of the focaccia colors a deep rusty red. Cool on a wire rack. Serve warm or at room temperature.

Crispy Crepes and Savory Half-Moons
Crespelle e Soffiatini

MAKES ABOUT 30

Although the word *crespelle* is generally used to describe crepes in Italian, here Antonio uses it to refer to small pieces of dough rolled out and flattened into disks about the size of a small crepe or pita bread and then fried to a delicious crisp in oil. We top the crespelle with anything from a sliver of hard cheese or a spoonful of creamy Gorgonzola, to thin slices of cured meat, such as prosciutto, bresaola, or speck, or a scattering of chopped arugula or herbs.

Soffiatini are made from the same dough as crespelle except that their fillings are hidden inside a crespella that has been folded in half. Soffiatini work best when their fillings are soft and moist—leftover meat ragù, sautéed zucchini, mushrooms, or eggplant are especially suited as fillings, as are soft cheeses and plum tomatoes. As the soffiatini cook, they puff up into half-moon-shaped cushions, concealing their flavorful treasures inside their steaming pockets.

These little treats are meant to be light and mouthwatering—the sort of thing that stimulates the appetite rather than overwhelms it—and so they require only a touch of topping or filling. We eat them *in piedi,* that is, standing up, and usually prepare an assortment of both when we make them for guests. You may either cut them into pieces or serve them whole.

The dough can be rolled out into disks, stacked between pieces of plastic wrap, then wrapped tightly and frozen for up to a month.

Dough Recipe for Crespelle and Soffiatini

1 cake compressed fresh yeast or 1 package active dry yeast
¾ cup warm water
2 tablespoons extra-virgin olive oil
Salt
3½ cups unbleached all-purpose flour, plus flour for dusting

For Frying

Ample amounts of corn or safflower oil

∽ Dissolve the yeast in a small bowl with ¾ cup warm water, then stir in the olive oil with a wooden spoon. Let the mixture stand for 10 minutes.
∽ Combine a pinch of salt with the flour, then pour the flour in a mound on a flat work surface or in a large mixing bowl. Make a large crater in the center of the flour and pour the

liquid mixture into it. Using the tips of your fingers, swirl the liquid around, slowly incorporating the flour from the edges and the inside of the crater. When the mixture has formed a cohesive ball, flatten it with your hands, then fold it in half. Continue this motion until the dough no longer sticks to your hands as you work it. Wash your hands and dry them well. Clean off your work surface, then dust it with flour. Knead the dough as you would knead bread dough until it becomes smooth and elastic (about 5 to 6 minutes).

⤲ Dust a clean mixing bowl with a bit of flour. Place the dough ball in it, cover with a dish towel, and leave it to rise in a comfortably warm spot for 30 to 40 minutes. The dough will rise faster or slower depending on the temperature of your kitchen. If you are making it on a scorching summer day, set the dough to rest in a relatively cool spot to avoid having it rise too fast and then collapse (or use a pinch less yeast). On a winter day, let the dough rise on top of your refrigerator or in some other warm spot.

Crespelle

⤲ After the dough has rested, flatten it down with your fists and then knead it for another minute or two. Cut off a golf-ball-sized piece of dough, dust it lightly with flour, and roll it out into a flat, round disk 5 to 6 inches in diameter. Continue rolling out as many crespelle as you plan to serve.

⤲ Heat ¼ inch of oil in a large skillet. Test the oil by throwing a crumb of bread into the skillet. If it begins to sizzle and fry upon contact, the oil is sufficiently hot. Don't let the oil smoke. You can quickly bring down its temperature by reducing the flame and adding additional oil.

⤲ Gently slip 1 or more crespelle (depending upon the size of your pan) into the oil. They will not remain perfectly flat as they fry but may curve up slightly on one side or form large bubbles on their surface. This isn't a problem—consider it just part of their homemade nature and what makes them look so interesting on a plate. When they are golden, turn them using both a spatula and a fork, taking care not to splatter any hot oil. When both sides are crisp and golden, drain with a slotted spatula and blot carefully between paper towels. Sprinkle with salt and dress them up with any of the following toppings (or any others that strike your fancy).

Toppings for Crespelle
(Per Crespella)

Bresaola, Shaved Parmesan, and Arugula
   1 slice Italian bresaola (salt-cured beef)
   1 wide shaving of Parmesan cheese
   Pinch of torn arugula leaves (tear into bite-sized pieces)
   Freshly ground black pepper

⌁ Lay the slice of bresaola on top of the crespella, cover with the Parmesan shaving. Sprinkle with arugula and a generous grinding of black pepper.

Smoked Salmon and Chives
   1 slice smoked salmon
   1 tablespoon sour cream
   Chopped fresh chives for sprinkling

⌁ Allow the crespella to cool slightly, then cover with a slice of salmon. Spoon a dollop of sour cream in the center and sprinkle with chives.

Gorgonzola Cheese and Walnuts
   1 tablespoon soft Gorgonzola cheese
   1 teaspoon chopped walnuts

⌁ Spread the warm crespella with the cheese, then sprinkle the walnuts over the top.

Cured Meats and Gherkins

    1 slice Italian prosciutto, speck, or salami

    1 gherkin, cut into thin slices

∾ Lay a slice of meat over a crespella. Cover with the slices of gherkin.

Soffiatini

∾ While the dough is resting, prepare any number of the fillings described below. When the dough is ready, flatten it down with your fists and then knead it for another minute or two. Cut off a golf-ball-sized piece of dough, dust it lightly with flour and roll out into a flat, round disk as you would for crespelle. Roll out as many disks as you wish soffiatini.

∾ Spoon a generous tablespoon of filling in the center of each flat disk, then gently fold the dough almost in half so that the bottom portion of the disk is slightly larger than the top. Seal the edges of the soffiatini by folding the bottom edge over the top edge and pressing down firmly with your fingers. You will end up with half-moons securely sealed around their curved edges.

∾ Heat ¼ inch of oil in a large skillet. Fry the soffiatini as you would crespelle, turning once or twice until they are golden on both sides.

∾ *Attenzione!* The inside of the soffiatini will be palate-scorchingly hot when they've just finished cooking. Let them cool down for a minute before serving.

Fillings
(Per Soffiatino)

Mixed Cheeses

    1 teaspoon Gorgonzola cheese

    1 teaspoon ricotta cheese

1 teaspoon grated Fontina, Muenster, or Edam cheese

1 teaspoon grated Parmesan cheese

∽ Combine the cheeses, then spoon onto the center of the flat circle of dough. Fold and seal the edges, then fry until golden on both sides.

Pizzaiola

2 tablespoons grated mozzarella cheese

2 tablespoon chopped canned Italian plum tomato

2 capers

Sprinkle of dry oregano

Pinch of crushed red pepper or chili powder, optional

∽ Place all ingredients in the center of the flat circle of dough. Fold and seal the edges, then fry until golden on both sides.

Marinated Artichokes and Taleggio Cheese

1 marinated artichoke heart, drained and thinly sliced

1 tablespoon Taleggio or other semisoft cheese

∽ Crumble the cheese and mix well with the artichoke. Spoon the mixture onto the center of the flat disk of dough, gently fold in half, seal the edges and fry until golden on both sides.

Mushrooms and Goat Cheese

1 tablespoon sautéed mushrooms (page 24)

1 tablespoon chopped canned Italian plum tomato

1 tablespoon goat cheese

∽ Spoon the ingredients onto the center of a disk of dough, fold and seal, then fry until golden.

Ricotta and Prosciutto

1 tablespoon ricotta cheese

1 tablespoon grated Parmesan cheese

½ slice Italian prosciutto cotto (cooked Italian ham)

Pinch of dried oregano

∽ Combine the cheeses, then place all the ingredients in the center of a flat circle of dough, fold and seal, then fry until golden.

SIMPLE DELICACIES: A LIST OF THINGS
THERE IS NO EXCUSE NOT TO EAT

The single scarcest resource in "modern civilization" seems to be time. Despite our efforts to save it, spend it well, and waste not a drop, most of us claim to be too busy to do the things we're convinced we would do if we only had the *time.* For whatever reason, eating well seems to be one of the first things sacrificed when our list of "things to do" becomes overwhelming. Instead, we zap something in the microwave, grab a sandwich at a stand, or open up one of the thousands of prepackaged treats hawked to us at every supermarket.

For the most part, Italians seem to have avoided the junk food deluge. Drive-through dining has yet to arrive and fast-food haunts are not lurking at every corner. Eating is done at meals instead of between them. True, a *bambino* might beg his mom for an ice cream or a chocolate Kinder egg, but he is just as likely to try to cajole her into buying a bag of ripe cherries at the greengrocer's or a wedge of juicy watermelon from a fruit stand.

So much food in America has been processed, packaged, and prepared in the name of "saving time" that we seem to have forgotten about some of the culinary world's purest treasures—things so totally delicious, so perfect in their simplicity, and so effortless to make that they rival even the most elaborately prepared feast, and leave junk food standing in the dust.

The following is *my* personal list of foods I have no excuse not to eat.

- New olive oil on toasted bread rubbed with garlic and sprinkled with salt
- Winter pears and aged pecorino cheese
- Wedges of fennel dipped in olive oil and vinegar
- A warm tomato fresh from a summer garden
- Ripe figs and thin slices of spicy salami
- Blackberries off the bush
- Fresh mozzarella cheese with basil, olive oil, salt, and pepper
- A bowl of cherries
- Roasted chestnuts in the winter
- Walnuts and soft Gorgonzola cheese
- A cold, juicy wedge of summer melon
- Raw baby artichokes pared down to their hearts and tender leaves
- Freshly shelled fava beans with fresh pecorino cheese
- Steamed asparagus dipped in mustard, lemon, and olive oil
- Radishes sprinkled with salt
- Spicy green olives
- Parmesan cheese and a glass of red wine
- Tea and toasted bread with butter and honey
- Anything at all eaten under a shady tree

Antipasti

SALADS

I grew up on "green" salads comprised of a few torn leaves of anemic, nearly tasteless iceberg lettuce tossed with one of the variety of bottled dressings that crowded the condiment shelf of our refrigerator. On special occasions, my mom would add a few cherry tomatoes, some sliced cucumber, and purple onion, and, if we were really lucky, a handful of packaged croutons.

The Italian *insalata verde* is a wondrous thing, made from tender cutting lettuces, chicory, or wild greens, and dressed only in olive oil and a few drops of lemon juice or vinegar. It is the essence of simplicity, accenting a meal rather than making it.

But both in America and Italy, "salad" has evolved to mean much more than the basic green. Lettuces or fresh vegetables are paired with things like chunks of roasted chicken, shrimp poached in wine and herbs, fresh cheeses, fruit, or nuts. Olive oil is flavored with herbs, shallots, sharp mustard, or wine. Almost any combination of foods is being chopped, sliced, roasted, toasted, or handled in any number of ways to become what, for lack of a better word, is still called "salad." Culinarily speaking, we think this is a good thing.

In this chapter, we've tried to give you the best of both worlds, from basics such as mixed wild greens in a herbed vinaigrette, and Locanda Veneta's signature salad of radicchio tossed with homemade croutons and an anchovy-laced dressing, to more substantial salads that are light meals in themselves.

Mixed Baby Lettuces
Lattughette Novelle
SERVES 4

We call them "cutting lettuces" or "baby lettuces." The Italians call them "twenty-four-hour lettuces," a reference to their extreme perishability, or perhaps to the speed with which the tender young leaves sprout up in the garden. You will find them in every Italian market, a dazzling mixture of textures, flavors, and colors, from delicate leaves tied into tiny bouquets to florets of young lettuces piled high in baskets. While once found exclusively in local farmers' markets, mixed baby lettuces have become a regular feature in many American markets. If you have trouble finding them, use the tender inner leaves of curly endive, escarole, and romaine instead.

Many Italians dress the leaves using nothing but a fine fruity olive oil and salt. Some will add a few drops of vinegar or lemon juice. Another delicious alternative is this herbed vinaigrette.

8 handfuls mixed baby lettuces
Freshly ground black pepper

For the Vinaigrette

2 tablespoons red wine vinegar
1 tablespoon Dijon mustard
1 tablespoon water
1 teaspoon snipped or finely chopped
   chives

1 basil leaf, finely chopped
3 tablespoons extra-virgin olive oil

~~ Wash the leaves well and dry them in a salad spinner. Whisk together the vinegar, mustard, and water. Sprinkle in the chives and basil, then pour the oil into the mixture in a steady stream, whisking continuously until the mixture is smooth.

~~ Toss the leaves with the dressing just before serving. Offer freshly ground black pepper.

Herbed Vinegar
Aceto Aromatico

Wine vinegar is as good as the wine from which it was made. Besides its obvious use for dressing salads, we use it in cooking, to pickle vegetables, and for marinades. I love the way a bouquet of herbs looks suspended in a bottle of white wine vinegar, and the subtle flavor it imparts when used with discretion. Find a pretty glass bottle to steep the herbs in, gather together a little bouquet of your favorite aromatic herbs, and make a couple of bottles for yourself and your friends.

Small bouquet of mixed fresh herbs, such as sage, oregano, rosemary, and tarragon
1 liter good-quality white wine vinegar

~~ Push the herb bouquet through the neck of a clean bottle or cruet. Pour the wine vinegar over the top, close with a cork tap, and allow to steep for 1 week before using.

HERB GARDENING
Le Erbe

Of all culinary gardening, herb gardening gives perhaps the greatest satisfaction for the least amount of effort. Just a few clay pots in a sunny windowsill or the tiniest square of earth is all you need to keep your kitchen herbally equipped.

For an Italian herb garden, you'll want to grow flat-leaf parsley, rosemary, sage, basil (of course, and why not more than one type?), oregano, thyme, and perhaps mint. Chives, known as *"erba cipollina,"* literally "little onion grass," grow wild throughout the countryside in Tuscany, especially in early spring between the tilled rows of grapevines. They are a delight snipped over leaf salads and a beauty in the garden with their great clusters of purple flowers. Another typically Italian herb is the delicately flavored, small-leafed wild mint known as *"nepitella"* or *"mentuccia."* A form of catmint, it grows wild throughout Italy. The best way to find it is to walk on wild grass—its delicate sweet scent will fill the air as soon as you tread on it. Use it to lightly flavor sautéed wild mushrooms, eggplant, or zucchini.

Rosemary, sage, thyme, mint, and chives are perennial and need to be planted only once. Parsley and basil need to be sown every year, but are extremely easy to grow. Other favorites from our garden are sweet laurel (which grows as a tree or shrub), wild fennel, tarragon, sorrel, and borage (whose tender leaves make a wonderful filling for ravioli). Every year, we bring dill and cilantro seed from America (the former is virtually unheard-of in Italy, while the latter is one of the only edible things of any kind for which Italians have an inexplicable loathing).

Having a little patchwork of herbs close to the kitchen adds a wonderful spontaneity to your cooking. You will never lack for places to use fresh herbs—cast a few sage leaves into a simmering pot of beans, add a sprig of thyme to a soup, scatter fresh basil leaves over juicy summer tomatoes, rosemary around a roasting chicken. . . .

Locanda Veneta Radicchio Salad
Insalata Locanda
SERVES 4

If there were a staple in any northern Italian vegetable garden, it would have to be radicchio, a type of chicory whose sharp, full flavor manages to be both sweet and bitter at the same time. It grows with long, thin pointed leaves (radicchio di Treviso), in compact heads marbled in shades of pink and cream (radicchio di Verona), or in little florets whose deep-green and red leaves return after each cutting (radicchio scoltellato). It can be grilled, sautéed, baked, or made into salads. This is the Locanda Veneta "house salad"—a kind of Venetian Caesar salad. It uses radicchio di Verona, the variety most commonly found in American markets.

3 small or 2 medium heads radicchio

For the Dressing

6 tablespoons extra-virgin olive oil

2 tablespoons red wine vinegar

1 tablespoon dry white wine

1 tablespoon mayonnaise

2 teaspoons anchovy paste

1 egg yolk

1 small clove garlic, minced

For the Croutons

2 cups cubed crustless white country bread, cut into ½- to 1-inch cubes

2½ tablespoons salted butter

1 teaspoon finely chopped fresh rosemary

1 teaspoon finely chopped fresh sage

2 tablespoons freshly grated Parmesan cheese

Freshly ground black pepper

∾ Preheat oven to 375°.

↩ Tear the radicchio into bite-sized pieces and soak in cold water for an hour, so that it becomes crisp and crunchy. Strain and dry in a salad spinner.

↩ *The dressing:* In a blender or by hand, mix the oil, vinegar, wine, mayonnaise, anchovy paste, egg yolk, and garlic until creamy.

↩ *The croutons:* Arrange the bread cubes on a baking sheet and bake until golden brown on all sides, turning occasionally. Warm the butter and chopped herbs in a medium skillet over a low flame. When the butter is melted but not brown and the herbs are fragrant and lightly toasted, remove the skillet from the flame and add the toasted bread cubes, tossing to coat evenly.

↩ Place the radicchio in a large salad bowl. Add the dressing and toss until the leaves are well coated. Sprinkle with the grated Parmesan, herbed croutons, and a generous grinding of black pepper. Serve immediately.

Spinach Salad with Pancetta Cracklings
Insalata di Spinaci e Ciccioli

SERVES 4

Ciccioli are the savory little morsels of crisp pork that remain in the frying pan after all the fat has melted away. We add them to our spinach salad—Italians eat them as is—hot, crispy, and undeniably delicious.

A note on the dressing: There's no getting around the fact that the dressing is most flavorful when made with at least 1 tablespoon, if not 2, of the rendered pork fat. If you simply can't fathom the notion of making your dressing this way, blend ¼ cup olive oil with the vinegar, mustard, and hard-boiled eggs instead. Stir in a couple tablespoons of water to adjust the consistency and season to taste with salt and pepper.

1 pound baby spinach, curly-leaf	6 ounces Italian pancetta, thickly sliced
Extra-virgin olive oil	3 tablespoons red wine vinegar

1 tablespoon whole grain mustard

2 hard-boiled eggs

2 tablespoons spring water

2 ounces Parmesan cheese, cut into thin shavings

Freshly ground black pepper

∼ Soak the spinach in cold water for 30 minutes, changing the water two or three times. Drain well, and inspect the leaves for dirt. Discard the stems and dry the leaves in a salad spinner.

∼ Warm 1 tablespoon of olive oil in a pan, add the pancetta and sauté over a medium-low flame until the fat melts away and the meat is browned and crispy (about 15 minutes). Use a slotted spoon to remove the cracklings from the pan, drain on paper towels and crumble into coarse pieces.

∼ Filter the pan drippings through a cheesecloth-lined tea strainer and use a paper towel to wipe clean your skillet. Return the skillet to the stovetop with 1 or 2 tablespoons of the strained fat and 1 tablespoon of vinegar. Heat for 30 seconds over a medium flame, stirring constantly, then add in the mustard and continue stirring for another 30 seconds. (The mixture will spatter a bit around the stove—this is hard to avoid.) Pour the resulting mixture into a small bowl to cool.

∼ Meanwhile, crumble the hard-boiled eggs by mashing them with the tines of a dinner fork. Add them to the vinegar-mustard mixture along with 3 tablespoons of olive oil, and 2 each of vinegar and spring water. Blend with a stationary or hand blender until smooth and creamy.

∼ Place the spinach together with the ciccioli and Parmesan shavings in a large bowl and toss with the dressing until they are well coated. Offer freshly ground black pepper.

Fennel, Orange, and Pecorino Salad
Insalata di Finocchio, Arance, e Pecorino

SERVES 4

When I think of the winter garden's modest bounty, things like broccoli and pumpkins, carrots and cabbage come to mind—delicious, but not the stuff from which light meals are made. While this salad takes its ingredients faithfully from the winter harvest, the crisp freshness of the fennel and the oranges' tart bite will leave you feeling that springtime is more than just around the corner. Try using Sicilian blood oranges if they are available where you live.

3 small or 2 large fennel bulbs, trimmed and cored

3 seedless oranges

4 tablespoons extra-virgin olive oil

1 tablespoon red wine vinegar

2 ounces aged pecorino cheese, cut into thin shavings

Salt

Freshly ground black pepper

∽ Trim the tops and root ends from the fennel, and remove the small core from the base of the bulbs. Remove the outer leaves if they are tough or stringy. Rinse the bulbs and cut them in half lengthwise. Place the fennel cut side down and cut crosswise into medium slices.

∽ Juice 1 orange, then set aside the juice for the dressing. Peel the 2 remaining oranges, removing the bitter white pith. Slice the oranges crosswise, then quarter the slices.

∽ In a small bowl, whisk together the olive oil, 2 tablespoons of orange juice, and the vinegar.

∽ Scatter the fennel, orange, and pecorino in a medium salad bowl. Toss lightly with the dressing and season to taste with salt and freshly ground black pepper.

Fresh Mushroom, Arugula, and Parmesan Salad
Insalata di Funghi e Parmigiano
SERVES 4

This salad has a wonderfully soft texture and taste—a nice departure from the crispy crunch that typifies most salads. The subtle earthiness of tawny brown mushrooms pairs up perfectly with Parmesan's ripe flavor—arugula adds a flash of color and bite. This salad can be made with any very fresh mushroom that can be eaten raw. Button and cremini mushrooms work well. To check for freshness, see that the stems are plump and the heads smooth and firm with tightly closed caps.

1 pound very fresh mushrooms, stems removed

6 tablespoons extra-virgin olive oil

3 tablespoons fresh lemon juice

1 teaspoon finely chopped Italian parsley

Salt

Freshly ground black pepper

4 ounces Parmesan cheese, cut into thin shavings with a potato peeler or sharp knife

1½ cups chopped arugula

If the mushrooms are fairly clean, wipe them off with a dry dish towel. If they are caked with dirt, then wash them under running water, pat dry, and slice the caps as thinly as possible.

Whisk together the olive oil and lemon juice until creamy. Sprinkle in the parsley, then season to taste with salt and freshly ground black pepper.

Gently mix the mushrooms, Parmesan, and arugula in a salad bowl. Lightly toss with the dressing and serve.

ARTICHOKES
Carciofi

My first few years in Italy a strange thing kept happening to my hands—every spring, the tips of my fingers became stained a black that no amount of washing would remove. It looked as if I'd just been fingerprinted and hadn't managed to erase the last traces of tell-tale ink. I figured it was just the rigors of country life wreaking havoc on my body. It would be three years before I was finally able to identify the culprit—artichokes.

The moment of illumination occurred when I happened upon my neighbor Bea working through a pile of *carciofi* she was preparing for a salad. Her hands were hidden in a pair of neon-yellow rubber gloves.

"Why the gloves?" I asked.

"So my hands don't turn black," she explained.

I asked myself why I hadn't faced this problem in America, where I'd cooked many mountains of artichokes. The answer was simple. Back home, cooking *carciofi* involved little more than soaking them for a minute in cold water and popping them into a pot to boil. Period. In Italy, I found myself handling the heck out of them—trimming, chopping, slicing, peeling back leaves, readying them to eat raw in salads or *pinzimonio* (seasoned olive oil used as a dip for raw vegetables), or cooking them in any of a vast number of ways.

Italian markets generally offer at least two types of *carciofi*: large, somewhat weathered *"mamme,"* as they are called in Tuscany (*"mammole"* elsewhere), which are most similar to the globe artichokes I grew up eating in California; and small, tender artichokes

whose furry chokes have yet to develop around their delicious hearts. Of the baby artichokes, the purply smooth-leaved variety is undoubtedly the best for eating raw, but any small immature artichoke will be more tender than its fully developed sibling.

Venice abounds with artichokes, from the famous *castraure*, or "castrated" artichokes grown in the lagoon's salty marshes and available only for a short time each year, to the *fondi di carciofi* (large artichokes cleaned down to their pale white hearts) floating in basins of water at the city's vegetable stands and eaten steamed, grilled, or fried.

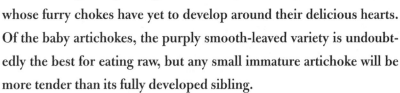

There are so many more things to do with an artichoke than simply boil it in water—and nobody knows this better than an Italian. Cleaned down to their edible hearts and tender leaves, artichokes are a wonder. They can be sliced thinly and sautéed in olive oil, garlic, white wine, and parsley; dipped in a light batter and fried; incorporated into the filling of a stuffed pasta or in a savory sauce for pasta; or used as the base for a delicately flavored risotto—and that's just for starters!

If you grow artichokes in your garden or happen upon them in the market with their stems intact, gather a bunch together and set them in a jug of water in the kitchen until you're ready to use them. They're as beautiful as flowers—but more delicious.

Baby Artichoke and Parmesan Salad
Insalata di Carciofi Crudi e Grana
SERVES 4

This is one of the best introductions to the wonders of raw baby artichokes—the heart and tender leaves are sliced into thin slivers, scattered with shavings of Italian Parmesan, and tossed in olive oil and lemon juice.

8 baby artichokes

Juice of 2 lemons

2 ounces Parmesan cheese, cut into thin shavings with a potato peeler or sharp knife

For the Dressing

4 tablespoons extra-virgin olive oil

2 tablespoons lemon juice

Salt

Freshly ground black pepper

Cleaning the artichokes: The object is to remove any tough, fibrous part of the artichoke that cannot be eaten raw. Begin by cutting off all but the top inch of the artichoke's stem (in America, artichokes are often sold without stems). Pare away the outer layer of the remaining stem, then peel off the outer leaves of the artichoke until you reach the tender yellow-and-purple-tinged inner leaves. Turn the artichoke on its side and cut off the tough green tops of the leaves until only the tender edible portion remains. Cut the artichoke in half lengthwise. If there are fibrous hairs surrounding the heart, run the tip of a small paring knife between the heart and the hairs, then scoop out the hairs with a spoon. Add the lemon juice to a large bowl of cool water and drop the artichokes in to soak once they've been cleaned.

Making the salad: Work with the artichoke pieces one at a time, picking them out of the soaking water to slice them and returning the slices to continue soaking while you cut up the remaining artichokes. Slice by laying the flat side of each halved artichoke on a cutting board and cutting it into paper-thin wedges. Leave the slices to soak for at least 30 minutes.

When you are ready to serve the salad, whisk together the olive oil and lemon juice until creamy. Add salt and freshly ground black pepper to taste.

Drain the artichokes and pat dry with a kitchen towel. Place the artichokes and Parmesan in a medium bowl. Toss lightly with the lemon vinaigrette, then portion onto individual salad plates.

CARCIOFI AND LEMONS

In order to prevent artichokes from turning black after they are cut, soak in a mixture of lemon juice and water. Antonio eschews rubber gloves when he's about to fondle a bunch of carciofi—he keeps his fingers clean by rubbing them with a half lemon instead.

Red Beet, Green Beans, and
Shallot Salad with Basil and Mint
Insalata di Barbabietola, Fagiolini, e Scalogno con Basilico e Menta

SERVES 4

It took planting a garden for me to realize just how wonderful and sadly underused beets are. They deserve a much better place at the table than we give them—they are sweet and yet taste of the earth. Buy your beets with their leaves still on if you can—you'll be assured of their freshness and you can cook the leaves separately as you would Swiss chard.

1 pound fresh beets, leaves removed

1 pound tender green beans, ends and strings removed

3 tablespoons extra-virgin olive oil

2 tablespoons red wine vinegar

Salt

Freshly ground black pepper

2 shallots, thinly sliced

Handful of fresh basil leaves, torn into small pieces

Sprig of fresh mint leaves, chopped

⌒ Wash the beets well and place in a medium saucepan. Cover them completely with cold water, then boil over a medium flame for about 1 hour. They are cooked when a fork inserts easily into the beet's center. Run them under cold water and slip off the outer skins. Cut off the root bottom and the top where the leaves were attached, then slice the beets and set aside to cool.

⌒ In the meantime, steam the green beans over an inch or so of simmering water until they are no longer crisp but are still quite firm (about 15 minutes).

⌒ Whisk together the oil and vinegar, add salt and freshly ground black pepper to taste.

⌒ Place all the vegetables and herbs in a medium serving bowl and toss well with the vinaigrette.

Butter-Braised Chicken Livers with Fresh Spinach in Balsamic Vinaigrette

Insalata di Fegatini, Spinaci, e Parmigiano al Balsamico

SERVES 6

I would normally hesitate to enter chicken livers in a culinary beauty contest, but this appetizer is gorgeous on the plate—the fresh green of the spinach leaves is a perfect backdrop for the rich, brown chicken livers and parchmentlike slivers of Parmesan. As always when purchasing offal of any kind, be sure to buy very fresh chicken livers—they should be moist and shiny. Soaking them in milk sweetens their flavor and maintains their freshness.

1 pound very fresh chicken livers (preferably organic, free range), trimmed of membranes and connective tissue

2 cups milk (approximately)

⅓ cup unsalted butter

18 whole, fresh spinach leaves

2 ounces Parmesan cheese

Salt

Freshly ground black pepper

6 tablespoons extra-virgin olive oil

2 tablespoons aged balsamic vinegar

Rinse the livers in cold water. Place them in a small bowl with enough milk to cover. Refrigerate overnight. When you are ready to use the livers, wipe them dry with a paper towel.

Melt the butter in a large skillet over a very low flame. Add the livers and gently cook, turning occasionally, until they are a deep, rich brown on the outside and tender pink on the inside (8 to 10 minutes). Leave them to cool in the butter.

Wash the spinach leaves and pat dry. Cut the Parmesan cheese into thin shavings with a potato peeler.

Arrange 3 whole spinach leaves on each serving plate. Remove the livers from the pan with a slotted spoon. Cut them in half or thirds and distribute them evenly over the spinach leaves. Add a couple of shavings of Parmesan to each spinach leaf and sprinkle with salt and a generous grinding of black pepper.

෴ Whisk together the olive oil and balsamic vinegar. Drizzle over the spinach leaves and serve.

MARKETING ITALIAN-STYLE

Marketing in Italy is an art form. Nowhere is it at the same time so satisfying yet so difficult to get your daily bread. If you wanted to, you could make your marketing last all day. Or, rather, all morning or afternoon, since not a shop is open during the leisurely Mediterranean lunch break.

It sometimes feels as if my first years in Florence were spent trying to figure out when and where I could buy the various essentials I needed to keep our kitchen going. You probably can't begin to imagine what I'm talking about if you happen to come (as I do) from a major American city where the supermarkets never close and even the local minimarket sells three different brands of olive oil.

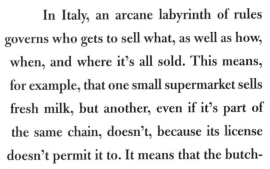

In Italy, an arcane labyrinth of rules governs who gets to sell what, as well as how, when, and where it's all sold. This means, for example, that one small supermarket sells fresh milk, but another, even if it's part of the same chain, doesn't, because its license doesn't permit it to. It means that the butchers can sell frozen, but not fresh, fish, and that they'll close on Thursday afternoons even though all the other food shops close on Wednesday afternoons. It means that the fishmonger is only open in the mornings. And, of course, it means that the entire complicated schedule changes completely during the summer.

Basically, there are three ways to get the shopping done:

- At the bustling open-air markets where itinerant merchants offer everything from fruits and vegetables, heaped in great, colorful piles, to meats, breads, cheeses, and all manner of housewares;
- At what are usually family-run specialty shops scattered throughout every town and city; and
- At the relatively new and ever-increasing battery of "modern" supermarkets.

   If you choose to market in the small shops, you ought to familiarize yourself with this nonexhaustive list of purveyors you might visit:

- The *ortolano* (also known as the *fruttivendolo*) for fruits and vegetables;
- The *alimentari* (sometimes called the *pizzicheria* or *pizzicagnolo*) for cheeses, cured meats, "deli" items, and various other sundries that may, but don't necessarily, include such things as fresh and dried pasta, rice, flour, bottled water, and more;
- The *pescheria* for fish and seafood;
- The *macelleria* for meat and poultry (and sometimes frozen fish);
- The *forno* or *panificio* for bread;
- The *pasticceria* for cakes and pastries;
- The *latteria* for milk, cheeses, yogurt, and usually also cookies, crackers, and cereals (on the theory that they go down well with milk?); and, finally,
- The *enoteca* or *fiaschetteria* for wine and grappa (but usually not beer or hard liquor).

   If traipsing in and out of seventeen shops is not your cup of tea, you'll probably head for the nearest supermarket. Beware. It's going to be a lot more work than you're used to. Take, for instance, the huge one fifteen minutes from my house. Just recently it began staying open from one to four, when everything else is closed. Tempting as it may be to get your shopping done at this usually "forbidden" hour, it's not such a good idea. Chances are there's only one checker and a line of customers twenty deep.

   These "supermarkets" are essentially still a bunch of markets within a market. You

take a number and stand in line to buy the better cheeses and cured meats. You do the same to buy fresh fish. The fun really starts in the produce section. Law requires that you don a disposable plastic glove to pick your veggies, which you then weigh and price at a scale that has drawings of what appears to be two hundred fruits and vegetables. You press the drawing that matches whatever you're buying. Kids love this. I don't. Playing the match-the-vegetable game in front of the small crowd waiting to use the scale seems to numb my brain, so that I'm never quite able to weigh and price everything with the efficiency befitting this modern, time-saving device.

When you finally make it to the checkout counter, you get to pack your own groceries, *and* pay for grocery bags (which is why many people bring their own cloth or reusable bags—not a bad idea for the rest of us).

Admittedly, shopping in open markets and small specialty stores saves little in the way of time or money. The payoff is of a subtler sort—a kind of quintessentially human experience with none of the sterile "efficiency" of the modern supermarket. Take a look at the gray-haired *nonna* ahead of you in "line" (a term I use loosely—order does not come easily to Italians). Chances are she has been buying from the same handful of purveyors for decades. She'll discuss what she's making, and how many people she's making it for. She'll weave her grocery list in among the running details of her life, punctuating her request for a loaf of bread *"cotta bene"* (well-cooked), or a few handfuls of baby lettuces *"bella fresca"* (nice and fresh), with accounts of her grandson's latest exploits and the effects of last week's hail on her tomato plants.

You might think she is at a disadvantage because she's not allowed to physically touch the fruits and vegetables in the small shops and open markets. That job is left to the vendors themselves. Actually, the setup suits her just fine. Her greengrocer knows he'll never hear the end of it if he sends her home with eggplants that are bitter or green beans that are past their prime. Of course, he might offer her some slightly overripe apricots at a discount, suggesting that she use them to make jam, or sell her twenty baby artichokes for the price of fifteen. Chances are he'll also remember that she likes her salad tomatoes on the tart side and prefers the local pale green ribbed zucchini to the ones that come from southern Italy.

There are few more valuable culinary learning experiences available for the enthusiastic cook than that of buying food in Italy's farmers' markets and small shops. Where else can you find someone to tell you how to cook a type of shellfish you'd only first seen that morning, advise you as to the best tomatoes to use for canning, or help you solve any one of a thousand gastronomic dilemmas? After a few visits to the same place, you will surely be asked your name, what it is you're doing in Italy, and how you like it there. You'll be offered centuries' worth of inherited culinary advice, a handful of cherries or a few tangerines for your kids—a generous dose of humanity in an increasingly user-unfriendly world.

Asparagus Giorgione-Style
Asparagi alla Giorgione
SERVES 4

Northern Italians (Antonio and Jean-Louis are no exception) have a real affinity for asparagus. Antonio especially loves the coveted white asparagus from his hometown, Bassano del Grappa. Jean-Louis is partial to the somewhat rougher-looking but ever-so-flavorful green asparagus that grows on the islands in the lagoon around Venice. You have free rein over which asparagus you use, the only requirement is that they be fresh and crisp. Look for tightly closed tips and unblemished stems.

Antonio named this recipe after Giorgione, one of his favorite Venetian artists—perhaps the spears of asparagus are meant to be reminiscent of paintbrushes, and the creamy yellow sauce in which they are dipped as paint. For a springtime lunch, we like to blanch the asparagus and serve them crunchy and cold; for dinner, we're more likely to cook them until tender and serve warm. "Sauce" is a bit of a misnomer for the creamy egg mixture that accompanies the asparagus, for it is much denser than a true sauce—which is why it's best served in little ramekins nestled next to the asparagus.

32 thin or 20 large asparagus

For the Dipping Sauce

6 hard-boiled eggs (made from very fresh eggs, preferably from free-range chickens)

4 tablespoons extra-virgin olive oil

2 teaspoons white wine vinegar

2 teaspoons Dijon mustard

3 tablespoons finely chopped cornichons

2 tablespoons finely chopped pearl onions (packed in vinegar)

2 teaspoons chopped capers

1 teaspoon finely chopped parsley

Freshly ground black pepper

Kitchen string
4 small ramekins

✑ Put a large pot of unsalted water on the stove to boil.

✑ Chop off the fibrous white ends of the asparagus spears. (The stalk is most tender at the tip and toughest at the base.) Use a potato peeler to pare away any part of the remaining stalk that is still tough and fibrous so that the entire spear will be tender and wholly edible once it is cooked.

✑ Divide the asparagus spears into 4 equal bunches and tie each bunch at the base with kitchen string. Place the asparagus, tips up, in the boiling water and cook for 4 to 6 minutes (depending on the thickness of the asparagus you are using). If you want to serve them cold, plunge the cooked stalks into a large bowl of icy water.

✑ Mash the eggs lightly between the tines of a dinner fork once they have cooled and place them in a blender or food processor together with the olive oil, vinegar, mustard, cornichons, onions, capers, and parsley. You can make the mixture as smooth and creamy or chunky as you wish. Antonio prefers his chunky, Jean-Louis and I usually opt for creamy. Blend the mixture at medium speed for 5 seconds at a time until you've reached a consistency that appeals to you. Add freshly ground black pepper to taste.

↶ Untie the asparagus bundles and place them on individual serving plates. Spoon the egg mixture into the individual ramekins and place 1 ramekin on each plate with the asparagus.

Grilled Marinated Summer Vegetables
Verdure Estive Grigliate
SERVES 6 TO 8

If you're lucky enough to find yourself with an hour to spare in the kitchen, you ought to consider preparing some grilled and marinated vegetables. They'll keep well in the refrigerator for 3 to 4 days and can be used throughout the week in various delicious ways. Many fresh, seasonal vegetables work for this recipe. Our favorites are zucchini, eggplants, mushrooms, carrots, scallions, and red and yellow peppers. Once grilled then marinated for a couple of hours, they can be used as you wish—colorfully arranged on a platter as an appetizer, over mixed lettuces, or with prosciutto, salami, or a fresh, milky mozzarella.

↶ *Variations: Experiment with your marinade—try adding a couple of teaspoons of chopped capers, or using additional fresh aromatic herbs such as Italian parsley, tarragon, or mint.*

For the Marinade

½ cup extra-virgin olive oil

2 cloves garlic, finely chopped

2 tablespoons coarsely chopped fresh basil leaves

2 teaspoons snipped or finely chopped fresh chives

Salt

Freshly ground black pepper or a pinch of crushed red pepper

Vegetables for Grilling

3 medium Japanese eggplants, green
   tops removed

3 medium zucchini, ends removed

6 young carrots, with their green tops

2 red or yellow peppers

½ pound button or cremini mushrooms,
   stems removed

6 scallions

∽ Prepare a medium-hot charcoal or wood barbecue, or heat a stovetop grill over a medium flame.

∽ Combine the olive oil, garlic, herbs, salt, and pepper with a fork. Set aside.

∽ Cut the eggplant and zucchini lengthwise into ¼-inch slices and grill for 3 to 5 minutes on each side until they are cooked through but still firm.

∽ Peel the carrots and cut off all but the first inch of their green tops. Slice the carrots in half lengthwise, drop them in boiling water for 3 minutes, then cool them immediately in a large bowl of ice water. Pat dry, then grill for 1 minute on each side.

∽ Roast the peppers either over a gas flame or under a broiler. To roast over a gas flame, set a pepper directly on top of the burner and turn it frequently until the skin is blackened evenly. Cool the peppers in a sealed container or paper bag for 10 minutes. Peel away their charred skins, remove the seeds, and cut the peppers into 2-inch-wide strips. Alternatively, heat a broiler to very hot and place the peppers on a baking sheet on the top rack of the oven, turning them frequently until they are evenly charred. Cool peppers and prepare as above.

∽ Wipe the mushroom heads with a damp dish towel or, if they are very dirty, rinse them under running water and towel dry. Grill the mushrooms for a couple of minutes on each side until they are cooked through (cooking time will vary depending upon the size of the mushroom).

∽ Cut the roots and tips from the scallions and grill, turning frequently, for a couple of minutes.

∽ Brush the vegetables lightly with the marinade and leave them to rest at room temperature for a couple of hours. Arrange the vegetables on a large platter to serve or store each vegetable separately in the refrigerator.

Terrine of Robiola Cheese
Terrina di Robiola

SERVES 4

If there is one recipe that makes me wish this book had color photos, this is it. Imagine creamy, herbed robiola cheese hidden under a brilliant casing of golden and red peppers, roasted summer zucchini, and fresh basil. Robiola is a soft, creamy cheese usually made from cow's milk. Locanda Veneta chef Massimo Ormani was ecstatic when his cheese supplier told him it was now available in American markets. This is the recipe he created to showcase its delicate, buttery flavor.

1 red pepper, roasted, skinned, and seeded (opposite)

1 yellow pepper, roasted, skinned, and seeded (opposite)

2 zucchini, thinly sliced and grilled (opposite)

1 pound fresh robiola cheese or ½ pound each whipped cream cheese and fresh goat cheese

1 tablespoon chopped fresh thyme leaves

Pinch of salt

Freshly ground black pepper

4 leaves fresh basil

3 cups torn arugula (tear into bite-sized pieces)

6 tablespoons extra-virgin olive oil

4 tablespoons lemon juice

4 ramekins or straight-edged coffee cups, approximately 3½ inches in diameter

⤳ Roast the peppers and grill the zucchini. Set aside to cool.

⤳ With a fork, whip the robiola or the cream cheese and goat cheese, thyme, salt, and pepper until well blended.

⤳ Line the bottom of each ramekin with a layer of roasted peppers. At Locanda Veneta, we cut out little half circles of red and yellow peppers that we match together to form a whole circle covering the bottom of the ramekin. Cut the half circles with a cookie cutter, knife, or with the rim of a glass of roughly the same size as the base of the ramekin.

⌒ Line the sides of each ramekin with 1 or 2 slices of grilled zucchini. Spoon the herbed cheese into each ramekin and refrigerate until ready to serve.

⌒ To serve, turn each ramekin upside down on a salad plate, let the roasted vegetables and cheese slip out of the mold, and place a fresh basil leaf on top. Surround with a scattering of arugula leaves drizzled with olive oil and lemon juice and any extra roasted vegetables remaining.

Eggplant Rolled with Mozzarella and Parmesan
Fagottini di Melanzane

SERVES 4

A *fagotto* is a bundle. These little bundles of eggplants and mozzarella cheese bathed in tomato sauce have been a favorite at Locanda Veneta since the restaurant opened in 1988.

2 large purple eggplants (about
   1½ pounds)
Salt
8 ounces mozzarella cheese, drained
   well if packed in water

1 tablespoon olive oil for panfrying
Generous handful of fresh basil leaves
1½ cups tomato sauce (page 99)
⅓ cup freshly grated Parmesan cheese

⌒ Remove the green tops of the eggplant (where the stem was attached). Cut the eggplant lengthwise into ¼-inch slices, discarding the first and last slices, which are primarily the outer purple skin. Sprinkle the eggplant with salt and place in a colander for 30 minutes to 1 hour while it expels a bit of water and any bitterness it contains. Rinse the eggplant under water and pat dry.

~ While the eggplant is "resting," cut the mozzarella into finger-sized rectangular pieces as long as your eggplant slices are wide. Cut as many pieces of cheese as you have eggplant slices.

~ The eggplant can either be grilled or lightly panfried. Antonio prefers grilling—a couple of minutes on each side over a medium-hot stovetop or outdoor grill—and no added fat is necessary. Leave the eggplant just slightly undercooked so that they're easier to handle. They'll finish cooking in the oven. Remove them carefully from the grill with a metal spatula, taking care not to tear the slices. To panfry, heat 1 tablespoon of olive oil in a nonstick frying pan and cook the eggplant over a medium flame for a couple of minutes on each side.

~ *The assembly:* Preheat oven to 400°. Place a piece of mozzarella and a couple of basil leaves crosswise at the center of each slice of eggplant, then roll the eggplant up like a cigar. Place the little "bundles" in a shallow glass or ceramic baking dish and bake in the oven for 10 minutes. Spoon the tomato sauce over the top, sprinkle with Parmesan cheese and return to the oven for 3 to 5 minutes or until the Parmesan has turned a golden brown and the tomato sauce is bubbling.

~ Serve immediately—3 or 4 *fagottini* per person.

Baked Goat's Cheese Wrapped in Crispy Smoked Pancetta with Sautéed Spinach
Formaggio di Capra alla Pancetta Affumicata e Spinaci Saltati

SERVES 4

This recipe comes from the menu at Ca' Brea, where it has been a favorite with customers for years. We use smoked Italian pancetta or high-quality local bacon to wrap around a savory blend of soft and grated cheeses. Traditional Italian pancetta does not work well with this recipe for it is too highly salted. The cheeses can be blended and wrapped in pancetta up to a day in advance, then cooked at the last minute. The only trick with this recipe is to make very sure that your broiler is extremely hot when you cook these savory morsels and that the cheese has been well chilled—otherwise, the bacon will melt rather than become crisp and brown, and the cheese will come oozing out the side. If your oven has a weak broiler, try broiling in a toaster oven.

6 ounces ricotta cheese, drained

6 ounces soft goat cheese

6 ounces freshly grated Parmesan cheese

24 strips thinly sliced smoked pancetta
　or bacon

1½ pounds fresh spinach

2 cloves garlic, sliced

2 tablespoons extra-virgin olive oil

Salt

12 toothpicks

～ Combine all the cheeses in a mixing bowl to make a paste. Shape the mixture into 12 golf-ball-sized spheres.

～ Wrap each ball of cheese tightly in 2 slices of smoked pancetta, which should completely conceal the cheese. Insert a toothpick through the center of each ball to secure the pancetta in place. Place the balls on a tray and refrigerate for a minimum of 2 hours.

～ When you are ready to cook the pancetta-wrapped cheese, preheat the broiler to high and place a wire oven rack about 3 inches below the broiler element.

～ In the meantime, wash the spinach well, then drain it in a colander without drying the leaves. If your spinach is young and tender, with fine stems and ribs, use the entire leaf, otherwise remove the stems and ribs. Warm the garlic and olive oil in a nonstick skillet over a medium flame. Add the spinach leaves and sauté them lightly until they wilt. Salt to taste.

～ Place the pancetta-wrapped cheese on a shallow baking sheet and broil them, turning once or more, until the pancetta is crispy and evenly browned (8 to 10 minutes). Don't worry if a bit of cheese leaks out.

～ Arrange the spinach on a serving platter. Place the crispy pancetta balls on top (drizzle with a bit of the rendered fat from the baking pan if you're feeling decadent) and serve.

AN ARGUMENT FOR PLANTING A GARDEN

I sort of opted into my first vegetable garden. Jean-Louis had returned to Florence six months before I finished my senior year of college. As soon as school was out, I headed off to Italy to join him. We lived in a somewhat shabby apartment on the edge of town with a small rectangular garden out back. One of the things Jean-Louis had done in my absence was plant a garden. A humble little patch of mixed lettuces, zucchini, tomatoes, and herbs, where he disappeared for entire afternoons to weed, water, snip, and generally provide the tender loving care needed to coax nature into doing its thing.

I barely acknowledged the garden's existence—not out of animosity but rather out of total lack of interest. My culinary repertoire was so limited that I couldn't make much use of its small bounty anyway. The only thing I really paid attention to was the fig tree tucked behind the neat little rows of vegetables. The Fig Newtons of my childhood hardly prepared me for the sweet, lush flavor of a ripe purple fig eaten straight off the tree.

Years later, and slightly older and wiser, the idea of growing my own herbs and vegetables began to appeal to me, the way writing appeals to you if you love to read. I had finally discovered the pleasures of the kitchen. What's more, we were living in our first little house, with our first little child. The thought of us tuning in to the seasons and to nature appealed to my newfound sense of nurturing.

With the usual zest that the novice brings to the unknown, I pored through seed catalogs and gardening manuals, searched for the best providers of seedlings and heirloom vegetable seeds, and began my garden. It didn't take long for me to realize the vast difference there is between the wanting of something and the doing of it.

The truth about gardening is this: For some, it holds a Zen-like appeal—the sweet, rich smell of humus, dewy leaves in the summer morning light, the sound of water as it trickles onto the soil, the hum of bees and insects, birdsong. Even as I write this, I think, "Ahhh." The reality is that, as the Italians say, *"La terra è bassa"* ("The ground is low"), and gardening involves an inordinate amount of stooping and bending. There's always something to do—fertilize, till soil, tie up vines, water, hoe, all in addition to a perpetual battle with the bugs, birds, and other creatures who want to share in your harvest. Your garden is like your child. It relies on you to do all those little things you wish it could do for itself.

The truth of the matter is that I need help in the garden, and get a far greater joy out of going out there with my basket and shears, looking as much like Martha Stewart as I ever will, and picking veggies or snipping small bunches of herbs than I do out of weeding, watering, and pruning.

Whatever your pleasure to pain threshold, do try to grow something. If you are just starting out and don't have loads of help, take it slowly. Plant the things you love to eat as well as things like tomatoes, which never taste quite as good as they do when they're eaten fresh from the garden. Plant things your kids will have fun with. Like peas. Or pumpkins.

Five pumpkin seeds will give you more pumpkins than you'll ever know what to do with. On the other hand, you need an unbelievable amount of pea vines to come up with a bowl of peas for a family of four. Try planting just a handful of peas— or, better yet, let your children plant them. Before you can say "Jack in the Beanstalk," your hungry little savages will be following you out to the garden to pluck sugary peas from their pods while you go about your horticultural business. They will gasp in delight at the brilliant orange pumpkins resting heavily in the garden. What's more, they will astonish you with the speed with which they learn to pick perfectly ripe cherry tomatoes, the sweetest peas, and whatever else appeals to their tender tastebuds.

If you live in a city and have no garden of your own, look into community gardens. If you don't have the time or inclination for major gardening, then buy a few small terracotta pots and get a miniature herb garden going in a sunny window.

Growing food connects you to the seasons, it gives you a sensitivity to flavors, and inspires you to create with what is right under your nose. One way or another, try to do it—even if only in the tiniest way.

Fried Zucchini and Zucchini Blossoms
Zucchini Fritti
SERVES 4 TO 6

Zucchini are some of the easiest and most satisfying plants to grow in a summer garden. At the beginning of the season, the sprawling vines are covered with a colorful blend of tender young zucchini with their small orangy-yellow blossoms still clinging to their tips, and showy large male flowers at the end of long, thin stems. The size, texture, and flavor of the male flowers make them best for eating—the female flower gives most of her essence to the squash. If you grow your own zucchini, pick the blossoms early in the morning, when the flowers are open and bathed in dew. At the market, look for blossoms whose petals, whether open or closed, look crisp and fresh.

For the Batter
1 egg, lightly beaten
½ cup milk
½ cup all-purpose flour
⅓ cup grated Parmesan cheese

For the Zucchini and Blossoms
16 zucchini blossoms
Corn or soy oil for frying
4 small, tender zucchini, halved crosswise, then quartered into sticks
Salt

The batter: Beat the egg and milk together in a small bowl. Place the flour in a separate bowl. Slowly pour in the egg and milk mixture, stirring continuously with a fork until you achieve a smooth batter. Mix in the Parmesan and allow the batter to rest for 30 minutes.

The zucchini and blossoms: Remove the stems from the blossoms, then cut down one side of the blossom so that you can open it flat like a hand with long, pointed fingers. Remove the pistils and then gently wash the blossoms in cold water and pat dry with paper towels.

Heat a large, heavy-bottomed skillet with ¼ inch oil. Coat the blossoms and zucchini sticks well with the batter. Drip off excess batter before frying. Test the oil by adding a drop of batter to the pan. It should sizzle on contact.

Fry the zucchini pieces first, adding them carefully to the pan so not to splatter the oil. Use 2 forks to turn them occasionally so that they color evenly. Use a slotted skimmer to remove them from the pan when they have turned golden. Place them on 2 or 3 layers of paper towels and blot free of excess oil. Sprinkle with salt.

Give the oil a minute to heat up again and use a slotted spoon to skim off any stray pieces of batter. Lay the zucchini blossoms flat in the pan, turning them over once or twice so that they brown evenly. Pick them gently out of the oil with metal tongs, allowing as much oil to drop back into the pan as possible, then blot free of excess oil on paper towels. Salt and serve with fried zucchini sticks.

Spring Artichoke and Sage Leaf Fritters
Carciofi e Salvia Fritta
SERVES 4 TO 6

Batter-dipped little wedges of artichokes fried until crunchy on the outside and wonderfully soft and steamy inside. Although the sage leaves certainly won't fill you up, each one of the crisp aromatic little fritters is laden with flavor.

For the Batter

¾ cup all-purpose flour

Pinch of salt

1 egg, separated

1 tablespoon extra-virgin olive oil

2 tablespoons dry white wine

⅓ cup cold water (approximately)

For the Vegetables

8 very fresh baby artichokes, cleaned
down to their hearts, stems, and
tender leaves (page 59)

1 lemon, quartered

30 large sage leaves

Corn or soy oil for frying

Salt

⌁ *The batter:* Pour the flour into a mound in a medium mixing bowl and make a well in the center. Sprinkle with a pinch of salt. Lightly beat the egg yolk, then add it with the oil and wine to the center of the well. Mix the ingredients with a wooden spoon to slowly incorporate the flour from the sides of the well. Gradually stir in enough cold water to form a batter that is smooth but not runny. Cover and refrigerate for at least 2 (but no longer than 12) hours.

⌁ Beat the white of 1 egg stiff and fold it into the batter just before using.

⌁ *The fritters:* Slice the cleaned artichokes into wedges (4 to 6 wedges per artichoke) and squeeze with lemon juice. Wash the sage leaves and pat them dry. Heat a large, heavy-bottomed skillet with ¼ inch oil. Coat the artichokes and sage leaves well with the batter. Drip off excess batter before frying. Test the oil by adding a drop of batter to the pan. It should sizzle on contact but not burn.

⌁ Fry the artichokes first, adding them carefully to the pan so as not to splatter the oil and using 2 forks to turn them occasionally so that they color evenly. Use a slotted skimmer to remove the artichokes from the pan when they have turned golden. Place them on 2 or 3 layers of paper towels and blot free of excess oil. Sprinkle with salt.

⌁ Line a small basket with paper napkins. Give the oil a minute to reheat and use a slotted spoon to skim off any stray pieces of batter remaining in the oil. Lay the sage leaves flat in the oil, turning them over once or twice so that they brown evenly. Use a slotted skimmer to lift them out of the oil, drain on paper towels, and salt.

〜 Transfer the fried artichokes to the basket, scatter with the fried sage leaves, and serve immediately.

Belgian Endive and Radicchio with Aged Balsamic Vinegar
Indivia e Radicchio al Balsamico

SERVES 4

Good aged balsamic vinegar is like a fine old wine—smooth and mellow, infused with rich, complex flavors. Inexpensive, mass-produced balsamics are sugary and acidic, they aren't suitable for this recipe, which relies on the ripe flavor of age. Grilling radicchio brings out its bitterness, and although we prefer the sharper flavor of long-leafed radicchio di Treviso, if you wish you may substitute with the milder flavored round heads of radicchio from Verona.

3 small Belgian endives

2 medium radicchio di Treviso or 2 small, tight heads of radicchio di Verona

2 tablespoons extra-virgin olive oil

Salt

Freshly ground black pepper

¾ cup freshly grated Parmesan cheese

3 tablespoons aged balsamic vinegar

1 ounce Parmesan cheese, cut into thin shavings

〜 Preheat your oven to broil.

〜 Halve the endives lengthwise and quarter the radicchio. Do not core the radicchio as the core is what will hold the leaves together once you cut it. Paint the outer leaves with olive oil and sprinkle with salt and pepper.

Heat a large nonstick skillet over a medium flame. Lay the endive and radicchio pieces side by side in the pan and cook until lightly brown on all sides, turning carefully to allow for even cooking, and taking care not to allow the leaves to burn. Depending on its size, the radicchio may take slightly less time to cook.

Transfer the endive and the radicchio to a baking pan, sprinkle the grated Parmesan evenly over the top, and put the pan under the broiler for a couple of minutes until the cheese turns golden brown.

Arrange the vegetables on a serving dish, sprinkle with the balsamic vinegar, scatter the shaved Parmesan over the top, and bring to the table immediately.

THE RIALTO FISH MARKET

8:00 A.M. Just off the Canal Grande, steps from the Rialto Bridge, Venice's fish market is coming to life.

Whack, whack, chop, chop, chop. The youngest fishmongers go through buckets of fish—hacking off heads and tails with rhythmic efficiency.

"Oh, Marco!" shouts a voice. "Marco!" echoes another, in part of the endless running conversation that ricochets from stand to stand throughout the marketplace.

Jean-Louis and I walk from counter to counter, overwhelmed by the sheer abundance and variety of the offerings. There surely is more seafood in this one tiny square than in all of Tuscany—tables are heaped with fish, shellfish, eels, some things familiar, others strange and exotic. The first thing I notice is the movement—fish flopping over and over; shrimp waving their tiny legs; long flat *canocchie* or mantis shrimp flexing their muscles; lobsters trying to snap their claws. It is spring, and the lagoon crabs, *moeche*, have shed their shells and crawl over each other, nearly naked and wholly edible. There are pink shrimp and almost colorless shrimp, some so tiny they look more like insects than crustaceans.

Signs everywhere compete to draw our eyes to the local fish—*"pesce nostrani."* There are *sgombri* or mackerel, with bright, shiny backs and iridescent waves of blue-green stripes along their slick bodies; brutish-looking *san pietro,* whose lower jaws are thrust forward in seeming defiance of their fate; *seppie* or cuttlefish covered in black ink; warriorlike *scorfani* used in fish soup; elegant *dentice,* and *orate,* the acknowledged queens of the sea, as beautiful on the plate as on the palate.

The bountiful tables of Rialto's *mercato di pesce* have inspired us immeasurably both at home and in our restaurants—make the market a required stop if you ever find yourself in Venice.

Venetian Seafood Salad
Insalata di Mare
SERVES 4

Some version of this salad is a standard in many Venetian restaurants. The flavors are best when the shellfish are still warm. Serve with a crusty country bread and a well-chilled bottle of Pinot Grigio or other crisp white wine.

1 red pepper, roasted, peeled, and seeded (page 68)

1 yellow pepper, roasted, peeled, and seeded (page 68)

12 black mussels, scrubbed and debearded

12 manila or littleneck clams, soaked for 2 hours in several changes of lightly salted water

12 medium bay scallops, without shells and rinsed

12 medium shrimp, peeled and deveined

6 ounces calamari, cut into strips

½ cup olive oil

¼ cup fresh lemon juice

2 teaspoons finely chopped garlic

Pinch of crushed red pepper

Salt

Freshly ground black pepper

6 imported marinated artichoke hearts, drained and quartered

A few fresh basil leaves, torn into small pieces

∾ Cut the roasted peppers into thin strips. Set aside.

∾ Poach the seafood separately in simmering salted water. Mussels and clams should be cooked 5 to 7 minutes, until their shells open. Discard any unopened shells. Scallops, shrimp, and calamari should be cooked 5 to 7 minutes, until opaque. Drain all the seafood and let cool. Set aside until ready to use.

∾ In a small bowl, whisk together the olive oil, lemon juice, garlic, and red pepper. Season to taste with salt and freshly ground black pepper.

∾ Combine the cooled seafood (keeping the mussels and clams in their shells), peppers, artichokes, and basil in a large bowl. Pour the dressing over the top and mix to coat thoroughly. Serve immediately.

Fresh Clams Poached in Tomatoes, White Wine, and Garlic

Vongole ai Pomodori e Profumo d'Aglio

SERVES 4

Venice's Lido, like most Italian beaches, does its best to provide all the comforts of home at the seaside—private wooden cabanas to dress or rest in, fancy lounge chairs, large umbrellas, and, of course, a bar and restaurant. Locanda Veneta is a far cry from the lazy pleasures of the Adriatic. But when the waiter sets before you a glass of cold white wine and a bowl of tiny clams, smelling of the sea, garlic, and wine, you might just feel like you're there. If you don't have the time to make tomato sauce, just eliminate it from the recipe and enjoy the clams steeped in garlic and wine.

NOTE: Fresh clams should have an appealing, saltwater scent and tightly closed shells. As luck would have it, most clams that aren't fit for eating do not open their shells when cooked. They should be discarded. Very occasionally, a bad clam does open during cooking. Although it may be hidden among several pounds of shells, it will identify itself in the stock pot by a sharp, unpleasant odor. You don't need to throw the whole batch of clams away. Instead, spread them out on a large platter and use your nose to identify the culprit. Discard the offending clam and serve the rest.

2 pounds fresh manila or littleneck
    clams in their shells
⅓ cup olive oil
8 cloves garlic, sliced, plus 2 cloves to
    rub on bread
1 tablespoon finely chopped Italian
    parsley
½ glass dry white wine

1 small red chili pepper, broken into
    small pieces, or a pinch of crushed
    red pepper
1 cup tomato sauce (page 99)
4 thick slices country bread, toasted to a
    golden brown and cut in half
Extra-virgin olive oil for drizzling

Rinse the clams. Soak them for 1 hour in several changes of lightly salted water. Drain.

Heat the olive oil in a large saucepan and add the garlic. When it turns a light golden color, add the clams, parsley, white wine, and chili pepper. Stir for a minute while the alcohol evaporates. Add the tomato sauce, stir, then cover the pan and cook until the clam shells open (3 to 4 minutes), shaking the pan occasionally. Do not overcook or the clams will become rubbery.

Divide the clams among 4 shallow bowls. Discard any unopened clams. Serve with toasted country bread rubbed with fresh garlic and drizzled with extra-virgin olive oil.

Fried Baby Whitebait
Bianchetti Fritti

SERVES 4

This simple recipe became one of Locanda Veneta's signature dishes when the restaurant first opened. Our customers couldn't get enough of the tiny fish, fried to a golden crisp and eaten whole. The hardest thing about this recipe is actually finding the whitebait. Get chummy with your local fishmonger and ask him or her to find you whitebait no longer than 1 to 2 inches.

12 ounces whitebait, no greater than 2 inches in length
1 cup all-purpose white flour
2 cups corn or soy oil
Salt
2 lemons, cut into wedges

～ Pat the fish dry with paper towels. Just before frying the whitebait, place them in a large bowl with the flour. Toss to coat lightly, then transfer the fish to a mesh colander and shake gently over the sink to remove as much excess flour as possible.

～ In the meantime, heat 2 inches of oil in a tall, heavy-bottomed saucepan. Test the oil for readiness by dipping 1 whitebait into the pot. The oil should sizzle on contact with the fish but should not smoke.

～ Fry the fish in 2 or 3 batches until golden (2 to 3 minutes), allowing the oil to reheat between batches. Be prepared for the oil to bubble up dramatically each time the fish is added to the pot. Drain between several layers of paper towels. Sprinkle with salt and serve hot with wedges of fresh lemon.

Mixed Fry of Squid and Summer Vegetables
Frittura di Calamari e Verdure

SERVES 4

When Antonio gave me this recipe, I was sure it wouldn't work. How on earth could all the vegetables go into the oil at once? Surely, the paper-thin sage leaves would be burned to a crisp while the carrots were still raw and crunchy. I decided to follow his instructions to the letter, devising the revised recipe in my head while I worked. To my great surprise (as is always the case when I am wrong), I *was* wrong. Each vegetable was cooked to perfection while retaining its own texture and flavor—from crisp and crunchy to soft and steaming hot.

1½ pounds fresh squid, preferably small, bodies cut into ½-inch rings, tentacles left whole

3 eggs

Abundant corn or soy oil for frying

2 cups all-purpose flour for dredging

1 carrot, peeled and quartered lengthwise

1 zucchini, quartered lengthwise

2 artichokes, cleaned down to their hearts and tender leaves and quartered (page 59)

4 broccoli florets

4 cauliflower buds

4 asparagus spears

4 1-inch-wide strips of red or yellow pepper

4 spring onions, roots and tip ends removed

12 whole garlic cloves, peeled

12 whole sage leaves

Salt

2 lemons

〜 Rinse the squid pieces under cold water and dry *thoroughly*.

〜 Beat together 3 eggs with an equal amount of water. Set aside.

〜 Heat 1½ inches of corn or soy oil in a pot approximately 12 inches wide and 4 to 6 inches deep. The oil should be hot but not smoking. Test it for readiness by dipping a small piece of squid into the pot. The oil is hot enough when the squid sizzles immediately upon contact.

∽ Fry the vegetables first. Dip them in the egg for 30 seconds, then in the flour until coated. Shake off any excess flour and put all the vegetables in to fry together until golden. Remove the cooked vegetables with a mesh or slotted skimmer and blot between paper towels. Salt.

∽ While the oil is reheating, dredge the squid in the flour only, shaking off any excess.

∽ When the oil is hot, add the squid, frying it until it reaches a light golden color. Remove with a skimmer, strain, blot between paper towels and sprinkle with salt.

∽ Arrange the vegetables and squid on a large platter. Garnish with lemon wedges and serve immediately.

TWO TIPS FOR FRYING SQUID

- *Squid should be dry when dredged (coated with flour) and fried immediately thereafter. Otherwise, the moisture from the squid combines with the flour and the squid loses its lightness and becomes heavy and gluey.*
- *Do not overcook squid or they become chewy.*

Marinated Sardines
Sarde in Saor
SERVES 8

Almost every restaurant in Venice offers some form of *antipasto mare* to whet the appetite. At its best, it is a plateful of gifts from the sea, describable by a lexicon rarely used outside the Adriatic. There may be *moscardini* (tiny octopus, the smaller the better, sautéed in olive oil or simply fried); *tartufi di mare* (small, delicate clams, reputed to have aphrodisiac properties); *bottarga* (dried tuna or gray mullet roe); or *canocchie* (the Rialto fish market is filled with these flat, opaque mantis shrimp). You are virtually assured one or two "sarde in saor"—most obviously because sardines are so plentiful and inexpensive but, above all, because they are so wonderfully delicious prepared this way. Remember to make them a couple of days in advance so they can marinate.

2 pounds very fresh, cleaned sardines (have your fishmonger remove the heads, fins, and innards so that only the 2 small fillets joined by the skin will remain)

White flour for dredging

Abundant corn or soy oil for frying

Salt

2 cups olive oil

2 pounds white onions, cut crosswise into thin rings

½ cup white wine vinegar

∽ Coat the sardine fillets with flour and set them aside. In a large skillet 4 to 6 inches deep, heat 1½ inches of corn or soy oil until hot but not smoking. Test the temperature by dipping the tip of a sardine into the pot. The oil is hot enough when the fish sizzles immediately on contact.

∽ Fry the sardines, turning them once until they are golden on both sides. Blot between paper towels, then salt well.

∽ In a separate skillet, heat the olive oil over a low flame. Add the onions and sauté gently until they become soft and translucent (8 to 10 minutes). Stir in the vinegar and continue cooking for 5 more minutes.

∽ Cover the bottom of a 3-inch-deep glass or terra-cotta dish with a layer of sardines. Coat with a layer of onions in their sauce. Continue layering the dish with the rest of the sardines and onions, then cover with the remaining oil.

∽ Cover and marinate in the refrigerator for 2 days. Remove from the refrigerator a couple of hours before serving. Eat and enjoy on the second and third day.

"MEATBALLS"
Polpette, Polpettine, e Polpettoni

Some words are harder than others to translate. *Polpetta,* despite the neat eight-letter English definition ("meatball") contained in my *Dizionario Inglese,* is one of those words. The English "meatball" makes me think of red-checkered tablecloths, candles dripping wax over straw-covered fiaschi that once held cheap Chianti, and tangled mounds of overcooked spaghetti swimming in tomato sauce and crowned with enormous round globs of hashed meat. *Polpetta* makes my mouth water.

Polpetta derives from the word *polpa,* a piece of meat without fat or bone. It can be used to describe any bit of ground meat, vegetable, fish, or shellfish, seasoned with anything from onions, garlic, mushrooms, herbs, spices, lemon, cheese, or nuts, and bound with milk-soaked bread, potatoes, rice, egg, or béchamel. This is only the most *basic* description. When they are quite large or shaped like a loaf, they become *polpettone;* when they are rolled into delicate little balls, they might be called *polpettine.* More often than not, the classic *polpetta* is not even ball-shaped, but rather rolled into a golf-ball-sized sphere and pressed down into a thick, succulent patty. A *polpetta* might be dipped in bread crumbs or flour, or splashed with wine before it is panfried, baked, or slowly stewed in tomato sauce, lemon juice, or stock. *Polpettine* might find their way into a sauce for pasta or gnocchi. *Polpettoni* would usually appear as a main course.

At our restaurants, we've always called our *polpette* "dumplings" rather than meatballs—most likely because they bear so feeble a resemblance to what Americans associate with the word "meatball." We offer them as antipasti, made from shrimp and crabmeat and served with wedges of lemon, or from duck and chicken and accompanied by an onion confit.

Oh, yes. And then there are Jean-Louis's *"polpette di Thanksgiving,"* which he constructs with the remnants of Turkey Day by combining leftover roasted turkey with equal amounts of herbed stuffing and mashed potatoes. Perhaps an egg or two to help them bind, a pinch of Parmesan if he's in the mood. Shaped into small patties, doused with white wine, and then panfried. *Buonissimo!*

Meatballs in Tomato Sauce
Polpette al Sugo di Pomodoro
SERVES 4

Spaghetti and meatballs without the spaghetti! Actually, the "balls" are flattened into thick patties, coated with bread crumbs and then lightly fried before finishing off their cooking in tomato sauce. You may use only ground beef if you wish, but the pork adds a somewhat sweeter flavor, which we prefer. They may be eaten hot or at room temperature.

For the Meatballs

1 cup cubed day-old country bread, crusts removed

½ cup milk

12 ounces lean ground beef

6 ounces ground pork

2 eggs, lightly beaten

½ cup grated Parmesan cheese

1 shallot, minced

1 clove garlic, minced

2 tablespoons finely chopped Italian parsley

½ teaspoon salt

Freshly ground black pepper

Pinch of nutmeg

Cooking the Meatballs

1 cup bread crumbs

1 cup red wine

¼ cup extra-virgin olive oil

1 recipe tomato sauce (page 99)

Making the meatballs: Place the bread cubes and milk in a small mixing bowl. Push the bread down into the milk with your fingertips, then leave the bread to soak for about an hour. The mixture will turn into a heavy paste. Break up any solid pieces of bread with your fingers. If the paste is at all watery, form it into a ball and squeeze out as much liquid as you can.

◠ Use a wooden spoon or your hands to combine the meats well in a large mixing bowl. Add the bread-and-milk mixture, eggs, Parmesan, shallot, garlic, parsley, salt, pepper, and nutmeg and combine to form a homogenous paste.

◠ *Cooking the meatballs:* Pour the bread crumbs onto a plate. Dip your hands in the wine and use your palms to gently shape the meat into balls of about 1½ inches in diameter, then flatten them into thick patties and coat them with bread crumbs.

◠ Heat the oil in a large skillet over a medium flame. Panfry the patties for about 2 minutes on each side so that they are lightly browned on the outside but still pink inside. Blot lightly with paper towels.

◠ Pour half of the tomato sauce into a large skillet, distribute the meatballs evenly over the sauce, then spoon the remaining sauce over the top. Simmer uncovered over a medium-low flame for 3 minutes, then turn the meatballs over, cover with sauce, and cook, covered, for another 3 minutes. Turn off the heat and leave the meatballs to rest, covered, for 5 minutes before serving.

Shrimp and Crab Cakes
Polpettine di Gamberi e Granchio

SERVES 4

We like these seafood cakes best with a simple salad of wild greens dressed with olive oil and lemon juice.

1 small onion, minced	1 egg, lightly beaten
2 tablespoons olive oil	1 clove garlic, minced
1 pound medium shrimp, shelled and deveined	1 tablespoon minced Italian parsley
	1 teaspoon salt
8 ounces lump crabmeat, fresh or frozen	Freshly ground black pepper
1 cup bread crumbs	2 lemons, cut into wedges
Corn oil for frying	

Place the minced onion and olive oil in a small pan over low heat and cook until the onion softens and becomes transparent, but does not brown (5 to 6 minutes). Set aside to cool.

In the meantime, rinse the shrimp under running water, then pulse blend in a food processor or use a sharp kitchen knife to chop almost to a pulp. Combine with the crabmeat and egg, then add the chopped cooled onions, garlic, and parsley and season with salt and freshly ground pepper.

Roll the mixture into golf-ball-sized spheres, flatten to a ½-inch thickness and coat well in the bread crumbs. Cover with wax paper or plastic wrap and refrigerate for 2 hours.

To cook the cakes, heat ¼ inch of oil in a large heavy-bottomed skillet over a medium-low flame. When the oil is hot but not smoking, carefully place the cakes into the pan and fry, turning every minute or so until both sides are golden brown and the interior is pale white all the way through (4 to 6 minutes). You may want to cut into one to check for doneness. Take care not to overcook or they will dry out.

Drain on several layers of paper towels. Salt lightly and serve with lemon wedges.

Chicken and Duck Dumplings with Onion Confit
Polpettine di Pollo e Anatra

SERVES 4

We serve this as an appetizer at Locanda Veneta—just double the recipe if you want to serve it as a main course. You can use any combination of ground chicken and duck thigh. The duck makes the polpettine more moist and flavorful, but you can use a combination of dark and light ground chicken with similar results.

1 cup cubed day-old country bread, crusts removed

⅓ cup whole milk

½ pound ground chicken

¼ pound ground duck thigh

2 small eggs, lightly beaten

2 cloves finely chopped garlic

2 tablespoons finely chopped parsley

2 tablespoons grated Parmesan cheese

Pinch of nutmeg

½ teaspoon salt

Freshly ground black pepper

All-purpose flour for dredging

¼ cup corn or soy oil for frying

½ recipe onion confit (recipe follows)

◦ Place the bread cubes and milk in a small mixing bowl. Push the bread down into the milk with your fingertips, then leave the bread to soak for about an hour. The mixture will turn into a heavy paste. Break up any solid pieces of bread with your fingers. If the paste is at all watery, form it into a ball and squeeze out as much liquid as you can.

◦ Add the ground meats, eggs, garlic, parsley, Parmesan, nutmeg, salt, and pepper. Work the ingredients with your hands or a wooden spoon until they form a homogenous paste.

◦ Shape the mixture into golf-ball-sized balls, dust them with flour and then flatten slightly into small, thick patties.

◦ Heat the oil over a medium flame in a heavy-bottomed 12-inch frying pan. Panfry the dumplings, turning them every few minutes until they are cooked through and golden brown on both sides (about 10 minutes; cut into the center of one of the dumplings if you are unsure). Blot between paper towels.

◦ Place a ramekin of onion confit in the center of a serving plate. Arrange the dumplings around it and serve.

Onion Confit
Confit di Cipolla
MAKES ABOUT 2 CUPS

Antonio explained to me that the secret to this confit is to "suffocate" the onions in their own moisture, which is done by sautéing them gently and then cooking them covered in their own juices. The balsamic vinegar adds a mellow sweetness that is not at all sugary and the onions take on the texture of a savory marmalade. At Locanda Veneta, we use this confit to accompany our duck and chicken dumplings. Try it on roasted meats or spread on thinly sliced toasted bread.

4 white or yellow onions, halved lengthwise, then thinly sliced
4 tablespoons olive oil
2 tablespoons balsamic vinegar
Salt

 Place the onions and olive oil in a medium heavy-bottomed saucepan. Gently sauté over a medium flame, stirring quite often while the onions sweat out their moisture and soften.

 After 10 minutes, stir in the balsamic vinegar and cook uncovered for 3 minutes, stirring well. Reduce the flame to low, and add salt to taste. Cover the pot and cook for an additional 30 to 35 minutes, checking every so often to make sure that the onions don't dry out completely and begin to burn. You can add a bit of water to the pot as necessary.

 Transfer into a small bowl or several ramekins or refrigerate for up to 3 days to use as needed.

COOK LIKE A KID

Why is it such a pleasure to watch Antonio work? Because he is a sensualist. He does nothing by rote—not the shopping, not the blending together of ingredients, not even the stirring of a simmering pot of sauce. His approach to cooking is at once both childlike and adult. Adult because when he describes to Jean-Louis and me how he rolls and shapes dumplings there are moments when it's not quite clear whether he's veered from the topic of conversation to the wonders of his lover's body. Childlike because he is incapable of cooking without unleashing his full range of senses.

"Don't let anyone tell you that cooking isn't a messy business," he announces. "When you think kitchen, don't think sterile laboratory—think kindergarten art class. Or sit and watch a toddler for a bit . . . then cook like he plays."

"Just what would a kitchen look like where the 'grown-ups' cooked with the curiosity and sensual abandon of children?" I ask Antonio.

"Ah! Just imagine a roomful of children happily immersed in an art project," he answers. "They will have smocks on—you will have an apron. Their smocks will be dotted with splashes of color, smudges of paint, *signs of creativity*—your apron really ought to look like someone has actually cooked in it. The kindergartners won't be able to resist putting down their paint brushes every so often to actually explore the paints or their canvases with their hands. If your kitchen and your hands are clean, *use* them! A wooden spoon doesn't have one little sensor on it—your hands, your taste buds have what—thousands, millions?"

I think of the day I spent at Jean-Louis's cooking class at the Capezzana winery. They were making local cookies called *biscottini di Prato*. Jean-Louis warned his students that the cookies were very literally *handmade* and they watched as first the flour and salt, then the eggs and other ingredients were poured onto the clean, marble work table, then mixed by hand with the occasional help of a pastry scraper. The students each got a chance to work (and taste) the dough themselves so that they would learn to *sense* when its weight and texture was just right.

Engaging your senses in the kitchen is like enlisting a small but highly skilled army of helpers, each with its own particular contribution to make. Touch, taste, smell and watch what is going on. Taste a pinch of dough (yes, I try it even when it has raw eggs in it—you do your own risk calculation), dip your finger in the batter or a spoon in the sauce to see how it's coming along before you commit to popping your cake in the oven or pouring your sauce over the pasta. The earlier the stage, the easier it is to correct things. You'll be able to decide if the gnocchi needs a pinch more nutmeg or a tad more salt, whether the pasta sauce could use a few more leaves of basil or a touch of hot red pepper.

Enlist your senses when you cook. *They* will be able to tell you more than even the best cookbook.

Primi

ANATOMY OF AN ITALIAN MEAL

For anyone who grew up on some variation of the single-course "meat, potatoes, and green vegetable" dinner, a full-scale Italian meal is nothing less than astonishing. A wedding banquet can last as long as five hours and might include twice as many courses. Even a simple "business lunch" is really nothing of the sort—in most cases, not a word of business is even spoken until dessert plates are cleared and the grappa or whisky brought out.

The gargantuan nuptial feasts directors love to depict in film are only slightly exaggerated parodies of the real thing: two years ago, Jean-Louis's cousin Stefania was married in a small town in the Veneto. Our children fidgeted their way through the pomp and solemnity of the ceremony—an hour of indecipherable Latin, a mile-long serpentine of faithful waiting in line to receive communion, an interminable Kodak moment in front of the church memorializing the event.

Lunch was in the conservatory of a gorgeous Palladian-style villa. And it seemed to never end. There were tiny plates of smoked fish and shellfish from the Adriatic, assorted pâtés and spring vegetables dipped in batter and fried. Then the "first" courses, which were served in small, though not minuscule, portions: two different pastas (one stuffed, one not) and a risotto of wild mushrooms.

Somewhere after the second pasta course every child under the age of twelve had left the table. Through the streaked panes of leaded glass, I watched them run across the garden or crouch behind the labyrinth of manicured hedges and stone fountains in a game of *nascondino,* the Italian version of hide-and-seek. The "grown-ups" were only halfway through the meal. There was still a grapefruit sorbet (purportedly to refresh the palate, although mine seemed beyond hope at this point), fillet of sole with artichokes, duck with new potatoes, and a leafy green salad. It was dusk by the time we called the kids in from the garden and cut into the wedding cake. It takes days to recover from such a feast.

Of course, not every Italian meal is a multicourse gastronomic extravaganza. Still, even the simplest Italian lunch or dinner tends to be played out in more than one act. If there are guests, a meal will almost always begin with some kind of *antipasto*—anything from a simple platter of cured meats to poached clams, marinated vegetables, or one of a thousand other choices. Then the *primo* or first course, which most non-Italians assume will be a pasta of some sort. Never assume anything—a *primo* in Florence is just as likely to be a thick, flavorful soup as it is a pasta. Northern Italy abounds with risotto and polenta. Gnocchi are found throughout Italy, though they will differ depending on what part of Italy you find yourself. Nonetheless, by almost any standard, it is the *primo* that defines the meal, if not Italian cooking itself.

As logic would have it, the *primo* is followed by the *secondo,* or the main course, usually a meat or fish of some kind. Although *contorni* or side dishes exist in Italy as they do in America, their function is far less important. Because American meals are usually focused around one course and a salad, the side dishes are used to round out and balance the main dish. A traditional Italian meal needs very little balancing once you've taken into account the fact that you are also eating an appetizer and/or first course. Restaurants rarely accompany a main course with a side dish, you must order it separately, the most common being sautéed spinach or chard, roasted potatoes, and, at least in Tuscany, small white beans known as "cannellini." A simple green salad is eaten with the main course or just following it. *Il dolce* or dessert can be something as simple and refreshing as a bowl of cherries or as sumptuous as vanilla custard. Finally, a bottle of grappa or digestive liquor (a ghastly herb-flavored alcohol I have yet to acquire a taste for) is brought to the table, tiny cups of espresso are poured into demitasses, and the curtain comes down.

THE POETRY OF PASTA

What culinary staple is better suited for the frantic pace of modern life than commercially made pasta? Its beauty comes from its simplicity and that it requires so very little to be happy—a bit of olive oil, a clove of garlic—and it is on its way to pleasing most every palate. Just a pound of penne, rigatoni, spaghetti, or more unusual shapes like corkscrews, bow

ties, shells, or snails, will get you through most gastronomic emergencies. And though it is delicious almost naked, quality Italian dried pasta is just as good with the strong, bold flavors found in a fiery hot tomato sauce or inky black olive pesto; and it holds up beautifully to more substantial sauces like the one with lentils, roasted tomatoes, and spinach that is a favorite at Locanda Veneta.

Homemade pasta is an entirely different creature. A relic from another time—when there was time . . . and pleasure derived from the *act* of cooking as well as from its results. "*Pasta fresca,* especially stuffed pasta like ravioli and tortelloni, is the poetry of Italian cooking," Antonio says with uncharacteristic wistfulness. "I can think of no more satisfying way to express yourself in the kitchen than by making stuffed pastas. They add a wonderful element of complexity to the traditional equation of 'pasta plus sauce.' You can fill a pasta with anything from the most basic ricotta cheese stuffing, or any combination of vegetables, cheeses, meats, and seasonings, to delicacies like lobster or crab. Your sauce can complement your filling, such as artichoke half-moons covered with sautéed baby artichokes, or contrast it the way the freshness of crabmeat is highlighted by the mellow richness of a creamy saffron sauce."

Whether you only have the time to throw together a quick but intensely flavorful spaghettata with balsamic vinegar or would revel in the fun of a few hours with your hands in dough, there are few areas of Italian cuisine that offer more potential for whimsy and delight—both in the making and the eating.

GENERAL TIPS FOR PASTA

- *Ribbed or rough-textured pastas, such as penne rigate and hand-rolled fresh pasta, hold their sauce better than smooth, slippery pastas.*
- *Always salt the pasta water just after it comes to a boil, then add the pasta once the water returns to a boil. Test the pasta after several minutes when it has begun to soften and add more salt to the water if necessary.*
- *Reserve a bit of the cooking water to add to the pasta if it appears dry once you've tossed it with the sauce. (Fresh egg pasta absorbs much more liquid than store-bought semolina pasta.)*
- *Unless either your pasta or your sauce is very delicate, toss the pasta with the sauce in a large skillet over a medium flame for a minute before serving. The flavor of the sauce will distribute best this way and a smaller amount of sauce will go a lot further.*
- *If you are not tossing your pasta in a skillet, then fill a serving bowl with very hot water to warm it while the pasta boils. Pour out the water just before draining the pasta and toss the pasta with its sauce directly in the serving bowl.*

THE PERFECT TOMATO SAUCE

Great debates have been had in the world of Italian cooking over how to make the perfect tomato sauce. The two major bones of contention are whether it's even worth making tomato sauce with canned, as opposed to fresh, tomatoes; and whether or not it's heresy to add sugar to the sauce to reduce its acidity. You'll find celebrated Italian cooks in separate camps on both of these issues. Often these doyennes of Italian cookery hold their beliefs so steadfastly that they seem to be part of their genetic makeup (which may indeed be the case).

In any event, we will cast ourselves into the fray and offer you our own reasoned contribution to the ongoing debate.

On the question of canned versus fresh tomatoes: There are few things better than a ripe, juicy summer tomato. There are few things more insipid than impostor tomatoes  grown in hothouses or continents thousands of miles away, picked green and ripened en masse in corporate storehouses. Evaluate your choices—if you have before you the real thing, then by all means rejoice and make a big pot of sauce with fresh tomatoes. If not, in our opinion, your time and money is better spent seeking out high-quality canned plum tomatoes (we like Italian San Marzano best). You will end up with a fine tomato sauce. Really.

Regarding sugar: We don't mind a slightly acidic tomato sauce, but many people do. While we wouldn't make a habit of adding sugar to the sauce (just as we wouldn't salt our soup before tasting it), we have no disdain whatsoever for the wise cook who dips a spoon into the sauce after it's simmered awhile and decided, then and there, whether or not it could stand a bit of "mellowing."

Locanda Veneta Tomato Sauce
Sugo di Pomodoro alla Locanda Veneta
MAKES ENOUGH SAUCE FOR PASTA FOR 6

Though the following recipe makes ample sauce for a pasta for six people, we would almost always double the recipe and freeze what's left or keep it in the refrigerator to be consumed by the spoon or cupful in any number of ways over the next two or three days.

3 tablespoons extra-virgin olive oil

1 small onion, finely chopped

1 carrot, peeled and finely chopped

1 stalk celery (leaves and strings removed), finely chopped

2 cloves garlic, peeled and finely chopped

2½ pounds ripe Roma tomatoes, skin
and seeds removed, or a 28-ounce can
of peeled plum tomatoes
A few leaves of fresh basil

Salt
Freshly ground black pepper
Pinch of sugar, optional

Heat the olive oil over a medium flame in a medium, heavy-bottomed saucepan. Add the chopped onion, carrot, celery, and garlic and sauté, stirring frequently until the onions are golden and the carrots and celery are soft (about 15 minutes). You may add a couple of tablespoons of water to the pan during the cooking if the vegetables appear very dry.

Add the tomatoes and basil, reduce the heat to low, and simmer uncovered for 20 minutes. Season to taste with salt and freshly ground black pepper, and if the sauce is too acidic for your taste, add a pinch or two of sugar. Simmer an additional 10 minutes, then blend the sauce until smooth with a hand or stationary blender.

Try this: In the wintertime, omit the basil and add a sprig of rosemary to the sauce during the final 10 minutes of cooking. Remove before pureeing.

Penne with Spicy Tomato Sauce
Penne al Pomodoro e Peperoncino
MAKES 6 LARGE PORTIONS

I should be embarrassed I've ordered this so often at Locanda Veneta. There is something about the spicy, garlicky combination I find hard to resist. It did even more for my childhood friend Stacia, who is convinced that her favorite pasta sent her into a timely labor with her first child! Use penne rigate if you can find them—they are shaped exactly like traditional tube-shaped penne but with a lightly ridged surface that soaks up the sauce wonderfully.

½ cup extra-virgin olive oil

3 medium red onions, finely chopped

2 medium carrots, finely chopped

1 large stalk celery (leaves and strings removed), finely chopped

3 cloves garlic, peeled and finely chopped

One 14½-ounce can Italian plum tomatoes

1 teaspoon crushed red pepper

Handful of fresh basil leaves

Salt

Freshly ground black pepper

1½ pounds imported penne pasta

¼ cup finely chopped Italian parsley

∽ Heat the oil in a medium, heavy-bottomed saucepan. Add the onions, carrots, celery, and garlic and cook over a medium-high heat, stirring frequently, until the vegetables are soft (about 15 minutes). You can add a bit of water to the pot as vegetables cook if they appear very dry.

∽ Add the tomatoes and red pepper, then reduce the heat to medium-low and simmer gently for another 30 minutes, stirring occasionally.

∽ Add the basil leaves and continue simmering for a couple of minutes. Season to taste with salt and freshly ground black pepper, then blend the sauce until smooth with a hand or stationary blender.

∽ Meanwhile, bring a large pot of water to a boil. Add salt, return the water to a boil, then cook the pasta until al dente (10 to 12 minutes). Drain and return the pasta to the pot. Pour the sauce over the pasta and toss well for a minute over a low flame.

∽ Ladle into individual pasta bowls, garnish with chopped parsley, and serve.

Meat Ragù
Ragù di Carne

MAKES AMPLE SAUCE FOR PASTA FOR 6

There are so many variations and uses for meat sauce. It is extraordinary with homemade tagliatelle noodles or over potato gnocchi. Antonio likes the flavor of this ragù best when made with equal amounts of lean ground beef and pork. It can be made with or without tomato, and this recipe gives you the option of doing either. The hardest thing about the preparation of this sauce is making it into the kitchen a couple of hours before dinner to get it on the stove—otherwise it is extremely easy to make and even more delicious to eat. It is well worth doubling the recipe and freezing half of the sauce or using a bit of sauce over the next couple of days in other recipes.

Always offer freshly grated Parmesan at the table with this sauce.

½ ounce dried porcini mushrooms

3 tablespoons extra-virgin olive oil

1 large carrot, finely chopped

1 celery stalk, finely chopped

½ onion, finely chopped

1 clove garlic, minced

3 fresh sage leaves

Sprig of fresh rosemary

½ pound lean ground beef

½ pound lean ground pork

Freshly ground black pepper

½ cup dry white wine

1½ cups cold water

1 clove, wrapped in a bit of cheesecloth

1 bay leaf

Salt

One 14½-ounce can Italian plum tomatoes, crushed, optional

Soak the dried porcini mushrooms in a small bowl of warm water for 20 minutes. Drain and finely chop.

In the meantime, warm the olive oil in a large, heavy-bottomed saucepan. Sauté the carrot, celery, onion, and garlic over a medium flame until soft, stirring often (about 15 minutes).

- Wrap the sage leaves around the length of the rosemary sprig, and secure them with a piece of kitchen twine.

- Add the ground meat to the pan, breaking it into small pieces with a wooden spoon. Distribute the meat evenly over the surface of the pot and let it sit for a minute before stirring. Add the herb bouquet and a generous grinding of black pepper. Increase the flame to high and stir the pot well. When the meat is evenly browned, add the chopped mushrooms and wine. Cook until the wine has almost evaporated, then stir in 1½ cups of water, the clove, and bay leaf, taking care to scrape the bottom and sides of the pot so that nothing sticks. When the liquid reaches a boil, reduce the flame to low and partially cover the pot. Simmer very gently for 45 minutes, stirring from time to time, then adjust the seasonings with salt and freshly ground pepper.

- *Without plum tomatoes:* Remove the lid and finish cooking at a gentle simmer for 30 minutes or until the sauce has reached a medium-thick consistency and is a warm light brown. (You may add a bit of water to adjust the consistency.) Remove the herb bouquet and clove.

- *With plum tomatoes:* Remove the lid, stir in the crushed tomatoes and simmer very gently for 45 minutes, or until the sauce has reached a medium thickness. Remove the herb bouquet and clove.

Porcini Ragù
Sugo Finto
MAKES 6 LARGE PORTIONS

Sugo finto. Fake sauce. A Tuscan would never stoop to calling something "meatless ragù." His is the land of the silver-tongued poet—Dante, Petrarch, the neighborhood butcher, the local farmer. Words, like everything else around those parts, are chosen with care . . . and humor. *Sugo finto* gets its name from its resemblance to traditional Bolognese-style meat sauce (which Florentines refer to simply as "*sugo*"), usually made with finely chopped onions, carrots, celery, and some combination of proscuitto, ground beef, and tomatoes. Here, fresh or dried porcini mushrooms take the place of the meat. Fake or not, this sauce is absolutely delicious in its own right. Use it over pasta, or as we do at Locanda Veneta, as a smoky red sauce for braised artichokes.

Of course, fresh porcini are so hard to come by in the United States that you might think it heresy to blend them—in that case, chop them roughly and sauté them separately for 10 minutes in a couple of tablespoons of olive oil over a medium flame. Prepare and blend the sauce as directed, then stir in the porcini at the end, simmer over a low flame for 3 minutes, and serve.

¼ pound fresh or 1 ounce dried porcini mushrooms

1⅓ cups water (if using dried mushrooms, use the water they have soaked in)

½ cup extra-virgin olive oil

1 large red onion, finely chopped

2 carrots, peeled and finely chopped

2 stalks celery, finely chopped

One 14½-ounce can peeled Roma tomatoes

Generous handful of fresh basil leaves

Salt

Freshly ground black pepper

1½ pounds penne, rigatoni, or other tubular pasta

Freshly grated Parmesan cheese for the table

൹ Wipe fresh porcini mushrooms with a soft, clean towel or, if they are covered with soil, rinse them clean and pat them dry. Thinly slice the stems and caps.

൹ If you are using dried porcini, leave them to soak in a bowl of warm water for 1 hour, then squeeze the water out of them (into the bowl where they soaked) and chop them finely. Reserve 1⅓ cups of soaking water (since the soil and sediment will have fallen to the bottom of the bowl, either skim the liquid off the top or strain it through a cheesecloth).

൹ Heat the olive oil in a medium, heavy-bottomed saucepan over a medium-low flame. Add the onion, carrots and celery and sauté gently, until the vegetables have softened but not browned (about 10 minutes). Stir in the mushrooms, coating them well with the aromatic vegetables and sauté for 3 minutes. Add the tomatoes and basil, stir the pot well, then add the 1⅓ cups water (or soaking water from the mushrooms).

~ Let the sauce simmer uncovered over a low flame for 10 to 15 minutes, stirring occasionally, then season to taste with salt and freshly ground black pepper. Blend the sauce lightly until it reaches a coarse texture. (You may also choose to blend until smooth . . . or not to blend at all!)

~ Boil the pasta in salted water until cooked but still firm. Strain into a large serving bowl, and stir in the sauce. Offer grated Parmesan cheese.

Rigatoni with Chicken and Radicchio
Rigatoni con Pollo e Radicchio
SERVES 4 TO 6

This pasta sauce can just about be made in the time that it takes the pasta to cook. Large-tube pastas like rigatoni are a perfect pairing for this wonderful mixture of flavors. Use round heads of radicchio if the long-leafed variety is unavailable.

½ pound long-leafed radicchio
  di Treviso
3 tablespoons extra-virgin olive oil
2 cloves garlic, finely chopped
1 pound chicken thigh meat, diced
½ cup dry white wine

One 14½-ounce can Italian plum tomatoes
1 pound Italian rigatoni pasta
Salt
1 tablespoon butter
¼ cup freshly grated Parmesan cheese,
  plus Parmesan for the table

~ Quarter the long heads of radicchio lengthwise, then slice the radicchio very finely crosswise. Wash and drain well.

~ Warm the olive oil and garlic in a large skillet over a medium flame. When the garlic is lightly golden and fragrant, add the chicken and stir it in the pan so that it colors evenly. When the chicken has lost its pink color on all sides, pour in the wine. When the alcohol has evaporated, add the tomatoes and crush them in the pan with a wooden spoon. Cook for 3 to 5 minutes over a medium flame, adding ¼ cup of water if the sauce looks dry. Remove the pan from the fire and add the chopped radicchio, stirring well to mix it with the rest of the sauce.

⌒ Boil the rigatoni in abundant salted water until cooked but still al dente (10 to 12 minutes). Drain and transfer to the skillet with the sauce. Add the butter and Parmesan and toss the pasta with the sauce over a medium-high flame for 1 minute. Serve immediately.

AN EMBARRASSMENT OF RICHES

All at once the tomatoes are ripening, their tart, sassy green turning varying shades of red. Late spring's orderly rows of plants, whose tender stalks we tied to a rough trellis of bamboo shoots, have conspired to become summer's untamed jungle of peppery leaves and luscious fruits of every size and persuasion, from grapelike clusters of sweet cherry tomatoes to gargantuan, grapefruit-sized beasts that look like something out of Jack and the Beanstalk.

Wedged in the corner of the garden are a few plants with tiny, yellow pear-shaped tomatoes that hang from their stems like Christmas ornaments. There are bushels and bushels of salad tomatoes. For cooking and preserving, there are both plum tomatoes and the local *pomodori fiorentini,* whose dense, sugary pulp is hidden beneath a thick, ruby skin that gathers at the stem in an accordion of pleats. And then there are the tomatoes in my daughter Michela's garden. Three perfectly tended plants dwarfed by a patch of towering sunflowers. It is an embarrassment of riches, an exercise in plenty. And it is overwhelming.

I am relieved to discover that ours is not the only family drowning in tomatoes. The weekly farmers' market under a canopy of trees in nearby San Casciano displays an astonishing array of canning paraphernalia—mountains of jars, lids, ladles, and labels, as well as huge metal cauldrons for simmering tomato sauce. I've been told that in parts of Italy, especially in the south, entire villages converge for one day of canning, basket upon basket of tomatoes transformed by collective effort into a year's worth of *conserva*. No such luck for us. We will be doing our canning *da soli*—all by ourselves.

We load the car up with Mason jars (called Bormioli here), mostly of the 250- and 500-ml variety, which corresponds roughly to ½-pint and pint jars—anything larger instills too great an apprehension of botulism in my American soul, since the risk of "trouble" increases with the size of the jar. Even still, every year around this time, I am hit with a fear akin to the one that threatens to ruin every Thanksgiving feast (i.e., fear of salmonella versus fear of turkey jerky).

I pore over our books on canning. The Italian ones resemble typical Italian cookbooks with instructions the equivalent of "cook in a hot oven until done." The American books tell us that our loved ones will likely perish if we take one misstep during the process, and are filled with bold-typed admonitions warning us of what we must *never* and *always* do. . . .

"DO NOT SHORT-CUT ANY STEP" . . . "NEVER RETIGHTEN SCREW-BAND LIDS . . . *EVER*" . . . "DESTROY SUSPECT CONTENTS SO THEY CANNOT BE EATEN BY PEOPLE OR ANIMALS". . . .

Surely the inherent dangers in canning (and the fact that between the cost of growing the tomatoes and buying the jars, each ½ pint of homemade *conserva* costs three times its store-bought equivalent) should be enough to dissuade us from the whole process. But it isn't. In the end, we can away. It seems a shame not to. We make the same decision every year, and as of this writing have yet to suffer any dire consequences (knock on wood). Jean-Louis has eaten home-canned tomatoes his entire life, and derives a kind of primordial pleasure out of pulling a jar of home-canned tomato sauce from the pantry in the dead of winter when fresh tomatoes seem the stuff of dreams.

We send Julien and Michela off to the garden with large baskets, clippers, and explicit instructions as to which *pomodori* are to be picked and which are to be left alone. They have been coerced into the task by our promise to give them each a chance to crank the Spremidoro—a contraption that comes down from the black hole above the refrigerator once a year and magically transforms whole, cooked tomatoes into a river of red juice, free of seeds and skin, that spurts out the end of a metal sieve.

Jean-Louis and I sterilize our jars and caps in boiling water, then carefully wash the tomatoes, eliminating any that are blemished or bruised. We place the tomatoes that have passed inspection in a huge pot of boiling water for a couple of minutes, strain them in a colander and leave them alone until they are still hot but cool enough to handle. The kids  take turns popping the tomatoes into the Spremidoro's gaping mouth and cranking the beast until we have filled several large pots with the juice, which we simmer to an appropriately saucy consistency and ladle ("carefully") into jars containing a couple of basil leaves each. We make sure to leave the requisite amount of air space in each jar. We screw on the lids ("firmly but not too forcefully") and process the jars in a boiling-water bath for half an hour as instructed.

Inevitably, somewhere into the process (when it's too late to turn back), I find myself alone in the kitchen. Jean-Louis is watching a movie. The kids have gone to bed. The room is like a subtropical sauna. I stand over the stove drenched in sweat while two huge pots of sauce bubble and thicken, and three even larger pots of rollicking water sterilize way-too-few jars at a time. It seems there is an element of masochism involved in attempting such a task during the height of a Mediterranean summer (which is, of course, the *only* time that tomatoes are in such extravagant abundance). And yet we do it every year. Perhaps it's more like childbirth—if you really remembered what it was like, you'd never do it more than once.

It is nearly two in the morning when I set the last of the ruby jars to cool on the kitchen counter. The house is quiet except for the occasional satisfying "plink" of a pliant metal lid being sucked down by the vacuum created inside the jar. I will not go to sleep until the Spremidoro has been washed and retired for another year, until the only sign of the evening's enormous toil is the sea of jars cooling on the kitchen counter. I am exhausted, but quietly triumphant—we've bottled our riches and will store them for the winter, each jar a kiss of summer past.

Anna's Raw Summer Tomato Sauce
Sugo Crudo di Anna
SERVES 4 TO 6

Our friend Anna, who lives on the Lido of Venice, makes this sauce every summer when even her tiny vegetable garden produces a wild abundance of tomatoes and basil and the weather is too hot and steamy to do much cooking. Since raw garlic in large amounts has a heavy cloying flavor that can stay with you all day, Anna uses just the smallest hint of it— you barely know it's there, but the flavor's not the same without it.

For the Sauce

1 pound fresh plum tomatoes,
   quartered and seeds removed
4 tablespoons extra-virgin olive oil
Handful of fresh basil leaves

⅓ clove garlic
Salt
Pinch of crushed red pepper

1 pound imported dried spaghetti or other pasta

Place all the sauce ingredients in a stationary blender and blend at a medium speed until smooth. Pour the sauce into the bottom of a large serving bowl. Cook the spaghetti or other pasta in abundant boiling water until al dente, drain and toss well with the sauce. Serve immediately.

Whole Wheat Pasta with Olive Pesto and Smoked Mozzarella

Pennette di Grano Saraceno al Pesto d'Ulive e Provola di Bufala

SERVES 4 TO 6

꧁꧂

Whole wheat pasta can take some getting used to—it has a coarse, almost grainy texture, a light brown color, and a flavor decidedly less subtle than its more popular sibling (which, at least in Italy, is made from refined durum wheat). Nonetheless, many of my favorite restaurants in Italy have at least one whole wheat pasta dish on their menus. This recipe is well worth a foray into the world of whole wheat pasta—the smoky flavor of the mozzarella and earthiness of the olive paste are a perfect match for a pasta you can really sink your teeth into.

½ cup extra-virgin olive oil

1 clove garlic, finely chopped

6 ripe medium-sized tomatoes, cut into
    small dice

Handful of fresh basil leaves

3 ounces olive paste

Salt

Freshly ground black pepper

1 pound whole wheat penne, spaghetti,
    or other whole wheat pasta

6 ounces smoked mozzarella cheese,
    diced

꙰ Heat the olive oil over a medium flame in a large, heavy-bottomed skillet. Add the garlic, diced tomatoes, and basil and cook over a medium flame for 10 to 15 minutes until the tomatoes are soft. Stir in the olive paste and season to taste with salt and pepper.

꙰ Cook the pasta in abundant salted water until al dente, then drain in a colander and transfer to a heated serving bowl. Add the tomato-olive sauce, sprinkle with the mozzarella cheese, and toss well.

꙰ Serve at once.

"Spaghettata" with Balsamic Vinegar
Spaghettata al Balsamico
SERVES 4 TO 6

Italians are masters of culinary improvisation. You will never be sent home hungry from an Italian home with the excuse that the cupboard is empty—every Italian (including those men who don't know how to cook one other thing) knows how to throw together *una bella spaghettata*—which, loosely translated, means a "good plate of spaghetti." It's the sort of thing you would eat with friends on a late summer night when you've come home from a movie or dancing. A midnight snack. The classic late-night, last-minute spaghettata is *"olio, aglio, e peperoncino,"* made by lightly heating olive oil and infusing it with garlic and spicy red pepper while spaghetti is already boiling in the pot. Since there is no true "sauce" to speak of, it is more important than ever that the pasta be cooked al dente so it can carry the flavored oil. This recipe is Antonio's variation on the traditional "aglio, olio" theme, only it relies on the simplest mixture of olive oil, herbs, and vegetables, and a last-minute splash of balsamic vinegar to get its wonderful flavor.

4 tablespoons extra-virgin olive oil

¼ white onion, thinly sliced crosswise

1 shallot, thinly sliced

1 fresh sage leaf

1½ tablespoons butter

1 large carrot, finely chopped

1 tablespoon finely chopped Italian parsley

1 teaspoon tomato paste

Salt

Freshly ground black pepper

1 pound imported Italian spaghetti

1½ tablespoons aged balsamic vinegar

∽ Put a large pot of water for the pasta on the stove to boil.

∽ Heat 2 tablespoons of olive oil in a very small saucepan over a low flame. Add the sliced onion, shallot, and sage leaf and cook, stirring frequently, until the onion and shallot are soft and translucent.

Warm the remaining olive oil and butter in a small skillet over a low flame, then add the carrot, parsley, and tomato paste. Cook over a low flame, stirring frequently. After 10 minutes, add ½ cup water and salt and freshly ground black pepper to taste. Continue cooking until the carrots are soft (about another 5 minutes), then stir in onion and shallot mixture. Continue cooking over a very low flame for another 3 to 4 minutes while the flavors meld. Remove the sauce from the heat.

Boil the spaghetti in abundant salted water, until it is still very firm to the bite. Drain well, then toss with the herb and vegetable mixture. Splash with the balsamic vinegar, quickly toss and bring to the table.

Spaghetti with Lentils, Roasted Tomatoes, and Spinach
Spaghetti con Lenticchie, Pomodori, e Spinaci
MAKES 8 LARGE PORTIONS

Winter in Los Angeles is somewhat of an oxymoron. Nonetheless, on those days when the weather is crisp and blustery or gray and damp, you can be sure that the dining room at Locanda Veneta is filled with people feasting on bowls of spaghetti laden with lentils, roasted tomatoes, and spinach. This recipe makes an ample amount of sauce. If you are only cooking for 4, don't reduce the recipe, but set aside the extra sauce to add to a vegetable soup, or eat cold with a salad straight from the fridge. Brown, green, or the tiny bluish *"Puy"* lentils from France can be used for this recipe. Brown or *Puy* lentils keep their shape best—the larger green lentils tend to disintegrate and get mushy when cooked.

For the Lentils
2 cups dry lentils

2 tablespoons extra-virgin olive oil

1 medium onion, finely chopped

6 cups cold water

1 clove garlic, crushed

1 bay leaf

½ teaspoon salt

Freshly ground black pepper

For the Tomatoes

6 ripe plum tomatoes

¼ cup finely chopped Italian parsley

2 cloves garlic, minced

1 tablespoon finely chopped fresh
   oregano or 1½ teaspoons dried
   oregano

Salt

Freshly ground black pepper

Extra-virgin olive oil

The Rest

2 tablespoons extra-virgin olive oil

1 pound fresh spinach, stemmed,
   thoroughly washed, then steamed
   until wilted

2 pounds imported dry spaghetti

Freshly grated Parmesan cheese for the
   table

The lentils: Rinse the lentils well, removing any stones. Warm 2 tablespoons of olive oil in a large saucepan over a medium flame, add the chopped onions and cook until they are soft and translucent, stirring frequently. Add the lentils, 6 cups of water, the crushed garlic clove, and the bay leaf. Bring to a boil, stir, then reduce heat and simmer covered, stirring occasionally, for 45 minutes or until the lentils are cooked but still firm and have absorbed most of their cooking water. Season with salt and a generous grinding of black pepper three quarters of the way through the cooking time.

The tomatoes: Preheat the oven to 400°. Cut the tomatoes in half and lay them cut side up in a medium baking pan. Scatter with the parsley, garlic, and oregano, sprinkle with salt and pepper, then drizzle lightly with olive oil. Roast in the oven for 20 to 30 minutes, until the tomatoes are soft but not leathery.

The pasta: Bring a large pot of salted water to a boil.

In the meantime, heat 2 tablespoons of olive oil in a large saucepan or pot. Add the steamed spinach and the tomatoes. Sauté over a medium-high flame for 1 minute, then stir in the lentils, reduce the flame to medium, and let everything cook together for 4 minutes, stirring regularly.

〜 Boil the pasta in the salted water until al dente. Drain, then pour into the pot with the sauce and toss well over a medium flame for 1 minute.

〜 Offer fresh grated Parmesan.

FRUIT OF THE VINE
Il Vino

The Tuscan hills are a glorious patchwork of grapevines, olive groves, woods, and fields, dotted with farmhouses, small villages, and gently winding roads. From the rich soil come grapes with names like Trebbiano and Malvasia, and olives that are pressed each fall into fragrant, green oil.

It is late February, and a pale winter sun is pushing the countryside toward spring. There are signs of life on hillsides quiet since the last of autumn's red and golden leaves fell from the vines. The annual cycle is about to begin anew—tender stalks climbing out of each gnarled grapevine will be neatly tied down with willow branches; the earth in the vineyard will be tilled; delicate green leaves will begin to sprout along the vines whose limbs stretch and curl around anything within their grasp; clusters of grapes will grow heavy and ripe under the hot summer sun; farmers will pray for some rain, then lots of sun, and then, please God, no rain at all while the grapes are harvested.

But for now the hills are mostly dormant and the supple stalks are bare. It is hard to believe that in a few months the vineyards will be thick with climbing vines and lusty bunches of ripening grapes. By mid-August, while the rest of Italy is off at *il mare,* the grapes begin to turn from light, bright green to various shades of purple. There are few sights in the countryside more lush and exquisitely beautiful than grapes ripening on the vine—each cluster for a brief gorgeous moment a mixed palate of greens and purples, colors so breathtaking you know they could only exist in nature. The grapes themselves are covered in a fine, opaque powder like sugarplums out of a child's fairy tale. This is not purple prose. It is simply impossible to exaggerate such ephemeral beauty.

Then it is September and a moment that feels like a second spring. The thick white summer sky has turned pale blue. High white clouds float along to their private destinations, casting uneven shadows over the landscape. The grapes are almost ripe, but still on the vine gathering their last drops of sweetness from the sun and soil before they are picked. Butterflies flutter around the garden. The roses are once again in bloom. It has rained and there are signs of tender green shoots sprouting where last month the soil was parched and dusty. But there is no sign yet of fall. The leaves are still green, and the cycle still feels like one of growth rather than decline.

The *vendemmia* or grape harvest begins when the fruit hangs heavy under the shade of its wide, green leaves, and has turned as sweet as the sun is strong. Jobs picking the year's harvest are available to anyone with the time and inclination. It isn't easy work and the pay is negligible. The days are still long and hot and the riot of fruit to be gathered appears inexhaustible. Still, almost everyone here has worked harvesting grapes at least once in their lives, if only for the pleasure of sharing a celebratory feast at one long crowded table when the picking is finally done.

By late September, when the country roads are crowded with carts ferrying grapes to the winepress and you can literally smell the must in the air, you begin to understand how seductive the whole grape-to-wine cycle can be. Soon local restaurants and shops will post handwritten signs letting you know that *vino novello,* this year's young wine, has arrived. In the meantime, more complex, robust wines slowly age in wooden casks inside dusky, cool cellars.

We had an acre or so of grapevines for a few years—overgrown and underpruned, but, still, real Chianti vines from which we tried our hardest to make wine. Our neighbor Beatrice watched, bemused, as her husband, André, Jean-Louis, and our gaggle of kids traipsed among the vines, snipping clusters of grapes into large red buckets. She knows a bit about the process herself—her family has been making outstanding wines for generations, and their Capezzana estate produces everything from light, young Chiantis to exquisite full-bodied reds like Ghiaie della Furba.

While Capezzana is known for their success in having woven modern enological innovations with time-honored techniques, our approach to winemaking at home was more primitive, some might say "traditional." The *bambini* were responsible for the first step, which they attacked with relish. Muddy shoes cast aside, socks off, feet washed with soap under the garden hose, they stomped on the grapes until their tiny feet were purple and the heavy clusters of fruit were reduced to a deep red juice. We poured the must into demijohns, which we stored amongst a tangle of farm implements. Every week or so, the men would disappear for a bit, presumably to stir, recite incantations, or otherwise endeavor to help the juice along. I'm sure we were the last people in all of Italy still making wine this way.

Months later, Jean-Louis and André declared the wine as fit to drink as it would ever be. Bea and I got together a loaf of county bread, some local salami, and a bowlful of olives, while our husbands poured some "wine" into a jug.

How to describe the taste of our wine? Like nothing you've ever sipped at before. And sip was all we could do, because, really, the stuff was barely palatable. The men bravely drank on while Bea and I semidiscreetly switched to one of her family's wines.

We've since pulled out our wine grapes and replaced them with about sixty fruit trees, everything from old standards like apples, pears, and plums to quince, pomegranate, and a couple of unusual vines that produce grapes that look more like huge black olives. There are two rows of heirloom grapes that form a leafy arbor down the middle of our kitchen garden. But, otherwise, we have become observers of, rather than participants in, the winemaking process.

Our daily walks take us past small farms where winemaking, even small-scale, is treated as the art—and work—that it is. And while our adventures in winemaking were hardly successful by objective standards, we *did* have fun. More than anything, we developed an enormous respect both for those who take their winemaking seriously and for the ancient alchemy that transforms *uva* into *vino*.

Pennette with Winter Squash
Pennette alla Zucca
SERVES 4 TO 6

Venetian pumpkins are the ugly ducklings of the squash family, especially when compared to their outrageously oversized American cousins. However, inside their green gnarled skin is a brilliant orange flesh, smooth, sweet, and not at all watery. In the Veneto, it makes its way into soups, risotti, pasta, and gnocchi. For Antonio, it was a special childhood treat—roasted whole in the kitchen fireplace, the pumpkin's sugar caramelized and left the house smelling like a candy shop. The best substitutes for Venetian pumpkins are calabaza, kabocha, butternut, and acorn squash.

1 pound winter squash, flesh only

2 tablespoons butter

3 tablespoons extra-virgin olive oil

1 small onion, finely chopped

1 clove garlic, finely chopped

1 cup cold water

2 tablespoons finely chopped Italian parsley

Salt

1 small red chili pepper, broken into pieces, or a pinch of crushed red pepper

1 pound imported pennette

¼ cup freshly grated Parmesan cheese

꙳ Cut the squash into finger-length strips.

꙳ Warm the butter and oil in a large saucepan over a medium flame. Add the onion and garlic and sauté until the onion is translucent and the garlic is lightly golden. Add the squash, stir it around in the pot to coat with the onion, and sauté gently for a couple of minutes over a low flame. Add the water, parsley, a generous pinch of salt, and cook over a low flame for 20 minutes, stirring occasionally. The squash will take on the consistency of a chunky puree.

꙳ Add the red chili pepper and stir well.

Boil the pasta in salted water until al dente. Drain, reserving a cup of cooking water. Return the pasta to the pot, pour on the sauce and toss well over a low flame for a minute, adding some of the reserved cooking water if the sauce is dry or pasty. Stir in Parmesan and serve immediately.

Locanda Veneta Linguine with Rock Shrimp, Asparagus, and Tomato

Linguine della Casa con Gamberi, Asparagi, e Pomodori

SERVES 4 TO 6

This recipe began as a Locanda Veneta special one spring when Executive Chef Massimo Ormani found himself with an abundance of fresh rock shrimp and crunchy asparagus. It was such a hit that it is on the menu whenever the ingredients are available.

¾ pound fresh, thin asparagus

4 tablespoons extra-virgin olive oil

3 cloves garlic, peeled and finely chopped

1 pound rock shrimp or other large shrimp, peeled and deveined

¾ pound plum tomatoes, cut into a small dice

Salt

Freshly ground black pepper

1 pound Italian linguine pasta

Chop off the fibrous white ends of the asparagus spears. Use a potato peeler to pare away any part of the remaining stalk that is still tough and fibrous. Cut the stalks into 1-inch pieces, leaving the tips whole. Steam over simmering water for 5 to 6 minutes, until tender but not soft. Set aside.

Warm the olive oil and garlic in a large, heavy-bottomed skillet. When the garlic is lightly golden, add the shrimp, stir briskly to coat the shrimp in the oil, then add the tomatoes, asparagus, and salt and pepper to taste. Sauté for a couple of minutes until the shrimp is opaque all the way through (test by cutting into one of the shrimp). Take care not to over-cook.

~ Boil the linguine in abundant salted water until cooked but still al dente. Drain the pasta, then add it to the skillet with the sauce (reserving ½ cup of the pasta's cooking water to add to the sauce if it appears too dry). Toss the linguine with the sauce over a medium flame for 30 seconds. Serve immediately.

Spaghetti with Shellfish and Garlic-Laced Tomato Sauce
Spaghetti ai Frutti di Mare
SERVES 4 AS A MAIN COURSE OR 6 AS A FIRST COURSE

To my mind at least, there are few things as inviting to the senses as a shallow bowl of thick, tangled spaghetti heaped with an assortment of seafood cooked in garlic, wine, and tomato. Scallops and tender rings of calamari to eat daintily with a fork; clams and shrimp to pick up with the fingers and suck out of their shells; firm thick strings of pasta to soak up the extraordinary blend of flavors. And yet, for all its sensory extravagance, if you have a bit of tomato sauce already handy (always a good idea), this sauce can be made in the time it takes the pasta to boil. Serve this dish to people you are comfortable eating with—you'll want to be able to use your hands as well as your fork to make your way through the abundance before you.

Salt

1 pound thick spaghetti

½ cup extra-virgin olive oil

12 cloves garlic, finely chopped

1 pound fresh manila or littleneck clams, soaked for 2 hours in several changes of lightly salted water

½ pound sea scallops

½ pound small calamari, tentacles whole, pouch cut into rings

½ cup dry white wine

1 tablespoon finely chopped parsley

1 cup tomato sauce (page 99)

16 large shrimp in their shells (you may substitute shelled shrimp)

Freshly ground black pepper

Pinch of crush red pepper, optional

Have all your ingredients chopped or otherwise prepared before beginning to boil the pasta. Heat a large pot of water to boiling. Add salt and then the spaghetti.

While the pasta is cooking, heat the olive oil and garlic over medium heat in a stockpot. When the garlic has colored slightly, add the clams, scallops, and calamari, stirring well to coat with the fragrant oil. Add the wine, sprinkle with parsley, and continue stirring for a minute while the alcohol reduces. Stir in the tomato sauce and shrimp, then season with a grinding of black pepper and, if you wish, a pinch of red pepper. Stir well for a couple of minutes. Cover the pot and turn off the heat. (You may add ¼ cup of water if the sauce appears too thick.) The residual heat in the pan will finish cooking the seafood while the pasta finishes boiling. The sauce is ready when the clamshells have opened.

Drain the pasta when it is al dente (10 to 12 minutes). Serve the pasta immediately in individual bowls, then spoon a portion of sauce and shellfish onto each bowl. Discard unopened shells. (Italians, incidentally, would never use Parmesan on a tomato-based seafood pasta.)

Lasagna with Bell Peppers, Eggplant, Zucchini, and Mushrooms
Lasagne alle Verdure Estive
SERVES 8

This is an especially wonderful treat for vegetarians—the flavors are sumptuous and full, a well-deserved respite from the ubiquitous "mixed vegetable plate" that for years seemed to be the only thing restaurants could muster up to offer their vegetable-loving friends. There's no denying that this recipe requires a bit of work to prepare. The good news is that you can assemble the lasagna hours before it actually needs to go into the oven.

Salt

Extra-virgin olive oil

9 lasagna sheets (13 by 3 inches each)

2 red or yellow peppers

1 small round eggplant, halved crosswise, then thinly sliced

1 medium zucchini, halved crosswise, then thinly sliced

½ cup all-purpose flour for dusting

8 ounces button or cremini mushrooms, thinly sliced

¼ small onion, finely chopped

Freshly ground black pepper

3 cups tomato sauce (page 99)

12 ounces mozzarella cheese, drained and sliced

1 cup freshly grated Parmesan cheese

⸱⸱⸱ Bring a large pot of salted water to a boil. Add 1 tablespoon of olive oil to the water (this will keep the sheets of lasagna from sticking together). Cook the lasagna sheets in two batches for 5 to 8 minutes, until they are pliant but still undercooked. Drain, then drape the sheets of pasta over the sides of a colander or your pasta pot.

⸱⸱⸱ Roast the peppers over a gas burner or under the broiler, using tongs to turn them frequently so that they roast evenly. When the peppers are charred on all sides, place them in a sealed container or paper bag for 10 minutes. Peel away their skins, remove the seeds, and slice the peppers into thin strips. Set aside.

⮑ Preheat the oven to 350°.

⮑ Dust the eggplant and zucchini slices with flour, keeping the 2 vegetables separate. Heat 2 tablespoons of olive oil over a medium flame in a heavy-bottomed skillet, then lay the eggplant slices in 1 even layer in the pan. Cook until lightly golden, about 2 minutes per side. Sprinkle with salt and set aside. Add a bit of oil to the skillet and cook the zucchini as you did the eggplant, so that they are firm but lightly golden on both sides. Sprinkle with salt and set aside.

⮑ Sauté the mushrooms and onion in 2 tablespoons of olive oil over a medium flame until soft (about 8 minutes). Season with salt and a generous grinding of black pepper.

⮑ *Assembling the lasagna:* Pour ¾ cup of tomato sauce into a 9 by 13-inch baking pan. Lay 3 sheets of lasagna over the sauce to cover. Top with the slices of eggplant, half of the roasted peppers, half of the mozzarella, half of the Parmesan, and 1 cup of tomato sauce. Place another layer of lasagna sheets over the top, then cover with the zucchini, mushrooms, remaining peppers, and remaining mozzarella cheese. Cover with a last layer of lasagna sheets, the remaining tomato sauce, and remaining Parmesan cheese.

⮑ Cover with aluminum foil and bake for 40 minutes. Remove the foil and bake for another 10 minutes until the Parmesan has turned a golden color. Remove the dish from the oven and leave to rest for a couple of minutes before serving.

"LESSON NUMBER ONE"

Julien, Michela, and I were still under the veranda mulling over a late summer breakfast when we saw the ancient black Mercedes-Benz with California license plates lumbering up the rutted dirt road leading to our house, a billowing trail of dust in its wake.

"Tony! . . . Vanessa!," my kids shouted, springing up from their chairs and racing off to greet the car. Antonio had arrived for a week of recipe testing, his friend Alessandra and his two kids, Antonio ("Tony" to avoid confusion) and Vanessa, in tow. The little group was drenched in sweat and panting like a pack of overheated dogs, the result of the car's failed air-conditioning unit and what Italian newspapers were billing as "The Hottest July in the Last 600 Years!!!" Exactly what meteorological records were consulted to back up this assertion I cannot even begin to imagine. Nonetheless, substantiated or not, it sure *felt* like the hottest summer this millennium. Certainly not the sort of weather anyone in their right mind would choose for a week in the kitchen, burners all aflame and the oven roaring like a furnace.

Upon seeing each other, the *bambini,* as *bambini* do, recovered instantly from their heat exhaustion and sped off to jump on the trampoline and careen around the garden on bicycles. They would happily keep each other company while we sliced, sautéed, simmered, and sweated out a week-long culinary marathon. Jean-Louis, unfortunately, would miss all the "fun"—he was back in LA manning the restaurants in the air-conditioned comfort that one can only dream of in the Tuscan countryside.

We spent the morning drinking tall glasses of iced peach tea and plotting our strategy for the week. Antonio roamed around the garden and poked through the cupboards and refrigerator to see what raw ingredients I had to offer. It certainly wasn't the first time he had cooked in our kitchen—but, until now, he had never cooked there with the degree of earnestness it would take to make our way through the gigantic menu we had scrawled out on the kitchen blackboard.

We decided to begin by making fresh pasta dough, first from white flour and egg, then from a mixture of bread crumbs and flour. Antonio would show me how to gauge the dough's moisture, and how to roll it out and cut or shape it into tagliatelli, tagliolini, ravioli, agnolotti, tortelloni, and several other forms I had never before encountered, much less attempted to execute. We would make a dozen or so fillings to stuff the scalloped-edged squares and crescents we cut out with a rolling metal pasta blade. Then we would move on to gnocchi, made with varying combinations of potatoes, pumpkins, and bread and topped with tiny meatballs, crumbled sausage, butter and sage, or one of any number of sauces that would be simmering on the stove in the coming days.

We compiled a shopping list, set off for the market and returned home, a couple of hours later, arms loaded with the essential ingredients necessary for our enterprise. As we began to unpack our purchases, I noticed a subtle shift in Antonio's demeanor. It dawned on me that for the moment at least Antonio was no longer my old friend preparing to cook a casual meal in my kitchen. He was a *chef,* it was *his* kitchen—and he had no intention of cooking in it until it was set up in a way that made culinary sense to him.

He opened the cupboards, I assumed (naïvely) to put things away. Instead, he began to pull things from the shelves, consult their freshness dates, and query me as to when they had been opened. I watched as he slowly and methodically dismantled my entire pantry. When he had finally finished, he stood accusingly next to the long marble work counter now heaped with seven or eight opened bags of polenta, an equal number of flours, an embarrassing jumble of herbs, spices, and tins (more than a few way past their expiration dates), and a collection of small paper bags and pouches containing still more spices and powders, a few of which were completely unidentifiable (baking powder, baking soda, cream of tartar???).

"*E allora?*" he asked rhetorically. In this humiliating context, I took the question to mean something between "What do you have to say for yourself?" and "What are we going to do with this mess?"

"Not a lot," was my silent response to the first question. "I don't know," my answer to the second.

In the end, we opened a couple of industrial-size trash bags and filled them with whatever Antonio, who was now clearly in charge of this operation, deemed unfit for the kitchen. I was assigned the task of wiping the bare cupboards with an alcohol-drenched rag, while Alessandra used a vinegar-soaked cloth to rub clean the bottles and jars that had passed inspection. I was then dispatched to the nearest town to fetch a battery of clear glass jars, canning labels, and a couple of rectangular woven trays. Tail between my legs, I scurried off to Impruneta, my chosen destination not only because of its proximity to my house but also because the local café, Bar Italia (half the towns in Tuscany seem to have cafés bearing this unimaginative name), makes the best gelato to be found outside Florence. Truth be told, I was in much need of a little break and relieved to have a respite, however brief, from the dissection of my kitchen.

"Get out your pen and paper," Antonio directed me hours later, after we had poured rice, polenta, pasta, flour, cookies, crackers, spices, and herbs into neatly labeled jars; filled one tray with a selection of cereals, cookies, and various sundry items to bring out each morning at breakfast, and the other with open flours, leavenings, sweeteners, and any other dry goods used for baking. We had not cooked a thing. Actually, dinner was going to be a pizza with the kids at a little restaurant down the road. The *bambini* had left us surprisingly at peace during "Operation Cleanup," most likely out of some juvenile sense of enlightened self-interest (i.e., fear of being recruited into the effort). In any event, what I had thought was going to be a day-long cooking extravaganza had turned into a summer-spring cleaning the likes of which would have made even my mother-in-law proud.

"Lesson number one," Antonio dictated. "Keep track of what you have in the kitchen; group ingredients logically so you'll never find ten bags of the same thing open at once; finish what you have opened before opening something new; and use jars and baskets to help organize your kitchen."

"*Hai capito* . . . understand?" he asked, smiling. I was puzzled by the smile, and by his general good humor. After all, he had just spent an entire hot summer afternoon doing for someone else's kitchen what most people I know find any excuse to get out of doing for their own. I nodded my head in earnest. "*Bene,*" he answered. "Tomorrow we can start cooking."

Ruminating over this little episode later that night, I asked myself whether Antonio's passion for culinary order and organization was something typically Italian or simply a result of his having organized professional kitchens for nearly all of his adult life. Nature or nurture? I would have to say *both*. He is a chef, but above all he is Italian, and like most of his compatriots does everything he can to pull off the delicate balancing act of keeping the kitchen stocked with only the freshest ingredients while avoiding culinary waste of any kind. No doubt he has elevated the simple act of organizing a kitchen to an art form, but I for one am not complaining—my *cucina* has never looked better!

HOMEMADE PASTA
Pasta Fatta in Casa

When making dough of any kind, most Italians combine flour and liquid using the "volcano" method. The dry ingredients (usually just flour and salt) are poured into a mound on a wooden or marble work surface. The center is hollowed out to accommodate the wet ingredients, such as eggs, milk, and/or oil, which are slowly swirled around in the center of the volcano in order to pick up the dry ingredients from the sides. When all goes well, just the right amount of flour is slowly and evenly incorporated into the dough. When things go less well, as is often the case with first-time pasta makers, the volcano gets unruly and leaks liquid out the side, and the gentle swirling becomes a frantic race to stop the runny eggs from flowing off the work surface onto the floor.

For this reason, we suggest that first-time fresh pasta makers put a lid on uncontrolled eruptions by combining the ingredients using the volcano technique in a mixing bowl rather than on a flat, open surface. After a few successful batches of dough, you can switch to the traditional wooden or marble work surface.

The Basic Recipe

MAKES ENOUGH DOUGH FOR ABOUT 6 PORTIONS OF PASTA

Many recipes for pasta dough require 1 or 2 large eggs per cup of flour. Antonio finds that the excessive use of egg whites makes the pasta too elastic to the bite. He prefers using only 1 whole egg and adds flavor, softness, and moisture to the dough with a combination of egg yolks, olive oil, and milk. Use eggs from free-range chickens if they are available where you live.

3 cups all-purpose flour, plus flour for
    dusting
Pinch of salt
3 large eggs

3 egg yolks from large eggs
1 tablespoon extra-virgin olive oil
1½ tablespoons milk

Pour the flour in a mound into a large mixing bowl or onto a wooden or marble work surface and make a well in the center. Sprinkle with a pinch of salt. Break the eggs into the center of the well, add the egg yolks and olive oil and lightly beat with a fork. Use one hand to swirl the egg mixture in a circular motion so that the flour is incorporated from the sides of the well. When about half the flour has been incorporated, add in the milk and continue incorporating flour from around the sides of the well.

⌒ If you are using a mixing bowl, remove the dough from the bowl when it forms a mass. Pour the loose flour remaining in the bowl onto a wooden or marble work surface and place the ball of dough on top. If you are making the dough directly on a flat work surface, shape it into a ball when it forms a mass and set it on top of the loose flour.

⌒ Use both hands to work the remaining flour into the dough. Continue incorporating the flour until the dough just barely stops sticking to your fingers if you press them deeply into the dough. Remember that the amount of flour you ultimately will need will vary according to the size of your eggs, the ambient humidity, and other factors that will vary on any given day, with any given batch of ingredients.

⌒ Use a pastry scraper to clean your work surface completely of all bits and pieces of dough and flour. Wash your hand thoroughly and dry them well.

⌒ Dust your work surface lightly with flour and knead the dough, pushing it away from you with the heel of your hands, then gathering it up with your fingers, folding it in half and turning the dough slightly. Continue kneading until the dough becomes smooth and elastic (6 to 8 minutes), adding additional flour in small increments if the dough is sticking to your hands.

⌒ You may begin rolling out the dough immediately if you are using a pasta machine. If you will be rolling the dough by hand, wrap and set it on the counter to rest for 20 minutes. (You may leave it to rest for up to 3 hours.)

Rolling and Cutting the Dough with a Pasta Machine

By "pasta machine" we are not referring to an elaborate contraption that combines the raw ingredients into a dough, then pushes out finished noodles. These machines are costly and unreliable and produce a poorly textured pasta unworthy of even the minimal effort required to make it.

A type of "pasta machine" worth its small investment, and the one we will refer to below, is a small, hand-cranked metal device with two adjustable rollers that thin and lengthen the dough in lieu of hand rolling. Special cutting rollers are then attached to the back of the instrument that cut the pasta into varying widths, from thin tagliolini noodles to wider tagliatelle or fettuccine. Relatively inexpensive motors can usually be purchased as an accessory to attach to the crank mechanism and power it electrically.

⌒ Mix and knead the dough as described on pages 126–127. Divide the dough into 5 or 6 small balls. Cover the dough sections with a layer of plastic wrap. Spread clean kitchen towels over the work space next to the pasta machine to lay the strips of pasta once they have been rolled.

To Thin and Cut Tagliolini, Tagliatelle, Fettuccine, and Lasagne

⌒ Place the rollers on the widest setting. Take one of the pieces of dough and flatten it into an oblong shape with your hands. Run the dough through the machine. (Lightly dust it with flour if it sticks to the rollers.) Fold the thinned dough in half or in thirds and run it through the rollers once again. Repeat four or five times. Folding and passing the dough through the rollers this way has the same effect as kneading and renders the dough soft and pliant. Lay the stretched dough over the kitchen towels and work through the remaining balls of dough in the same manner.

⌒ Change the setting on the rollers by one notch so that the rollers are brought closer together. Without folding the strip of dough, pass it through the rollers and lay it back on the towel. Repeat with the other pieces of dough. Move the setting by one notch to bring the rollers closer together and pass each strip of dough through the machine. The strips of pasta will lengthen as they are stretched. Let them hang over the side of the counter if you are running out of room. Continue progressively narrowing the space between the rollers, one notch at a time, and passing each strip of dough through the machine until each piece of dough has been passed through all but the narrowest setting.

⌒ To cut the pasta into noodles, allow the strips to dry for 8 to 10 minutes until they are still pliant but no longer sticky. For lasagna, use a straight-edged or fluted pastry wheel to cut 3 by 13-inch rectangles. For string pastas, most pasta machines have two cutters. Run the strips of pasta through the narrow cutters for tagliolini and the broad cutters for tagliatelle or fettuccine. Wrap the cut noodles around your hand to form several small nests. Set them on kitchen towels until ready to use.

⌒ Antonio advises against drying homemade pasta and storing it for lengthy periods of time because he finds the chances of toxicity due to mold development are too great. He recommends cooking homemade pasta the same day or drying it on kitchen towels and using it within 2 days.

To Thin and Shape Stuffed Pasta

ⴰ Pasta that will be stuffed, such as ravioli or tortelloni, needs to be slightly moister than pasta that will be cut into strings. For this reason, divide the kneaded dough into 5 or 6 portions and work with only 1 section at a time, keeping the remaining portions tightly covered in plastic. Pass a section of dough through the rollers on the widest setting exactly as you would for string pasta, folding the dough in half or thirds each time you run it through the rollers. Then run the dough through progressively thinner settings until it has gone through all but the thinnest setting.

ⴰ Lay the strip of dough over a work counter. Fill with stuffing as described on page 135. Cut into desired shapes and transfer to a lightly floured platter before thinning and stuffing the next strip of dough.

Rolling Out the Dough by Hand

ⴰ Hand-rolled pasta dough has a slightly textured, uneven surface that makes it a perfect vehicle for pasta sauce. In some parts of Italy, especially Emilia-Romagna, rolling out huge, paper-thin sheets of pasta is so common an art that home cooks seem to have acquired the technique through osmosis. Unfortunately, it is more of a visual art than a written one. Describing the unfurling of one gigantic, nearly transparent sheet of pasta to someone who has never seen it done is rather like giving written cycling instructions to someone who has never seen a bicycle in motion. Confusing . . . unmanageable . . . and ultimately frustrating.

ⴰ Grab the chance to watch a pro roll out pasta the traditional way. It is a skill worth mastering, and is really best acquired through a mixture of observation, practice, and patience. In the meantime, Antonio suggests you get into the habit of wielding your rolling pin by working with a smaller quantity of dough—you'll find it more manageable and you will reduce the chance that the dough will dry out during rolling and become impossible to stretch. The only equipment you need is a large, flat, preferably wooden work surface and a long wooden rolling pin (traditional Italian pasta rolling pins measure 2½ feet long).

⌒ Always let the dough rest for at least 20 minutes before rolling it out. This allows the gluten to relax and the dough to become more pliant and easier to work. Lightly dust your work surface with flour. Unwrap the dough, and cut it in half. Rewrap one half in plastic and knead the other half gently for a minute. Sprinkle a trace more flour on the work surface and on the rolling pin, and lay the dough ball in the center of the work surface. Work quickly and use additional flour sparingly or the dough will dry out and become unmanageable.

⌒ Pummel the dough with your hands into a thick, flat circle. Place the rolling pin slightly above the center of the circle and gently roll it away from you, toward, but not over, the far edge of the circle. Let the pin roll back to its original position and repeat this motion three times, working quickly. Rotate the dough a quarter of a full turn clockwise and repeat the above rolling motion until the dough has been rotated a full circle. Turn the dough over and repeat. The dough should roll out into a relatively uniform circle. The idea is to gently *push* the dough outward to expand the circle. *Do not* press the rolling pin down into the work surface—the dough will only stick. Continue rolling the dough from the center radiating outward in a succession of quick, light strokes without rolling over the outer edges of the dough. Turn the dough over and repeat. Continue gently but quickly rolling the dough this way until the entire sheet has been rolled to a uniform thinness. It will not have the near transparence of traditionally stretched dough, but it will be thin enough to perhaps still be the most wonderful pasta you have ever tasted.

Cutting Hand-Rolled Pasta

While ravioli, tortelloni, and other stuffed pastas must be filled and cut while the pasta is still moist, long strands of pasta such as fettuccine and tagliatelle must dry out slightly before being cut.

Cutting Long Noodles

The dough must be dry enough so that the sheet of pasta can be rolled up and cut without sticking to itself, but not so dry so that it cracks to pieces. Lay the flat sheet of pasta on a lightly floured cloth. Turn it over after about 5 minutes. The exact drying time will vary depending on the heat and humidity in your kitchen. Look for the moment when the pasta assumes the texture of supple leather.

When the sheet is dry but still supple, fold it loosely upon itself at 2-inch intervals so that you end up with a long, flat 2½-inch-wide roll. Use a large knife to cut the roll crosswise into the desired thickness. Pappardelle have a width of ¾ inch; tagliatelle and fettuccine should be cut to about ¼ inch wide; and tagliolini slightly thinner.

Once you have cut the strands, unravel them slightly and set them out on a clean cloth to use within 2 days.

TIPS FOR LEFTOVER BITS OF PASTA DOUGH:

One of the fundamentals of Italian cooking is that nothing ever goes to waste. Once you've rolled your dough and cut it into half-moons, ravioli, or whatever else has struck your fancy, you will find your cutting board littered with stray scraps and bits of leftover dough. Cut them into irregular diamond shapes, which Italians call maltagliati *(translation, "badly cut") and add them to a soup.*

Making Stuffed Pasta

In order for stuffed pasta to seal properly, it must be filled and cut immediately after the dough has been rolled into a thin sheet. See the section on stuffed pasta (p. 135) for specific instructions on creating particular shapes.

USING WONTON OR EGG ROLL WRAPPERS

There is an art to rolling out pasta to just the right thickness and cutting and stuffing it with any kind of efficiency and ease. That said, you needn't shy away from ravioli, tortelloni, and other stuffed pastas just because you've yet to master the intricacies of making fresh pasta. If you don't have the time or inclination to make the pasta yourself, you can make stuffed pastas using egg roll or wonton wrappers. Made from flour and egg and dusted with cornstarch, they are easy to handle and can be stored for several days in the refrigerator before using. They are sold cut into squares or rounds. You can use either. Because they are drier than freshly made noodles, egg roll and wonton wrappers need a bit of help to stick together. Add a tablespoon of water to a lightly beaten egg and paint the edges of the wrappers before folding them.

Tagliolini with Fresh Plum Tomatoes and Basil
Tagliolini con Pomodori Freschi e Basilico
SERVES 4 TO 6

The beauty of this pasta is in its utter simplicity—fresh tomatoes, bright green leaves of basil, and sweet butter over pale yellow homemade noodles. Italian cooking doesn't really get much better than this.

For the Pasta
1 recipe fresh pasta (page 126), cut into tagliolini (page 128), or
    1 pound store-bought tagliolini, tagliatelle, or fettuccine egg noodles

For the Sauce
2½ pounds ripe plum tomatoes, peeled, seeded, and crushed

Handful of fresh basil leaves

Salt

Freshly ground black pepper

3 tablespoons sweet butter

Freshly grated Parmesan cheese for the table

∿ Prepare the fresh tagliolini.

∿ Place the tomatoes in a medium heavy-bottomed skillet over a medium flame. Bring them to a simmer, stirring occasionally, then reduce the flame to low and simmer gently for 15 minutes. Add the basil leaves and season with salt and freshly ground pepper. Continue cooking for another 10 to 15 minutes, until the tomatoes thicken to a light sauce. Remove from the heat and stir in the butter.

∽ In the meantime, bring a large pot of water to boil. Add salt. Fresh pasta will take only 2 to 3½ minutes to cook. Dry egg pasta will take slightly longer and should be cooked according to the package directions. Drain the pasta (reserving ¼ cup of the cooking water) and add it to the skillet with the sauce. Toss well over a medium flame for 1 minute, adding some of the reserved cooking water if the pasta seems dry. Serve immediately.

∽ Offer grated Parmesan at the table.

Tagliatelle with Shrimp and Mushrooms
Tagliatelle ai Gamberi e Funghi
SERVES 4 TO 6

Shrimp and mushrooms are a favorite combination of Antonio's, who enjoys the marriage between the briny flavors of the sea and the musky richness of woodland mushrooms. The shrimp take only minutes to cook—as do the tagliatelle. Begin cooking the pasta the moment you add the shrimp to the sauce.

For the Pasta

1 recipe fresh pasta (page 126), cut into tagliatelle (page 128),
   or 12 ounces store-bought tagliatelle or fettuccine egg noodles
Salt

For the Sauce

1 pound fresh porcini mushrooms or
   ½ pound each stemmed shiitake and
   oyster mushrooms

1 shallot, finely chopped
2 cloves garlic, minced
1 bay leaf

¼ cup extra-virgin olive oil

1 tablespoon finely chopped Italian parsley

Freshly ground black pepper

⅓ cup dry white wine

1 cup crushed Italian plum tomatoes, with their juice

1 pound large shrimp, peeled and deveined

2 tablespoons butter

∾ Prepare the fresh tagliatelle.

∾ Bring a large pot of water to a boil. Add salt and return to a boil.

∾ Wipe the mushrooms clean with a soft cloth or paper towel. If they are quite dirty, wash them under running water and pat dry. Trim the stems (discard the shiitake stems entirely) and cut the mushrooms into medium slices.

∾ Place the shallot, garlic, and bay leaf in a medium pan with the olive oil and sauté over low heat until the shallots soften and the garlic colors a pale gold. Increase the flame to medium, stir in the mushrooms, parsley, and a grinding of black pepper and sauté until the mushrooms soften and release their water (about 6 to 8 minutes). Pour in the wine and allow it to reduce almost completely. Add the crushed tomatoes and simmer until the sauce thickens somewhat (5 to 6 minutes). Season with salt and additional black pepper if needed. Add the shrimp, reduce the flame to low, and cook until the shrimp are opaque all the way through (about 3 to 4 minutes). Remove the bay leaf.

∾ Begin cooking the tagliatelle as soon as you have added the shrimp to the sauce. Cook the pasta until it is tender but still al dente (3 to 4 minutes for fresh pasta, slightly longer for dried egg noodles). Drain, reserving ½ cup of the cooking liquid.

∾ Place the pasta in the skillet with the sauce, add the butter and a bit of the reserved water if the sauce seems dry. Toss quickly over a low flame and serve.

STUFFED PASTAS

Little squares and circles of pasta can be filled with a dollop of stuffing and folded in any number of ways. I learned the techniques of pasta folding from Antonio with a clean kitchen towel and a wadded-up paper napkin—the towel was the pasta and the napkin the stuffing. Not a bad way to practice your folding skills before trying them out on the real thing.

Keep in mind the following principles for stuffing any pasta:

- It doesn't take much filling to stuff a piece of pasta—count on anywhere from half a tablespoon to just over a tablespoon of filling per piece, depending on the particular shape.
- We spoon the filling into a wide-nozzled pastry bag at the restaurants (or just use the bag only without a metal nozzle at all). If you don't have a pastry bag, make one by snipping off the corner of a medium zip-lock plastic bag.
- Homemade pasta can be sealed closed by gently pressing the dough together or by brushing the edges with water. Store-bought wrappers should have their edges sealed with a mixture of beaten egg and a tablespoon of water.
- Stuffed pasta should be handled gently. There is no need to press heavily down on the edges to seal—firm, even pressure works best.
- Dust each piece of stuffed pasta very lightly with flour after shaping to keep the pieces from sticking to each other or the serving platter they rest on before they are cooked.
- Whether using hand-rolled or machine-rolled pasta, work with only 1 strip of pasta at a time, wrapping or covering the rest of the dough with plastic wrap.
- Invest in a fluted pastry wheel to cut the shapes with—not only will it give you beautiful edges, but the scalloped edge helps crimp the pasta closed.

Here is how to make the shapes we use most often for stuffed pastas at our restaurants:

Ravioli: Roll out a long strip of pasta, then use a straight-edged pizza cutter to trim it to an even 3-inch width. Dot the pasta with ½-tablespoon dollops of filling along the length of the strip, spacing the dots at 1½-inch intervals and setting them 1 inch up from the bottom edge of the strip. Brush a bit of water (or water and egg if you are using wonton wrappers) around each dollop of filling, then gently fold the strip over to enclose the filling. Seal around each mound of filling, gently pressing out any air with your fingertips. Use a fluted pastry wheel to cut 1½-inch filled squares. Serve 14 to 18 ravioli per person.

Ravioloni: Roll out a long strip of pasta, then use a straight-edged pizza cutter to trim it to an even 5-inch width. Dot the pasta with 1-tablespoon dollops of filling along the length of the strip, spacing the dots at 2½-inch intervals and setting them 2 inches up from the bottom edge of the strip. Seal as you would regular ravioli and use a fluted pastry wheel to cut 2½-inch filled squares. Serve approximately 10 ravioloni per person.

Mezzalune: Roll out a long strip of pasta, then use a straight-edged pizza cutter to trim it to an even 3-inch width. Dot the pasta with ½-tablespoon dollops of filling along the length of the strip, spacing the dots at 1½-inch intervals and setting them 1 inch up from the bottom edge of the strip. Brush with a bit of water (or water and egg if you are using wonton wrappers) around each dollop of filling, then gently fold the strip over to enclose the filling. Seal around each mound of filling, gently pressing out any air with your fingertips. Use a fluted pastry cutter to cut half circles around the enclosed filling so that the straight edge of the half-moon is the folded piece of pasta and the scalloped half circle is made by the pastry cutter. Serve 15 to 18 mezzalune per person.

Tortelloni: Place 1 tablespoon of filling in the center of a 3-inch square of pasta (or space the filling at 3-inch intervals and cut the squares with a straight-edged pizza cutter afterward). Brush the edges of the square with water or beaten egg, then gently fold the square in half at the corners to make a triangle and gently press any air out with your fingers. Place the tortelloni's folded edge toward you and take the 2 bottom ends of the triangle and join them together below the pillow of filling—a drop of water or beaten egg on the tips of the joined ends of the triangle will help them stick together. Serve 12 to 14 tortelloni per person.

Spinach and Ricotta Tortelloni with Pureed Asparagus Sauce

Tortelloni di Ricotta e Spinaci agli Asparagi

SERVES 6

Finely chopped greens and soft ricotta cheese are a favorite filling for stuffed pastas. The asparagus are cooked and blended until soft and creamy—but the tips cook along with the pasta and remain bright green and firm.

For the Filling

1 pound spinach or Swiss chard

6 ounces whole milk ricotta cheese

½ cup freshly grated Parmesan cheese

1 egg yolk

Pinch of ground cinnamon

Pinch of nutmeg

Pinch of salt

Freshly ground black pepper

For the Tortelloni

1 recipe basic pasta dough (page 126) or about 80 egg roll wrappers

For the Sauce

2 pounds fresh asparagus

4 tablespoons butter

2 onions, halved, then finely sliced

1 tablespoon olive oil

2 cups chicken broth (page 173) or 2 cups water

Salt

Freshly ground black pepper

Freshly grated Parmesan cheese for the table

The filling: Discard the stems and ribs from the greens, then wash the leaves in several changes of cold water. Drain in a colander. Steam the leaves until tender in just the water that has clung to their leaves (adding a bit of water to the pot if necessary). Chard will take a bit longer than spinach because the leaves are thicker. Allow the leaves to cool, then form them into a ball and squeeze out as much water as possible. Chop the leaves very fine, then once again squeeze out any additional water. Use a wooden spoon to combine the spinach or chard with the remaining filling ingredients to form a smooth paste. Transfer the filling to a large-nozzled pastry bag if you have one.

The tortelloni: Prepare the pasta dough. Roll out the dough and prepare the tortelloni (page 129).

The sauce: Wash the asparagus, then cut away the pale fibrous bottom of the stalk and use a potato peeler to shave off any remaining tough portions. Cut off the tips of the asparagus and set aside. Chop the remainder of the stalks into small pieces.

Warm the butter with the onions in a large, heavy-bottomed skillet. Cook over a low flame until the onions are soft and translucent, stirring frequently. Increase the flame to medium, add the chopped asparagus stalks, and sauté for a minute. Add the broth or water, salt and freshly ground pepper to taste. Cover and simmer gently until the asparagus becomes soft and begins to break apart (about 30 minutes). Blend until smooth with a stationary or hand blender.

Bring a large pot of water to a boil. Add salt, return the water to a boil, then add the tortelloni together with the reserved asparagus tips. When the tortelloni are firm but still tender and the tips are still bright green (test after 3 minutes), drain and toss with the sauce. Offer freshly grated Parmesan cheese.

Homemade Artichoke Half-Moons
with Artichoke Sauce
Mezzalune di Carciofi con Carciofi
SERVES 6

An artichoke lover's paradise! The artichokes are prepared two different ways—soft and smooth to fill the little half-moons, and sautéed with garlic and tomato for a fragrant sauce. The base for the filling is the recipe for puréed artichoke tapenade given earlier in the book. To give it some added body, Antonio adds Parmesan, nutmeg, and either ricotta cheese or potatoes. The former gives a "cheesier" flavor, the latter highlights the taste of the artichokes.

For the Filling

1 recipe artichoke tapenade (page 30)
½ cup freshly grated Parmesan cheese
Pinch of nutmeg
1 egg yolk
4 ounces whole milk ricotta cheese, drained, or 1 medium potato, boiled, then
    peeled

For the Pasta

1 recipe basic pasta dough (page 126) or approximately 100 egg roll wrappers

For the Sauce

Juice of 2 lemons
12 baby artichokes or 4 globe artichokes
⅓ cup olive oil
6 cloves garlic, crushed

4 ripe plum tomatoes, peeled, seeded, and chopped into small chunks

2 teaspoons finely chopped Italian parsley

1 cup chicken broth (page 173) or water

Salt

Freshly ground black pepper

Freshly grated Parmesan cheese for the table

The filling: Place all the filling ingredients together in a food processor; pulse blend until smooth. Pass the mixture through a sieve if it looks as if any fibrous parts of the artichoke are hiding in the paste. Transfer the filling to a large-nozzled pastry bag or a medium zip-lock plastic bag with a corner snipped off.

The dough: Prepare the pasta dough. Roll out the dough and prepare the mezzalune (page 128).

The sauce: Add the lemon juice to a large bowl of cold water. Remove all but the top 1½ inches of the artichoke stems, then use a small knife to pare away the outer layer of the remaining stem. Peel off the outer leaves of the artichokes until you reach the tender inner leaves. Turn the artichoke on its side and cut off the tough or pointed tips of the leaves. Cut half of the artichokes into small wedges and slice the remaining artichokes thinly. Soak the artichoke pieces in the lemon water for 20 minutes.

Drain the artichokes. Transfer them to a large, heavy-bottomed skillet with the olive oil and garlic and sauté for a couple of minutes over a medium flame, stirring often. Add the tomatoes, chopped parsley and broth, then season to taste with salt and freshly ground black pepper. Reduce the flame to low and cook, partially covered, until the artichokes are tender but the sauce is still juicy and slightly brothy (about 10 minutes).

Cook the mezzalune in abundant salted boiling water until they are tender but still firm, testing one after about 3 minutes. Drain, then add to the skillet with the artichoke sauce and toss well over a medium flame for 30 seconds. Offer grated Parmesan.

Homemade Potato Tortelloni
with Mixed Cheeses and Walnuts
Tortelloni di Patate alla Crema di Formaggio e Noci
SERVES 6

This pasta is a blend of subtle, harmonious flavors—the honest simplicity of the potato filling coated with a soft and savory blend of cheeses. Don't be fooled by the humbleness of the ingredients—they come together to make an elegant pasta indeed!

For the Filling

3 medium potatoes

Salt

1 tablespoon extra-virgin olive oil

1 small onion, finely chopped

½ cup freshly grated Parmesan cheese

¼ cup whole milk ricotta cheese, drained

1 egg yolk

Pinch of nutmeg

Pinch of ground cinnamon

For the Pasta

1 recipe basic pasta dough (page 126) or about 80 egg roll wrappers

For the Sauce

12 ounces any combination of Taleggio, Fontina, Gouda, Brie, or Edam cheese (crusts removed), cut into small pieces

½ cup whole milk

1 cup freshly grated Parmesan cheese

⅓ cup chopped walnuts

❧ *The filling:* Boil the potatoes in their skins in ample salted water until they can be pierced easily with a fork (20 to 30 minutes). Remove them from the water and when they are cool enough to handle, peel away their skins. Set the potatoes aside to cool.

❧ In the meantime, gently heat the olive oil in a small saucepan, add the onion, and cook it over low heat until soft.

❧ Place all the filling ingredients in a food processor. Blend to a thick, stiff paste. Season to taste with salt, then spoon the filling into a large-nozzled pastry bag.

❧ *The dough:* Prepare the pasta dough. Roll out the dough and form the tortelloni (page 129).

❧ *The sauce:* Place the pieces of cheese in a heavy-bottomed saucepan with the milk. Heat over a low flame, stirring continuously until the cheese melts. Stir in half the Parmesan cheese and allow the sauce to simmer gently for just a minute. Transfer the sauce to a heated serving bowl.

❧ Boil the tortelloni in abundant salted water until they are tender but still firm (3 to 4 minutes). Drain then gently and toss with the cheese sauce, walnuts, and remaining Parmesan cheese. Serve immediately.

Eggplant, Zucchini, and Goat Cheese Ravioli in Thyme Butter
Ravioli di Melanzane e Formaggio di Capra al Burro e Timo
SERVES 6

Although these savory ravioli would be delicious in a light fresh tomato sauce such as the one described on page 99, the delicate flavor of the summer vegetables and cheeses comes through beautifully when accented simply with thyme leaves and sweet butter.

For the Filling

2 tablespoons extra-virgin olive oil

1 onion, finely chopped

1 clove garlic, finely chopped

2 medium eggplants, peeled and
   cut into small cubes

2 medium zucchini,
   thinly sliced crosswise

1 teaspoon finely chopped fresh thyme leaves

Salt

4 ounces fresh ricotta cheese

4 ounces soft goat cheese

1 egg

For the Ravioli

1 recipe basic pasta dough (page 126) or 90 to 100 egg roll wrappers

For the Sauce

6 tablespoons sweet butter

2 teaspoons fresh thyme leaves

½ cup freshly grated Parmesan cheese

∼ *The filling:* Heat the olive oil in a large skillet over a medium flame. Add the onion, sauté until it begins to soften, then add the garlic and sauté until the onion is golden and the garlic fragrant. Add the eggplant and zucchini and stir the pan well to mix all the ingredients. Sauté over a medium flame for 3 minutes. Add the thyme leaves, a pinch of salt, and 1 cup of water. Cook until all the liquid evaporates (20 to 25 minutes), stirring occasionally.

∼ When the eggplant and zucchini mixture has cooled, pass it through a food mill or blend in a food processor. Use a wooden spoon to combine the vegetable mixture, cheeses, and egg to form a smooth paste.

The ravioli: Prepare the pasta dough. Prepare the ravioli (page 129).

The sauce: Prepare the sauce while the ravioli are boiling in abundant salted water. Melt the butter in a small saucepan over a medium flame. Sprinkle in the thyme leaves and continue heating the butter over the lowest possible flame. When the ravioli are tender but still firm (begin checking after 3 minutes), pour the herbed butter into a heated serving bowl. Drain the ravioli well and toss with the herbed butter and grated Parmesan. Serve immediately.

Pumpkin Tortelloni with Cream and Parmesan
Tortelloni di Zucca alla Panna, Cannella, e Parmigiano
SERVES 6

Reducing cream through extended cooking causes it to lose its freshness and become heavy on the palate. Here Antonio warms the cream to just below a simmer, adds the fragrant cinnamon and allows the sauce to finish cooking while it is tossed with the hot pasta just before serving. Use firm fleshed pumpkins or winter squash (kabocha, butternut, or acorn work best) for the filling.

For the Filling

¾ pound pumpkin or winter squash, threads and seeds removed

¾ cup ricotta cheese

½ cup freshly grated Parmesan cheese

3 imported Amaretto di Saronno cookies, crushed

1 tablespoon bread crumbs

1 small egg

Touch of nutmeg

Salt

White pepper

For the Pasta

1 recipe basic pasta dough (page 126) or about 80 egg roll wrappers

For the Sauce

1 cup heavy cream
Pinch of ground cinnamon
1 cup freshly grated Parmesan cheese

✐ *The filling:* Preheat oven to 375°. Cut the pumpkin into thick slices and lay, skin side down, in a lightly oiled baking dish or cookie sheet. Cover with aluminum foil and bake until tender (this can take anywhere from 45 minutes to 1 hour and 15 minutes). Remove from the oven and allow to cool, then use a large metal spoon to scrape the flesh of the pumpkin from the skin. Mash the pumpkin with a potato masher or pass through a ricer. Add the other filling ingredients and blend together to form a homogenous mixture.

✐ *The dough:* Prepare pasta dough. Roll out the dough and prepare the ravioli (page 129).

✐ *The sauce:* Warm the cream in a small saucepan until it barely begins to simmer. Sprinkle in the cinnamon and turn off the heat.

✐ Boil the pasta in abundant salted water until it is firm but still tender. Test after 3 minutes, but it may take up to a couple of minutes more. Transfer the pasta and sauce to a large skillet over a medium flame. Sprinkle with the grated Parmesan, then gently toss the mixture for 1 minute before serving.

Homemade Chicken Ravioloni with Chanterelles
Ravioloni di Pollo ai Finferli
SERVES 6

For years, I assumed that chanterelles came only from France. Actually, *finferli,* also known as *"galinaccio," "giallino,"* or *"cantarello"* mushrooms, grow throughout northern Italy's deciduous woods and are a favorite accompaniment to polenta. They range in color from yellow to orange and are identifiable both by their trumpetlike shape and by the delicate perfume of apricots that characterizes them.

For the Filling

2 cups coarsely chopped roasted chicken, skin removed

3 ounces cooked ham, cut into small dice

3 ounces good Italian mortadella, cut into small dice

⅓ cup freshly grated Parmesan cheese

1 large egg

Pinch of nutmeg

Freshly ground black pepper

For the Pasta

1 recipe basic pasta dough (page 126) or 120 egg roll wrappers

For the Sauce

1 pound fresh chanterelle mushrooms

½ white onion, finely chopped

2 tablespoons butter

2 tablespoons olive oil

1 teaspoon fresh thyme leaves

⅓ cup white wine

Salt

Freshly ground black pepper

The filling: Blend the meats and cheese in a food processor until smooth and pastelike. Add the egg and blend well. Season with nutmeg and freshly ground black pepper.

The ravioloni: Prepare the pasta dough. Roll out the dough and prepare the ravioloni (page 129).

The sauce: Clean the mushrooms with a soft cloth or mushroom brush. Wash them quickly under running water if they are very dirty. Pat dry. Chop the mushrooms roughly into medium pieces.

Gently sauté the onion in the butter and oil over a low heat until it is soft and translucent. Increase the flame to medium, add the mushrooms and sauté for 1 minute only—chanterelles cook quickly and become tough if overcooked. Sprinkle in the thyme leaves and stir well, then pour in the wine. When it reduces add ⅓ cup of water to the pan and season to taste with salt and a grinding of black pepper. Remove the pan from the heat until you are ready to use the sauce.

Boil the ravioloni in abundant salted water until they are firm but tender (taste one after 3 minutes). Drain and toss with the sauce over a low flame for 30 seconds. Serve immediately.

Crabmeat Ravioli in Saffron Sauce
Ravioli di Granchio allo Zafferano

SERVES 4

This is not an everyday dish—but, then, saffron is not an everyday spice. Harvested from the pistils of a particular classification of small purple crocus, it takes thousands of flowers to produce one ounce of pure saffron. But what could tickle the senses more than the distinctive flavor of a spice harvested from the hearts of a field full of flowers? It takes only the tiniest pinch of saffron to both flavor and color a sauce—less is definitely more, since too much saffron will make a sauce bitter. The use of apple juice here is a trick Antonio learned years ago in France—the juice eliminates any subtle bitterness imparted by the pungent spice. If you can find them, use saffron threads (the actual stigma of the crocus) rather than powder, which is more readily available and unfortunately more easily adulterated. Crush the threads gently with your fingers before using them. Keep in mind that the golden-red saffron powder will tinge a sauce a pale mustard color immediately; the threads will take a few minutes longer.

For the Filling

1 tablespoon extra-virgin olive oil

1 shallot, finely chopped

⅓ cup dry white wine

12 ounces cooked crabmeat

1 small potato, baked, peeled, and cut into cubes

1 egg yolk

⅓ cup heavy cream

Salt

For the Pasta

1 recipe basic pasta dough (page 126—you will use only two thirds of the dough) or
   approximately 70 egg roll wrappers

For the Sauce

2 tablespoons butter

1 white onion, halved lengthwise and sliced very thin

⅓ cup dry white wine

½ cup unsweetened apple juice

1½ cups heavy cream

Pinch of saffron threads or ¹⁄₂₀-ounce vial powdered saffron

Salt

2 tablespoons freshly grated Parmesan cheese

The filling: Heat the oil and shallot in a sauté pan over a medium flame. Sauté until soft, then add the wine and reduce until the shallot is almost dry, stirring occasionally. Reduce the flame to low, add the crabmeat and potato, and stir for 1 minute to mix well. Remove from the flame and allow to cool. Mash the mixture well with a fork until it forms an even paste. Slowly fold in the egg yolk and cream. Season lightly with salt and cook over the lowest flame for 3 to 4 minutes, stirring continuously.

～ *The ravioli:* Prepare the pasta dough. Roll out the dough and prepare the ravioli (page 129).

～ *The sauce:* Melt the butter in a small saucepan. Add the onions and sauté over a low flame for 7 or 8 minutes while they soften. Pour in the wine and simmer until the liquid reduces completely. Continue cooking the onions until they are completely translucent and have released all of their stored moisture. (This step is very important, since the cream will curdle if the onions have retained any of their water.)

～ Add the apple juice and simmer over a low heat until the liquid has reduced roughly by half (about 8 minutes). Stir in the cream and allow the mixture to reach then sustain a low simmer for 2 minutes before adding the saffron. Salt to taste.

～ Simmer gently for 10 minutes, stirring regularly. Pour the sauce through a mesh strainer. It should be smooth and golden hued. (You may want to reserve the saffron-flavored onions to spread on thin slices of toasted bread.)

～ Boil the ravioli in abundant salted water until tender but still firm (3 to 4 minutes). Drain, then toss in the saffron sauce with 2 tablespoons of grated Parmesan cheese. Serve immediately.

Pasta Soufflé with Mixed Mushrooms
Timballo di Pasta ai Funghi
SERVES 6 TO 8

This elegant baked pasta alternates layers of fresh egg lasagna noodles with a savory mixture of sautéed mushrooms, creamy-textured milk-based béchamel, and freshly grated Parmesan. The colors are pale and harmonious, the flavors subtle and rich. It does take a bit of work to put together, but it makes a beautiful first course for a special occasion. Homemade lasagna noodles are incomparably light and delicate compared to their store-bought equivalent. They are the only noodles we would use for this dish.

This timballo can be assembled the day before and cooked just before serving. If you choose to do this, cook it covered for the first 20 minutes, then uncover and remove from the oven when the top of the timballo is lightly browned (10 or more minutes longer).

For the Béchamel

4 tablespoons butter

6 tablespoons flour

4 cups milk

1 teaspoon salt

Pinch of nutmeg

Pinch of cinnamon

White pepper

2 eggs, at room temperature (to be added to the cooled sauce as directed below)

For the Mushrooms

4 tablespoons extra-virgin olive oil

2 tablespoons butter

3 shallots, finely chopped

2½ pounds fresh mixed mushrooms, stems and caps thinly sliced

½ cup dry white wine

Salt

Freshly ground black pepper

For the Pasta

1 recipe fresh pasta dough (page 126)

1 tablespoon salt

Additional Ingredients

Butter for greasing the pan

Flour for dusting

2 cups freshly grated Parmesan cheese

The béchamel: Melt the butter over a low heat in a medium saucepan. Add the flour slowly, stirring continuously for about 2 to 3 minutes, until the mixture thickens and smells faintly of biscuits (this is known as a "roux"). Do not let the mixture brown. In the meantime, heat the milk in a separate saucepan to just below a boil. Pour the hot milk over the roux and whisk together until smooth (take care to mix well around the edges of the saucepan). Add the salt, spices, and white pepper. Cook the mixture over a low flame, stirring occasionally, until it forms a creamy sauce thick enough to flow from a spoon (3 to 4 minutes). Adjust the seasonings as necessary. The sauce should be flavorful and well seasoned. Remove the sauce from the flame, and set aside for 30 minutes or until cool. (After 5 minutes, lay a piece of wax paper directly on top of the sauce to keep it from forming a film.)

The mushrooms: Lightly heat the olive oil and butter in a large skillet. Sauté the shallots for 3 to 4 minutes, then increase the flame to high and add the mushrooms, stirring vigorously until they begin to soften and release their juices. When the pan is almost dry, pour in the wine, season with salt and a generous grinding of black pepper and allow the wine to reduce almost completely, stirring frequently. Reduce the flame to low and continue to sauté until the mushrooms have reduced substantially in volume (5 to 10 minutes).

The pasta: Roll out the dough by hand or shape the dough with a pasta machine into twelve 3 by 13-inch rectangles. Don't worry if the pieces are not perfectly uniform. The timballo will be formed with several layers of pasta, and each layer can be put together like a patchwork, filling in open spaces with smaller pieces of pasta, or slightly overlapping 1 strip of pasta with another. (No one will *ever* notice.)

Do not cook the sheets of pasta until you are ready to assemble the timballo. Bring a large pot of water to a boil, add 1 tablespoon of salt, and return to a boil. Fill a large mixing bowl with cold water. Cook the pasta 3 or 4 strips at a time for 1 minute only. Carefully scoop them out of the boiling water with a large skimmer and place immediately in the bowl of cold water to stop their cooking. (Don't worry if a strip of pasta tears apart. You will piece it back together in the pan.) Lay the pasta flat onto dish towels, and pat dry.

Assembling the timballo: Preheat the oven to 475°. Beat 2 room temperature eggs vigorously in a medium mixing bowl for a couple of minutes until their color and texture is light and fluffy. Fold in the cooled béchamel.

Generously butter a 9 by 13-inch earthenware casserole and then dust with flour. Cover the bottom of the casserole with 3 sheets of pasta to form an even layer (trim the sheets if necessary). Spread with a light layer of béchamel and sprinkle with Parmesan. Spoon a third of the mushrooms over the top, then layer with another 3 sheets of pasta. Repeat this layering sequence two more times. Cover with a final layer of pasta, the remaining béchamel, and a generous sprinkling of Parmesan. Don't worry if some of the edges and corners of the lasagna sheets aren't covered with the sauce or cheese. They will brown beautifully in the oven, and the crunchy, toasted edges will perfectly offset the soft bubbly center of the lasagne timballo.

Bake uncovered for 25 minutes or until the top of the timballo is lightly browned and bubbling.

CULINARY CREATIVITY

You may never write a poem, you may never paint a watercolor, but chances are, during the course of your lifetime you will find yourself making a meal, or more likely, thousands of them, and not just for yourself. How you live your culinary life is entirely up to you. You can pick at cold leftovers by the dim glow of your open refrigerator, spend hours fretting over even the simplest dinner party, or use the time spent in the kitchen, at the market, and at the table to create, satisfy, and inspire. The choice is yours.

Using your inborn creativity in the kitchen doesn't require you to completely disregard cookbooks, traditional recipes, and established methods of preparation in favor of reinventing the gastronomic wheel. It means leaving some space in the kitchen for your own voice and reminding yourself that recipes are nothing more than your teachers. A well-explained recipe will help you understand why something is cooked in a certain way. Make those lessons part of your own culinary baggage so that you can apply them as general principles to everything you cook. Italian cookbooks are notoriously vague and imprecise. I've come to believe that the reason for this is that the authors know their recipes will be followed only in the most approximate sense and that the home cook will brand each recipe with his or her own signature.

Cook with both sides of your brain. There's a place for the organizational right side, which makes detailed shopping lists, follows directions to the letter, and rationally prepares balanced meals. Just don't ignore the other side, the creative part, which is happiest playing freely with the flavors, aromas, textures, and colors in its midst. You'll have more fun, and you'll be delighted with yourself when you invent something of your own. If by some small chance an experiment falls short of your expectations, well, tomorrow is another day—and the day after that another. You have a lifetime of cooking ahead of you—make the most of it.

A CULINARY CREATIVITY PRIMER

- Open this book (or any cookbook you enjoy cooking from) to any page and make the recipe on that page. You may try something you never would have tried otherwise and give your taste buds a delicious surprise.
- Make a few risotti following a recipe and then invent your own with something you love to eat—asparagus, leeks, mushrooms, sausage, herbs—whatever appeals to you.
- Take a simple recipe that you enjoy and modify it slightly.
- Invite friends to stay for dinner when you think there's nothing to eat in the house. See what you can come up with. You'll be surprised.
- Try marketing without a shopping list and buying only what looks freshest and most appealing.
- Let your kids invent a recipe.
- Cook with a friend.
- Cook with leftovers.
- If you have a vegetable garden, base an entire meal around its bounty.

- Host a dinner party where everyone cooks a meal together. Watch and learn from each other. Shift your attention from the end results to the sheer pleasure of creating with friends.
- Listen to your taste buds. They have a lot to say!

RISOTTO

Few foods illustrate what is best about Italian cuisine as well as risotto.

It is accessible. At its base is one of the world's most humble and plentiful grains—rice.

It is unique. No other cuisine does to rice what the Italians, particularly northern Italians, do. Though risotto is unique to Italy, the method for preparing it is a simple one. It is made from specially cultivated starch-rich Italian rice (*arborio, vialone nano,* and *carnaroli* are the best varieties). The pearly white grains are short, plump, and much harder than their long-grained siblings. A risotto begins as most pasta sauces do, with a soffritto—finely chopped aromatic vegetables, usually onions or shallots, lightly sautéed in butter and/or oil. The rice (unwashed) is tossed into the pan and stirred vigorously for a minute to coat and lightly toast the grains. Often a splash of wine is added. The rice is then lightly covered in a small amount of simmering liquid (usually a meat, fish, or vegetable broth or bouillon) and stirred until the moisture is absorbed by the grains. A small ladleful of flavorful broth is stirred into the pot only after each previous addition of liquid has been absorbed. The rice is ready after it has cooked for 16 to 18 minutes and is tender but still firm to the bite. A bit of butter and Parmesan is often added at this point to help bind the flavors together, a process known as *mantecare.* We like the flavor of risotto best when it is left to sit for a couple of minutes before serving (keep in mind that the rice will continue to cook very slightly as it sits, absorbing a bit of liquid and softening just a touch).

Antonio, like most Venetians, prefers his risotto slightly fluid or *all'onda* ("with a wave"), as it is described in Venice. Other parts of Italy opt for a stiffer, less runny risotto.

It inspires creativity. Although the technique for making risotto always remains more or less the same, the variations are infinite—there are as many different risotti as stars in the summer sky. As a general rule, if it is edible, chances are it is suitable for a risotto—I've even heard of recipes for *risotto alle fragole* or strawberry risotto. More likely, you will flavor your risotto with meat or game of all kinds, seafood, vegetables, cheeses, or herbs.

You may find yourself influenced by the seasons, for there is nothing like a fall risotto flavored with woodland mushrooms, or a bright spring risotto made with tender peas, artichoke hearts, asparagus, and spinach. Or you may take your cue from whatever you have on hand, a bit of leftover roasted meat, ragù or pasta sauce, a head of crisp radicchio, or even something as simple as butter and Parmesan.

It requires you to cook with your senses. Although a recipe may call for 5 cups of broth and state that the rice will take from 16 to 18 minutes to cook, the final stage of a risotto is anything but scientific. It takes a bit of experience, and the use of all your senses to determine when the rice has lost the last of its hard interior; when just enough broth has been added for the consistency you prefer; and when the risotto could benefit from a touch more cheese or butter. Risotti are a wonderful tool to wean the recipe-dependent from the drudgery of following instructions by rote, to the artistry (dare I say "joy") of cooking.

It is delicious. Whether flavored with fresh spring asparagus, crumbled Italian sausage, saffron, or shellfish, a bowl of creamy, soft risotto is a joy to both the eye and the palate—each grain of rice plump and translucent, bound together in a savory mass, infused with the subtle flavors in which it has cooked. Italian cooking at its best.

ABOUT BOUILLON CUBES
A Proposito dei Dadi

Nothing really compares to a homemade broth that has simmered slowly over the stove for hours—certainly not a tiny foil-wrapped cube of compressed flavorings. Nevertheless, the fact remains that a slow simmer is a rare luxury for many home cooks whose agendas are filled with 1,001 other more urgent tasks.

The good news is that while American bouillon cubes used to find their flavor primarily from such dubious ingredients as monsodium glutamate, the newer bouillon cubes, available in health food stores and some supermarkets, take their flavor from dehydrated meats, herbs, and vegetables as well as a generous portion of salt and sometimes a bit of flour, yeast, and oil. We would always opt for homemade broth when given the choice (after all, it *is* extremely easy to make and freezes beautifully), and we'd never use bouillon cubes when the broth itself is the essence of a recipe (such as for *tortellini in brodo*). That said, we do find broth made from good-quality domestic or imported bouillon cubes to be perfectly adequate for risotti or wherever only scant quantities of broth are required.

You needn't even feel as if you're cheating—no Italian kitchen is without a healthy supply of *dadi* (literally "dice"), as they are affectionately known. Italian *dadi* taste astonishingly close to the real thing with a flavor that manages to be pronounced without being oppressive or cloying. Pick up a couple of boxes if you come across them at a specialty store.

Caveat: If you cannot come by high-quality bouillon cubes and are adverse to making broth, look for a good frozen or canned broth. Canned broth should be diluted with water (roughly ½ to 1 cup broth for every 2 cups water), as it is too salty and concentrated to use full strength.

Risotto with Early Spring Vegetables
Risotto con Primizie Primaverili
SERVES 4

Primizia is one of those wonderful Italian words that clues you in to just how attached the culture is to food. Roughly translated, it means "early vegetable" or "first fruit"—practically speaking, it refers to any fruit or vegetable at the very beginning of its season. To buy a *primizia,* which everyone does, is to splurge—there's usually a relatively hefty price tag attached to these earliest of vegetables. But imagine how inviting baskets of asparagus, unshelled spring peas, and the first tender artichokes look after a long winter of potatoes, broccoli, and cabbage.

For this recipe, use tender spinach leaves in addition to any combination of asparagus tips, peas, artichoke hearts, zucchini, and carrots. Later in the year, you can also use eggplant or small amounts of sweet red or yellow peppers (larger amounts would overpower the delicate flavor of the other vegetables).

If you don't have any tomato sauce handy, substitute with an additional cup of broth or bouillon added in small increments.

6 cups chicken broth (page 173) or 1 high quality bouillon cube dissolved in 6 cups
    simmering water
4 tablespoons butter
1 small onion, finely chopped
2 cups chopped fresh spring vegetables
2 handfuls spinach, leaves only, coarsely chopped
2 cups arborio or other Italian rice
1 cup tomato sauce (page 99)
⅓ cup freshly grated Parmesan cheese, plus additional Parmesan for the table
Salt
Freshly ground black pepper

∽ Heat the broth or bouillon to a low simmer over the stove.

∽ In a large, heavy-bottomed saucepan, combine 3 tablespoons of butter and the onion. Sauté gently over a low flame for a couple of minutes, then add all the remaining vegetables except for the spinach. Cook, stirring regularly, for 3 to 5 minutes, until the vegetables begin to soften, adding a few spoons of broth to the vegetables as they cook. Mix in the spinach and continue to sauté gently for a couple of minutes.

∽ Add the rice to the pan, stirring vigorously for a couple of minutes with a flat-bottomed wooden spoon to coat the grains with the butter and vegetables. Take care to scrape the bottom and sides of the pot so that the rice doesn't stick.

∽ Add a ladleful of broth to the rice, and stir frequently until the rice absorbs most of the liquid. Continue to stir the rice more or less constantly, adding additional broth as it is absorbed by the rice, until the rice has cooked for about 15 minutes.

∽ Stir in the tomato sauce and continue to cook, stirring constantly, for 2 or 3 more minutes. Add additional broth if necessary to keep the risotto slightly fluid.

~ Remove the risotto from the heat, stir in the remaining tablespoon of butter and the Parmesan, and adjust the seasonings with salt and freshly ground black pepper. Let the risotto rest a couple of minutes before serving. Offer grated Parmesan at the table.

Creamy Asparagus Risotto
Risotto alla Crema d'Asparagi
SERVES 4 TO 6

This risotto gets its creaminess from the asparagus itself—the tender stalks are blended smooth to give the risotto a velvety texture that is as light and fresh as spring itself.

5 cups chicken broth (page 173) or 1 high quality bouillon cube dissolved in 5 cups
    simmering water
1½ pounds fresh asparagus
6 tablespoons extra-virgin olive oil
2 medium shallots, finely chopped
2 cloves garlic, finely chopped
2 cups Italian arborio rice
½ cup dry white wine
¾ cup freshly grated Parmesan cheese
Salt
Freshly ground black pepper

~ Heat the broth or bouillon to a low simmer over the stove.
~ Put a large pot of water to boil on the stove. Trim away the white fibrous ends of the asparagus spears. Use a potato peeler to pare away any of the remaining tough outer stalk. Place the asparagus, tips up, in the boiling water and cook until the spears are tender (4 to 6 minutes depending on their size). Drain the asparagus, conserving ½ cup of the cooking

water. Cut off the tips and set them aside. Place the stalks in a food processor with 3 tablespoons olive oil and the reserved cooking water and blend until smooth.

Ꙭ Heat the remaining olive oil in a large, heavy-bottomed saucepan over a low flame. Add the shallots, stirring frequently, then 2 minutes later add the garlic. Continue to gently sauté until the shallots are lightly golden and the garlic fragrant. Increase the flame to medium, add the rice, stirring vigorously for a couple of minutes with a flat-bottomed wooden spoon. Pour in the wine and continue stirring for a couple of minutes while the alcohol evaporates.

Ꙭ Add a ladleful of broth to the rice, and stir frequently, until the rice absorbs most of the liquid. Continue to add small amounts of broth to the rice and stir constantly until the rice has been cooking for about 10 minutes.

Ꙭ Add the pureed asparagus to the rice and stir continuously for a couple of minutes while the risotto thickens. Continue adding small amounts of broth and stirring continuously until the rice has cooked a total of 16 to 18 minutes. Gently stir in the asparagus tips and test the rice for doneness. It should be cooked through, but still firm and textured.

Ꙭ Remove the pot from the heat, stir in the grated Parmesan, and season to taste with salt and freshly ground pepper. Allow the risotto to rest for a couple of minutes, then ladle into individual bowls and serve.

Risotto with Porcini Mushrooms
Risotto ai Funghi Porcini
SERVES 4

There are few better ways to savor the rich muskiness of porcini mushrooms than in this classic risotto. The grains of rice are infused with the flavor of the mushrooms and bound together with grated Parmesan and a hint of butter.

1½ pounds fresh porcini mushrooms or 1 pound button or cremini mushrooms
   and 1 ounce dried porcini mushrooms
6 cups beef or chicken broth (page 173) or 1 high quality bouillon cube dissolved
   in 6 cups simmering water
4 tablespoons butter
1 tablespoon olive oil
½ small onion, finely chopped
2 cloves garlic, finely chopped
2 cups arborio or other Italian rice
2 tablespoons dry white wine
4 tablespoons freshly grated Parmesan cheese

꩜ Wipe the fresh mushrooms clean with a soft towel, or, if they are covered with soil, rinse them clean under running water and pat dry. Do not soak. Trim away the woody base of the stems, then thinly slice the stems and caps.

꩜ If you are using dried porcini, soak them for 1 hour in a bowl with 2 cups of warm water. Squeeze the water out of them (into the bowl where they soaked) and chop them coarsely. Skim 1 cup of the soaking liquid from the top of the bowl and reserve.

꩜ Heat the broth or bouillon to a low simmer.

꩜ Warm 2 tablespoons of butter and the olive oil in a large, heavy-bottomed saucepan. Add the onion and garlic and sauté over a medium flame until the onion is colored a pale gold. Add the mushrooms, taking care to stir them regularly at first so they won't stick to the pan. If you are using a mixture of dried and fresh mushrooms, add ½ cup of the soaking water to the pot.

꩜ Sauté the mushrooms until they have released all of their liquid (or until the added liquid has evaporated), then add the rice, stirring vigorously for a couple of minutes with a flat-bottomed wooden spoon to coat the grains with the butter, oil, and mushroom mixture. Add the white wine and stir until the rice has absorbed all the liquid.

꩜ Begin adding broth little by little, just enough to cover the rice. Stir constantly while the rice absorbs the liquid. Continue adding additional amounts of broth (if you are using dried mushrooms, substitute ½ cup of the soaking water for ½ cup of broth). When the rice is tender but firm to the bite (16 to 18 minutes), remove from the heat and stir in the remaining butter, Parmesan, and a small ladleful of broth. Continue stirring for another minute. Cover and allow the risotto to rest for a couple of minutes before serving.

Risotto with Radicchio and Balsamic Vinegar
Risotto al Radicchio Profumato all'Aceto Balsamico
SERVES 4

This risotto has a lovely antique rose color on the plate. A dollop of butter is stirred into the pot just as the rice finishes cooking to bind the flavors together—here the contrast of balsamic vinegar's rich, woody flavor with the bright bitterness of the radicchio.

5 cups meat or chicken broth (pages 174 and 173) or 1 high quality bouillon cube
   dissolved in 5 cups of simmering water
6 tablespoons butter
1 medium onion, finely chopped
¾ pound radicchio, cored and coarsely chopped
2 cups arborio or carnaroli rice
2 tablespoons aged balsamic vinegar
Salt
Freshly ground black pepper
Freshly grated Parmesan cheese for the table

∽ Bring the broth or bouillon to a gentle simmer on the stove.
∽ Heat 2 tablespoons of butter in a large skillet. Add half the chopped onion and sauté gently for a couple of minutes as the onion softens. Add the radicchio and cook, stirring frequently, until it softens completely and takes on a deep burgundy color (about 5 minutes). Set aside.

Heat 2 tablespoons of butter in a large, heavy-bottomed saucepan. Add the remaining chopped onion and cook over low heat, stirring frequently, for 3 to 4 minutes, adding a touch of broth to the pan as the onions cook. Increase the flame to medium and add the rice, stirring vigorously with a flat-bottomed wooden spoon for a couple of minutes to coat and lightly toast the grains. Add enough broth to just barely cover the rice, then stir until the liquid is absorbed. Continue adding additional broth in small amounts, stirring almost continuously. When the rice has been cooking a total of 10 minutes, add the cooked radicchio to the pot and stir well. Continue adding additional broth and stirring continuously for about another 8 minutes or until the rice is tender but firm to the bite.

Remove the pot from the flame and stir in the balsamic vinegar and the last 2 tablespoons of butter. Correct the seasonings with salt and freshly ground black pepper. Cover and let the risotto rest for 2 minutes before serving. Offer freshly grated Parmesan.

Risotto with Prosecco
Risotto al Prosecco

SERVES 4

The vine-covered hillsides from Conegliano to Valdobbiadene are affectionately known in the north as "La Strada del Prosecco." The Prosecco Trail. Our good friend Bruno Bortolotti and his family have produced delightful sparkling Prosecco wines under their family label for the last fifty years. He offered us their recipe for a wonderfully subtle and elegant risotto using Prosecco DOC Spumante, Extra Dry. The consistency of this risotto should be smooth and fluid without being runny. The bubbles, of course, dissipate during the cooking—the delicate flavor of the Prosecco does not.

5 cups chicken broth (page 173) or 1 high quality bouillon cube dissolved in 5 cups simmering water

1 medium yellow onion, finely chopped

1½ tablespoons olive oil

3½ tablespoons butter

2 cups Italian arborio or carnaroli rice

1½ cups Extra Dry Prosecco Spumante

4 tablespoons freshly grated Parmesan cheese

☙ Heat the broth or bouillon to a low simmer.

☙ In a large, heavy-bottomed saucepan over a low flame, gently sauté the onion in 1½ tablespoons of olive oil and an equal amount of butter until it is soft and translucent. Increase the flame to medium and stir in the rice, using a flat-edged wooden spoon to mix the grains well with the onion and oil. After a minute, pour 1 cup of Prosecco into the pot and stir. It will bubble and foam dramatically, and then evaporate rather quickly.

☙ Add just enough broth to lightly cover the rice, and stir the mixture until most of the liquid has been absorbed. Continue adding small amounts of broth as it is absorbed, stirring almost constantly. When the rice has cooked for about 15 minutes, stir in the remaining Prosecco and 2 tablespoons butter. Stir well for a minute, then remove the pot from the heat. The consistency should be smooth and fluid but not runny. Stir in the grated Parmesan. Let the rice rest for 2 minutes and serve.

Risotto with Shrimp and Arugula
Risotto con Scampi e Rucola
SERVES 4

Antonio generally dislikes the strong flavor imparted by fish stocks when making risotto, using instead a good-quality vegetable bouillon for recipes such as this light and refreshing risotto with shrimp and arugula.

- 4 tablespoons butter
- 1 shallot, finely chopped
- 1 pound medium shrimp, shelled and deveined
- 2 cups Italian arborio or carnaroli rice
- ¼ cup dry white wine
- 1 vegetable bouillon cube dissolved in 5 cups simmering water
- 1 cup coarsely chopped arugula

Melt half of the butter in a large saucepan over medium heat. Add the chopped shallot and gently sauté until it is soft and translucent. Add the shrimp and turn them around in the pan for a couple of minutes until they color evenly. Remove only the shrimp from the pan and set aside. Add rice to the pan, stirring to coat the grains in the oil and juices from the shallots and shrimp. Douse with the wine and stir continuously with a flat-bottomed wooden spoon until the alcohol evaporates and the rice soaks up the butter and liquid.

Add a small ladleful of broth, reduce the heat to low and stir the rice continuously as it absorbs the liquid. Continue adding small amounts of broth and stirring the pot until the rice has been cooking for about 17 minutes.

Stir in arugula, shrimp, and the remaining butter. Let the risotto sit for a couple of minutes, then ladle into shallow bowls and serve.

Saffron Risotto with Lobster and Asparagus Tips
Risotto allo Zafferano con Aragosta e Punte di Asparagi
SERVES 4 FOR A MAIN COURSE OR 6 FOR A FIRST COURSE

Humble as the lowly grain of rice may be, here is one example of its transformation into an elegant and beautiful dish fit for any special occasion.

2 live Maine lobsters (1½ pounds each)

1 cup dry white wine

Salt

2 white onions, papery skins removed

2 carrots, peeled

Handful of Italian parsley sprigs

8 black peppercorns

4 tablespoons butter

2 teaspoons finely chopped onion

2 cups Italian carnaroli rice

20 asparagus tips

Scant teaspoon saffron threads or ½0-ounce vial of saffron

ᐧᐧ Bring a stockpot of water to a boil. Plunge the live lobsters into the pot and cover. When the water returns to a boil, add the white wine and 1 teaspoon salt. Boil for about 6 minutes so that the lobsters are almost, but not completely, cooked. Remove the lobsters from the pot and detach and set aside the tails and claws. Return the heads to the pot along with the onions, carrots, parsley, and peppercorns. Simmer uncovered for 1 hour.

ᐧᐧ Cut the tails down the middle, pull out the meat, and cut into 1-inch pieces. Crack open the claws, break apart the meat, and set aside.

ᐧᐧ Melt the butter in a large, heavy-bottomed saucepan. Add the onions and sauté them over a low heat until they are tender and translucent. Add the rice, and stir it well for a minute with a wooden spoon until the grains are evenly coated with the onions and butter.

ᐧᐧ Increase the flame to medium heat, and add the asparagus tips, saffron and a ladleful of broth. Stir more or less continuously while the liquid evaporates. Continue adding small amounts of broth and stirring for another 10 minutes.

ᐧᐧ Add the cut lobster tails and stir the mixture well. Continue adding broth and stirring until the rice is cooked but still firm to the tooth. The total cooking time will be about 18 minutes. Ladle the risotto into individual bowls, sprinkle with the meat from the lobster claws, and serve.

Risotto with Fresh Herbs and Chicken
Risotto alle Erbette e Pollo

SERVES 4

Venetians favor their risotti creamy and liquid as opposed to the somewhat stiffer stuff of places like Milan. Antonio, not surprisingly, follows the Venetian tradition and so the risotti at Locanda Veneta *"van' giù bene,"* which is to say, they "go down easy." This earthy, herb-laced risotto is no exception. We use a combination of light and dark meat, you may use any combination of either.

6 cups chicken broth (page 173) or 1 high quality bouillon cube dissolved in 6 cups
   simmering water
4 tablespoons olive oil
1 stalk celery, finely chopped
4 tablespoons chopped shallots
1 teaspoon finely chopped fresh rosemary
1 teaspoon finely chopped fresh sage
10 ounces boned raw chicken, diced
2 cups Italian arborio rice
½ cup white wine
1 cup grated Parmesan cheese
Salt
Freshly ground black pepper to taste

∽ Bring the chicken broth or bouillon to a low simmer.
∽ Lightly heat the olive oil in a large, heavy-bottomed saucepan. Add the celery and shallots and sauté them lightly over a medium flame for a couple of minutes. Stir in the herbs, saturating them in the aromatic vegetables, then add the diced chicken. When the meat has

colored on all sides, vigorously stir in the rice. After a minute, pour in the white wine, stir, and simmer until the liquid evaporates.

༄ Lightly cover the rice with the broth or bouillon and stir regularly until the liquid is soaked up by the grains. Continue adding small amounts of broth, stirring almost continuously as the rice absorbs the liquid, until the rice has cooked for 15 to 18 minutes and is tender yet firm to the bite. The consistency should be creamy and liquid, but not soupy.

༄ Remove from heat, stir in Parmesan and season to taste with salt and freshly ground black pepper. Allow the rice to sit for a couple of minutes before serving.

Savory Rice Layered with Eggplant, Ragù, and Mushrooms
Millefoglie di Riso, Melanzane, Ragù, e Funghi
SERVES 6

It's not that Italians eat so much more than Americans, it's that they prefer to eat a greater variety of things at one meal than many Americans are accustomed to. Almost any college student who has traveled to Italy has had the embarrassing experience of taking three helpings of spaghetti, only to find out that roasted pork, potatoes, sautéed spinach, and salad were still to come. Interestingly enough, these large, varied meals don't necessarily mean that the Italian home cook is a slave to the kitchen. Rather, the time in the kitchen is wisely spent, with sauces, meats, and vegetables made in quantity so they can be used over the next couple of days as a base for other dishes.

This millefoglie is an example of how an industrious home cook might put to use the remnants of a couple of past meals to create something entirely new and delicious.

Salt

5 medium Japanese eggplants, peeled and cut lengthwise into ¼-inch slices

¼ cup olive oil

Flour for dredging

6 cups chicken broth (page 173) or 1 high quality bouillon cube dissolved in 6 cups
    simmering water

2 tablespoons butter, plus additional butter for greasing the pan

1 shallot, finely chopped

2 cups arborio rice

1½ cups freshly grated Parmesan cheese

1 cup *funghi trifolati,* at room temperature (page 281)

1 cup meat sauce, at room temperature (page 102)

   Lightly salt the eggplant slices, layer them in a colander and set aside for 30 minutes. Rinse the slices under water and pat dry. Warm the olive oil in a large nonstick pan. Lightly dredge the eggplant in flour and fry until lightly golden on each side, turning once or twice. Blot between paper towels and set aside.

   Preheat the oven to 400°. Heat the broth or bouillon to a gentle simmer. Place the butter and shallot in a heavy-bottomed saucepan and sauté over a low flame, stirring regularly, until the shallots begin to soften. Increase the flame to medium, add the rice, and stir vigorously to coat the grains in the oil. Prepare a basic risotto, adding the broth in small increments and stirring almost continuously until the rice has cooked for 18 minutes and is tender but still quite firm to the tooth. Stir in ½ cup grated Parmesan and set aside.

   Generously butter a 9-inch round cake pan. Line the bottom and sides with an even layer of eggplant, laying the slices either horizontally or radiating out from the center. Cover with a thin layer of risotto, and sprinkle with half the remaining Parmesan. Spoon the mushrooms over the rice in 1 even layer, and cover with an additional thin layer of rice. Spoon the ragù evenly over the rice and sprinkle with the remaining Parmesan. Cover with any remaining slices of eggplant and the remaining rice.

   Bake in the center rack of the oven for 15 minutes, then cover with aluminum foil and continue baking for an additional 15 minutes. Remove the pan from the oven and let it stand for 10 minutes. Run a knife along the side of the pan, then set a large, round platter over the pan. Invert, then tap along the pan to unmold. Serve by slicing as you would a pie.

CULINARY ALCHEMY

The only time I ever really feel like a child anymore is when Jean-Louis's parents, Lino and Maria, come to visit. They come only infrequently, since it's a three-hour drive from their home in Vittorio Veneto to ours, and a much longer one if they travel all the way from the small town in the South of France where they spend part of the year.

Maria begins to lay siege on the house a couple of weeks before actually arriving. "Lori, save all your ironing for me to do when I come. And get together anything that needs mending, and any of Jean-Louis's shirts that are missing buttons," she instructs. I gladly acquiesce, knowing that next to cooking, sewing and ironing are her favorite pastimes. There was a time when I resisted my mother-in-law's offers to help—I needed to show her how capable I was at running our household. Nearly twenty years later, I am more than happy to temporarily hand over the reins and give myself a little break from the rigors of domesticity.

Lino and Maria arrive with all the tumult and clamor of a small three-ring circus, bringing very little in the way of clothing or personal effects, but extracting an astonishing array of food and other culinary paraphernalia from the car. Exactly what they bring will depend on whether they are coming from the Veneto or France. From northern Italy, there will be bags of polenta and borlotti beans from Lamon, several wedges of local cheese, a basket of vegetables their friend Gigi grew in his small garden, mushrooms if it is the season, and several jugs of *vino sfuso* (good unbottled wine that Lino has bought directly from the source). From France, there will be boxes of lentils from Le Puy and tisanes from the local herbalist, jars of tart, crisp cornichons and hot Dijon mustard, and here, too, a couple wedges of cheese and few liters of good unlabeled local wine.

They will also have packed the entire perishable contents of their refrigerator, down to the last half-consumed pint of milk, into a series of temperature-insulated bags. There will be fresh bread for us and bits and pieces of yesterday's bread that Maria will insist upon eating herself or using in a soup. She will have already spent a couple of days cooking at home to prepare for the visit. There will be two large plastic water bottles filled with pureed vegetable soup and four or five containers of things like homemade pasta sauce, *funghi trifolati,* sautéed spinach, and veal stew—just so she knows we won't all die of hunger before she manages to get the *cucina* up and running at full speed.

For the duration of their visit, my culinary responsibilities are limited to setting the table and showing up at said table at the required time (one sharp for lunch, eight for dinner) with a ravenous appetite.

Maria will invite our neighbors André and Beatrice for dinner at least once, as well as any friends of ours lucky enough to be at the house anywhere near mealtime. And although she will delight in planning an elaborate multicourse meal, and trying out recipes from the latest copy of her favorite food magazine, *Sale e Pepe,* she will extend an invitation to stay for dinner even if she has no idea what she'll be able to offer besides an abundant dose of hospitality.

Like the medieval alchemist who could miraculously transform common metal into something as precious as silver or gold, Maria has the gift of pulling together the most exquisite meal even when the cupboard looks bare. Where I see a refrigerator full of miscellaneous bits of leftovers, Maria sees the makings of a savory risotto. Where I see a cheese drawer that looks as if it should be emptied—into the cat's dish—she sees a delicate *pasta con quattro formaggi.* With a handful of kitchen staples, she can come up with an astonishing variety of things to eat. All she needs is a bit of dried pasta, rice, polenta, bread or beans, some olive oil, an onion, or a clove of garlic and she is in business.

My aversion to leftovers (which Maria neither refers to nor thinks of as such) was the source of some conflict when Jean-Louis and I were first living together. Our approach to things that had lingered in the refrigerator for a few days was hugely different. I grew up in a house where if you were asked to smell the milk for freshness, your response was to throw it out. In Jean-Louis's house, any doubts were resolved by boiling the milk, and if it didn't separate, using it for coffee. Not one morsel of edible food *ever* hit the wastebasket in the De Mori kitchen—a kitchen that has produced some of the finest meals I've ever eaten.

With a mixture of spontaneity, resourcefulness, and postwar aversion to waste, Maria manages to put something different and interesting on the table at every meal, using far less time and energy than most of the beleaguered home cooks I know. She actually plans on leftovers, counts on them, couldn't do without them. By this I do *not* mean that she makes a huge pot of soup and foists it on her family every night until its finished. It's just that while it may look as if she's in her kitchen making dinner, chances are she's also got in mind something for tomorrow's lunch, or the base for a soup she'll make later in the week. She'll extract every bit of usefulness from anything she makes. She knows her marinated vegetables will be even better in a couple of days, she plans on using her *funghi trifolati* for tomorrow's risotto, she'll add a bit of this or that to a sauce and turn it into something fresh and new.

Making something new from the remains of an earlier meal is one of the best ways to start cooking creatively. It's easier on the psyche to experiment with a bit of leftovers than to unleash your imagination on imported mushrooms and filet mignon. Learn to cook with whatever your kitchen has to offer. Make a big pot of chicken soup and save some broth for a risotto; eat a minestrone chunky one day and pureed and drizzled with olive oil and Parmesan the next; *always* make extra tomato sauce. Discover the art of culinary alchemy.

SOUPS

Midmorning yesterday I decided to make a soup with the stray remnants of the vegetable bin. There were just the most basic ingredients, and they were fresh, if not exactly exciting—two onions, a heart of celery, a carrot, a couple of zucchini, three almost overripe tomatoes, and a fistful of new potatoes.

I poured a bit of olive oil into a large soup pot, chopped up the onions, and lit the gas flame on the stove. I stirred somewhat absently for a couple of minutes while the onions sizzled and softened, then cut the remaining vegetables directly into the pot. I stood at the stove a bit longer, turning the vegetables over in the oil before covering them with water and throwing in a bay leaf, some peppercorns, and a generous handful each of lentils and barley.

After a few minutes the kitchen took on the tantalizing fragrance of sautéing onions and it smelled like something wonderful was cooking. I peered into the pot. What I saw looked a lot less like a soup than a bunch of ingredients sitting in some not-so-appetizing-looking murky water. It didn't possibly seem like my efforts were going to amount to much. I could only hope that a long, slow simmer would help my ingredients soften up and make friends with each other.

It did. But of course, this is what we love about soups—that from their inauspicious beginnings come perhaps the ultimate comfort food. They ask so little from us in the way of preparation, and yet few things make a kitchen more inviting than a pot of soup bubbling away on the stove. The recipes in this chapter range from savory broths to thick, hearty soups that ask for little more than a basket of crusty bread and a bottle of wine to complete the meal. Though each soup has its own "personality," the underlying principle remains the same: wonderful, homey flavor for very little work. Need I say more?

Chicken Broth
Brodo di Pollo

MAKES ABOUT 10 CUPS

We in America have convinced ourselves that chicken is the healthy alternative to red meat. Consequently, when we think broth, we think chicken broth. Most Italians opt to make their broths with the meat and bones of beef, believing that commercially raised chickens, with their tight living quarters and unnatural diets, produce a broth with less flavor and substance. Antonio is convinced that there's room in the kitchen for both beef and chicken and suggests using a free-range chicken if they are available where you live. Chicken broth, like meat broth, freezes well, and can be frozen in ice cube trays, then stored in airtight freezer bags to be used as needed. The meat is delicious eaten with the broth itself or shredded over salad.

One 3- to 4-pound stewing chicken
2 small onions, outer skins removed
3 carrots, peeled
1 celery stalk
Handful of fresh Italian parsley

3 black peppercorns
1 bay leaf
12 cups cold water
1 teaspoon coarse salt

Rinse the chicken well under running water. Put all the ingredients except the salt in a large stockpot and heat uncovered over a high flame almost to boiling. Skim off any impurities that rise to the top. Add the salt, reduce the heat to low, and simmer, partially covered, for 1 hour. Skim the fat off the top as it rises or when the broth cools and the fat solidifies.

Strain the broth in a colander, or for a very clear broth strain though a chinois or a cheesecloth-lined colander. Leave out to cool before refrigerating or freezing.

Meat Broth
Brodo di Carne
MAKES ABOUT 10 CUPS

Lesso is one of those things that Italians can't get enough of and Americans could live their whole lives without. Born of necessity and ingenuity, like the best Italian dishes, tough pieces of meat and flavor-giving bones are brought together with a few vegetables in a big pot to simmer all afternoon. The fork-tender meat is served with the cooked vegetables and usually a condiment such as herbed *salsa verde* (literally, "green sauce"), hot mustard, or fragrant olive oil. The broth is savored with fine threads of cooked pasta or tortellini, or used as a base for risotto or soup.

For the Broth

4 pounds beef chuck or brisket, with some bone in

2 small onions, outer skins removed

3 carrots, peeled

1 celery stalk

1 ripe tomato

3 black peppercorns

1 bay leaf

12 cups cold water

1 teaspoon coarse salt

For the Salsa Verde

1 bunch of flat-leaf Italian parsley, leaves only

Handful of fresh basil leaves

3 anchovy fillets, finely chopped

½ spring onion, white only, chopped

½ clove garlic

½ cup extra-virgin olive oil

1 tablespoon lemon juice

1 teaspoon Dijon mustard

～ *The broth:* Rinse the meat and bones well under running water. Put all the ingredients except for the salt in a large stockpot and heat uncovered over a high flame almost to boiling. Skim any foam off the top. Reduce the flame to very low, add the salt, and simmer partially covered for 3 to 4 hours. Add more water if necessary depending on how concentrated a broth you need. Skim the fat off the top as it rises or when the broth cools and the fat solidifies.

～ Strain the broth in a colander lined with cheesecloth. Cool before refrigerating.

～ *The salsa verde:* Place all the ingredients in a food processor and blend to a paste.

～ *Serving the meat:* Slice the meat and vegetables from the broth and arrange on a platter with some boiled potatoes and ramekins of *salsa verde* and Dijon mustard; or cut the meat into small pieces and serve over lettuce dressed with olive oil and a touch of red wine vinegar.

WASTE NOT, WANT NOT

Some of Italy's most interesting recipes are the fruit of centuries of dogged determination to avoid culinary waste of any kind. Sopa caoda *is a characteristically Venetian example of "leftovers" put to wise and delicious use. It can be made from any leftover bits of broth or roasted meats, whether beef or fowl. Sauté a couple of finely chopped carrots, potatoes, and onions. Chop or shred the meat. Layer a baking dish with thick slices of toasted day-old country bread. Cover the bread with the vegetables, meat, and a generous grating of Parmesan cheese. Cover with additional slices of bread and more cheese. Ladle broth over the whole thing and cook uncovered in a 350° oven for 1½ hours, adding a ladle of stock now and then. Serve in shallow soup bowls.*

Summer Minestrone with Three Sauces
Minestrone Estivo con Tre Salse
SERVES 6

The carrots, onion, and celery are used more as culinary herbs than as vegetables in this soup. The recipe calls for a small amount of cooked cannellini or white beans, but, if you can find them, by all means use fresh cannellini or white beans—they can cook in the soup pot with the rest of the vegetables (½ pound unshelled beans will give you 1 cup cooked). If you use fresh beans, increase the cooking time by about 20 minutes.

The three condiments—basil, tomato, and peperoncino—can be used in unison or separately (pages 177–78). Place them on a tray at the center of the table and let each person infuse their soup with the flavors of their choosing. Go lightly with the sauces, each has its own strong assertive flavor and only a touch is needed.

3 tablespoons olive oil

1 onion, chopped

1 carrot, chopped

1 small celery heart, chopped

8 cups water

4 new potatoes, peeled and diced, then set in a bowl of cold water until ready for
  the pot

½ pound green beans, trimmed and cut into 1-inch lengths

3 small zucchini, diced

¾ cup fresh or frozen peas

½ cup cooked cannellini or white beans

½ pound Swiss chard, ribs and leaves coarsely chopped

Salt

Freshly ground black pepper

↬ Warm the olive oil in a large soup pot over a medium flame. Add the onion, carrot, and celery and sauté gently for 3 to 4 minutes before adding to the pot 8 cups of water and all the vegetables except the chard.

↬ When the water begins to boil, add the chard and simmer gently for 10 minutes. Then reduce the flame, cover the pot partially, and simmer for another 20 minutes before adding salt and pepper to taste. (If you use fresh white beans, the soup will need to simmer for an additional 20 minutes, or until the beans are tender.)

↬ Ladle the soup into individual serving bowls. Put the 3 condiments on the table with a tiny spoon in each ramekin.

Basil and Garlic
Basilico e Aglio

2 large handfuls of fresh basil leaves
4 cloves garlic
4 sprigs of Italian flat-leaf parsley, leaves only
2 tablespoons extra-virgin olive oil
3 tablespoons butter
Pinch of salt

↬ Blend all the ingredients in a food processor until they form a creamy paste. Spoon into a ramekin.

Tomato
Pomodoro

1 spring onion, white part only, minced

3 cloves garlic, minced

1 tablespoon olive oil

¼ cup tomato paste

1 small rosemary sprig

Pinch of dried oregano

¾ cup water

In a small saucepan, gently sauté the onion and garlic in the olive oil, taking care not to burn the garlic. After a minute or two, add the tomato paste and cook for a few minutes, stirring constantly. The tomato paste will turn from a bright rusty red and will take on a mildly sweet aroma.

Add the herbs, ¾ cup water, and simmer gently until the mixture reduces itself to a thin paste (about 10 minutes). Remove the rosemary. Pour the sauce into a ramekin.

Spicy
Peperoncino

4 tablespoons cayenne pepper oil (page 28)

6 small dried red chili peppers, stem ends removed, finely chopped

4 tablespoons extra-virgin olive oil

Mix the ingredients together well. Pour into a ramekin.

Country Potato Soup
Minestra di Patate
SERVES 4

Even the barest cupboard is usually hiding at least a couple of potatoes and onions. Antonio likes the delicate flavor he gets by sweating the onions in equal parts butter and olive oil—this is typically northern Italian. A Tuscan cook would shudder to think of using anything other than unadulterated olive oil. For a wonderful variation, omit the marjoram and croutons and stir 1½ cups of sautéed mushrooms (page 281) into the prepared soup and simmer for 3 minutes.

1½ pounds baking potatoes

2 tablespoons extra-virgin olive oil

2 tablespoons butter

2 medium yellow or white onions, finely chopped

4 cups chicken broth (page 173) or high quality bouillon, heated to a low simmer

Salt

Freshly ground black pepper

1 tablespoon fresh, chopped marjoram or 1 teaspoon dried marjoram

2 thick slices country bread, cut into medium cubes

∽ Preheat oven to 375°.

∽ Wash and peel the potatoes. Cut them into small cubes.

∽ Put the olive oil, butter, and onions in a soup pot and heat over a low to medium flame, stirring the onions frequently until they are soft and translucent. Stir in the potatoes, coating them well with the sautéed onions. Cook them until they have colored slightly (about 10 minutes). Scrape the bottom of the pot frequently with a flat-bottomed wooden spoon to prevent the potatoes from sticking.

꜒ Add the chicken broth or bouillon, then season to taste with salt and freshly ground pepper. Simmer, partially covered, until the potatoes begin to dissolve. (The time will vary depending on the age and type of potato, but allow for up to 40 minutes.) Using a potato masher or a hand blender, break up some of the potatoes, leaving small chunks of potatoes in with the thick, creamy body of the soup. Sprinkle in the marjoram. Simmer for a couple more minutes.

꜒ In the meantime, toast the bread cubes, turning occasionally until they are evenly golden.

꜒ Ladle the soup into individual serving bowls and scatter with the toasted croutons.

Potage of Fresh Zucchini
Passato di Zucchini
SERVES 4

Anyone who's planted zucchini knows that there arrives a time in midsummer when it becomes nearly impossible to keep squash consumption up with production. This simple soup began as an effort to make a dent in our zucchini bounty, but the fresh green puree, flecked with the darker green of the skin and basil, is a beautiful way to spotlight one of summer's most abundant vegetables.

4 tablespoons extra-virgin olive oil, plus oil for drizzling

3 medium yellow or white onions, finely chopped

2 pounds small zucchini, cut crosswise into very thin slices

Large handful of fresh basil leaves, plus additional leaves for garnishing

4 cups chicken broth (page 173) or high-quality bouillon

Salt

Freshly ground black pepper

Lightly heat the olive oil in a medium, heavy-bottomed soup pot. Add the onions and sauté over a medium flame, stirring often, until the onions are soft and lightly golden.

Stir the zucchini into the pot to mix with the onions and cook over a low flame, stirring occasionally, until the zucchini softens and begins to break apart (about 20 minutes). Add in the basil leaves and continue cooking for another 2 to 3 minutes, then pour in the chicken broth or bouillon, reduce the flame to low, and simmer uncovered for 20 minutes, stirring occasionally.

Blend the soup with a hand or stationary blender to a smooth pale green flecked with darker green. Season to taste with salt and a generous grinding of black pepper.

Ladle the soup into individual serving bowls, drizzle with olive oil, and garnish with fresh basil leaves.

Asparagus and Barley Soup
Zuppa di Asparagi ed Orzo
SERVES 4

Rarely is barley the star of a soup—usually it's hidden somewhere inside a thick broth laden with meat, mushrooms, and vegetables. This beautifully delicate soup celebrates pearly white barley's toothy texture and subtle flavor. When made with the white asparagus of Bassano del Grappa, the soup is a palate of gorgeous whites speckled with parsley. Don't despair if you can't find white asparagus—fresh green asparagus work deliciously as well. If you do use white asparagus, remember that the outer skin of the stalk must be peeled away entirely—it is fibrous, bitter, and inedible (exactly the opposite of the sweet, tender interior).

½ cup pearl barley, soaked overnight in a large bowl of cool water
1 pound fresh white or green asparagus
1 tablespoon extra-virgin olive oil, plus oil for drizzling

1 small white or yellow onion, chopped

⅓ cup finely diced Italian pancetta

6 cups chicken broth (page 173) or good-quality bouillon

Freshly ground black pepper

Salt

2 tablespoons finely chopped Italian parsley

Freshly grated Parmesan cheese for the table

∽ Drain the barley and set aside.

∽ Chop off the fibrous bottoms of the asparagus. If you are using white asparagus, completely pare away the tough outer skin of the stalks. If you are using green asparagus, simply pare away any fibrous portion on the exterior of the stalk. Cut the pared stalks into a small dice, leaving the tips whole.

∽ Warm 1 tablespoon of olive oil in a soup pot over a medium flame, add the onion and pancetta and sauté until the onion becomes lightly golden in color and the pancetta has begun to melt its fat (6 to 8 minutes). Add the asparagus and the barley and mix well to coat with the pancetta and onion mixture.

∽ Add 5 cups of broth and a grinding of black pepper, raise the flame to high until the broth boils, then reduce to a simmer and leave the pot partially covered for 20 minutes, stirring occasionally.

∽ Correct the seasonings, adding additional salt and pepper if necessary. Add the last cup of broth if the soup looks too thick. Simmer for an additional 10 minutes or until the barley is cooked.

∽ Ladle into warmed soup bowls, sprinkle with chopped parsley, and drizzle with a good olive oil. Offer grated Parmesan.

SOME LIKE IT HOT
Butto La Pasta?

Americans tend to like their beers icy cold and their soups steaming hot. Europeans take a more moderate approach. Ask for a glass of water at any bar and you will be given the choice: room temperature or chilled? A refrigerator-cold drink will rarely be served with ice. If you ask, a bartender *will* ceremoniously drop two ice cubes, three at the very most, into your drink—but that won't stop him from wondering why on earth you are adding ice to something that is already chilled. As for *il latte,* Italians aren't big milk drinkers, but those who do drink it seem to prefer it *tiepido,* what we would (shudder to) call tepid—its cold edge removed at the bar by a quick blast with the cappuccino frother. (In the heat of the summer, ice cold drinks are considered to be positively dangerous—especially for children—the cause of "*congestione,*" one of those vaguely Victorian maladies whose symptoms I have never quite understood, most likely because in all my years here I have never actually seen them manifest themselves in any child.)

There is a well-founded belief in Italy that the flavors of most foods come through best at a somewhat neutral temperature. Fruits and vegetables are set out in bowls and baskets in the kitchen, rather than in the produce bin of the refrigerator (watermelon being an exception even in Italy—the colder the better). Artichokes and fresh herbs sit in pitchers of water on the counter. Tomatoes are eaten warm from the summer garden.

The approach is much the same on the other end of the temperature spectrum. Risotto is left to sit in the pot for a couple of minutes before it is ladled into shallow bowls and served. Even then, many people use their forks to spread the rice over the plate and allow it to cool even more.

In the summer, we make it a point to serve our soups warm rather than steaming hot. The obvious rationale is that a boiling mouthful of soup will do little to take the edge off a sweltering day. But the real reason is that the flavors seem to ripen as they reach a temperature that doesn't assault the palate. Of course, temperature is a matter of preference—and habit. Our penchant for warm soups caused a bit of confusion when they first appeared at Locanda Veneta. Many a bowl of soup was sent back to the kitchen to be heated, until we convinced our customers that we had served the soup comfortably warm *on purpose* and that they might actually like it better that way.

Ironically, the one thing Italians cannot tolerate cold or even at room temperature is that most *italiano* of foods: pasta. While you might come across a pasta salad in a tourist trap in the center of Florence, you will rarely be offered one in an Italian home. More likely, the meal will be timed around the exact moment the pasta hits the boiling water, where it will be cooked until appropriately al dente, drained, tossed with one of an infinite variety of sauces, then brought to the table as quickly as possible.

In fact, *"Butto la pasta?"* is probably the most common question that Jean-Louis and I find ourselves debating with our neighbors André and Beatrice. Once or twice a week, our two families have dinner together, and at least one of those meals is sure to include pasta.

The unspoken rule is that no pasta hits the water until everyone has been given fair warning—hence the question, *"Butto la pasta?,"* which literally translated means, "shall I throw the pasta?" One of us usually begs for five or ten extra minutes to finish something up. When the pasta is finally "thrown," another announcement circulates: "Ho buttato la pasta," i.e., "Wash your hands and get your body to the dinner table." If by chance you are late, *peggio per te.* All the worse for you. Someone will cover your bowl of pasta to keep it warm until you arrive, and everyone will ooh and ahh about how absolutely wonderful it was (and by implication what you missed by being late).

Temperature is a matter of preference—and habit. It contributes to the flavor of the food we eat as much as the herbs and seasonings to which we tend to devote a far greater share of our attention. Notice how the flavor of a peach, a tomato, a bowl of slowly simmered soup changes at different temperatures. You may still decide that you prefer a tart green apple cold and crisp out of the icebox, and your soup steaming and bubbling like some primordial brew. Just whatever you do—serve your pasta hot!

Chicken and Corn Chowder
Zuppa di Pollo e Granturco
SERVES 6

Somewhere along the way, our kids became part of our contingent of indentured recipe testers. Their voices were part of a larger chorus of opinions, suggestions, and (literally) gut reactions to the recipes they sampled. This hearty country soup was as huge a hit with our little ones as it has been with our customers at Locanda Veneta who have been enjoying it for years.

⅓ cup extra-virgin olive oil

1 medium red onion, finely chopped

1 carrot, peeled and finely chopped

1 stalk celery, strings and leaves removed, finely chopped

1 pound boned chicken thigh meat, cut into ½-inch dice

½ cup dry white wine

½ teaspoon salt

Freshly ground black pepper

1 pound potatoes, peeled, halved lengthwise, and thinly sliced

4 cups water

1 plum tomato, peeled and crushed

½ cup fresh, canned, or frozen corn

∽ Heat the olive oil in a large soup pot over a medium flame. Add the onion, carrot, and celery, and sauté until the vegetables are soft and golden (about 15 minutes).

∽ Add the chicken, stirring it in the pot with a flat-edged wooden spoon until it has colored lightly on all sides. Pour in the white wine and stir for a couple of minutes while the alcohol evaporates and the pan juices thicken. Season with salt and a grinding of black pepper, then add the potatoes, water, and tomato. Increase the heat to high, until the soup almost reaches a boil, then reduce to a simmer and skim any foam off the top.

∽ Simmer for 5 minutes, then add the corn. Cook over low heat until the potato begins to break apart easily (about 20 minutes). Stir the soup briskly with a wire whisk and serve.

Sweet Pepper Soup
Minestra di Peperoni
SERVES 4

We serve this thick potage at room temperature. The peppers soften and mellow during their slow simmer—you decide whether to use red or yellow.

2 tablespoons extra-virgin olive oil, plus oil for drizzling

1 large onion, finely chopped

3 shallots, finely chopped

1 pound red or yellow peppers, ribs and seeds removed, cut into bite-sized pieces

1 pound potatoes, peeled and cut into small cubes

4 cups water

Small handful of fresh basil leaves

Salt

Freshly ground black pepper

∽ Warm the olive oil in a soup pot over a medium flame. Cook the onions and shallots until they begin to soften, then add the peppers and increase the flame to high, stirring briskly. After a few minutes, when the peppers begin to soften and release their liquid, add the potatoes and stir the pot regularly with a flat-bottomed spoon for the next 5 minutes.

~ Add the water and the basil leaves to the pot and reduce the flame to medium. When the pot begins to bubble, lower the flame, add salt and freshly ground pepper to taste, then simmer gently for 1 hour, stirring often.

~ At the end of the cooking time, use a wire whisk to beat the soup briskly. The potatoes will have formed a thick, chunky broth. Let the soup cool to warm, drizzle with good olive oil, and serve.

Maria's Pasta e Fagioli
Pasta e Fagioli alla Maria

SERVES 4

Jean-Louis and I think his mother's *pasta e fagioli* is the best we've ever eaten. Of course, it may well be that everyone from the Veneto is convinced of the unassailable superiority of the *pasta e fagioli* they grew up eating. "It's all about the beans—which ones you use and how you cook them," Maria explained as I tried to get her to put into words something she has done instinctively for at least fifty years.

She uses *fagioli di Lamon,* which are widely acknowledged as the very best bean for this classic recipe from the Veneto. Venetian explorers brought the beans back from Mexico in the sixteenth century and they've been grown ever since in a tiny pocket of the Venetian countryside not far from Vittorio Veneto, where Jean-Louis's parents live. Maria uses them fresh in late summer and dried the rest of the year. Unfortunately, so great is the Venetian passion for pasta e fagioli that the limited cultivation from Lamon rarely makes it outside the Veneto.

Much more readily available are the speckled pink and red borlotti beans, whose pods are creamy white stippled with pink. You can find them in most Italian specialty stores both dried and canned. While the quality of canned precooked Italian borlotti is usually quite high, you won't get the classic thick and creamy consistency of a true *pasta e fagioli* unless you cook the fresh or dried beans yourself.

EVERYTHING MARIA TOLD ME ABOUT COOKING BEANS

- *The object is to cook the beans so that both the skin and flesh become soft and creamy.*
- *Shell fresh beans only right before you cook them, since their skins toughen up when exposed to air.*
- *Remember that fresh beans cook more quickly than dried and use somewhat less water.*
- *Simmer fresh and dried beans as gently as possible under the lowest flame necessary to keep the pot barely bubbling so that the beans won't break apart while cooking.*
- *For really tender beans, let the beans simmer for 30 minutes, then turn off the heat for 15 minutes and let the pot sit, simmer for another half hour, then turn the heat off once again for another 15 minutes. Continue cooking the beans until they are tender.*
- *Any additional water added to the beans when they are cooking should be hot so as not to reduce the temperature of the pot.*
- *Always salt beans toward the end of their cooking time.*
- *Blending half of the soup makes for a wonderfully thick and creamy broth.*

For the Beans

1 pound unshelled borlotti or cranberry beans or 1 cup dried borlotti or cranberry beans (soaked overnight in abundant lukewarm water)

Herb bouquet of 4 or 5 sage leaves, a sprig of thyme, 2 bay leaves, and the green tops of 1 leek, tied together with kitchen twine

2 cloves garlic, peeled and finely chopped

2 tablespoons extra-virgin olive oil

For the Base

3 tablespoons extra-virgin olive oil,
   plus oil for drizzling
1 leek, white top only, thinly sliced
1 carrot, finely chopped
1 celery stalk, finely chopped
1 ripe tomato, peeled, seeded, and crushed
Salt
Freshly ground pepper
Pinch of crushed red pepper, optional
4 ounces egg fettuccine,
   broken into short lengths
Freshly grated Parmesan cheese for the table

The beans: Shell and rinse fresh beans, or rinse soaked beans well. Place the beans in a large soup pot with the herb bouquet, garlic and 2 tablespoons of olive oil. Cover with 2 to 3 inches of cold water and simmer covered over a low flame until the beans are tender, stirring occasionally (40 to 60 minutes for fresh beans; 1 to 1½ hours for dried beans). For extra-tender beans, interrupt the simmering for two 15-minute periods as described above. When the beans are tender, turn off the flame and remove the herb bouquet.

The base: In the meantime, heat 3 tablespoons of olive oil in a large skillet. Add the leek, carrot, and celery and sauté over a medium flame until the vegetables are quite soft (15 to 20 minutes), stirring frequently. Add the crushed tomato and two ladles of the cooking water from the beans. Simmer for 5 minutes, then add the vegetables to the beans and season to taste with salt and a generous grinding of black pepper (or a pinch of hot red pepper if you want some spiciness). Simmer at the lowest possible heat for 30 minutes.

Pass half the soup through a food mill or lightly blend the soup with a hand blender. Return the soup to a low boil, then add the pasta and cook until al dente (5 to 7 minutes).

Ladle the soup into individual bowls, drizzle with olive oil, and serve. Offer grated Parmesan.

Variations: In the summer, Maria often adds 2 or 3 small, sliced zucchini and a handful of green beans to the sautéed leek, carrot, and celery. In the winter, she may add a couple of ounces of diced pancetta, ½ cup of diced winter squash, or a generous handful of chopped chard leaves to the sautéing vegetables.

White Bean Soup with Pasta and Shrimp
Zuppa di Cannellini con Gamberi
SERVES 4 TO 6

Allegria, our only beachside restaurant, has come up with its own take on the traditional Venetian *pasta e fagioli*, using tender white beans instead of borlotti and adding a generous portion of shrimp when the soup's almost ready to be served. Italians would never add Parmesan to this soup since it contains seafood—however, a drizzling of good olive oil is more than acceptable.

1 cup dried cannellini or white beans (soaked overnight in water)

3 tablespoons extra-virgin olive oil, plus oil for drizzling

1 tablespoon finely chopped onion

1 tablespoon finely chopped carrot

1 tablespoon finely chopped celery

1 tablespoon tomato paste

2 potatoes, peeled and cut into bite-sized chunks

Handful of fresh sage leaves

3 ounces prosciutto, cut into small dice

Salt

Freshly ground black pepper

1 pound large shrimp (about 20 shrimp), peeled and deveined

10 ounces pappardelle, fettuccine, or other flat egg noodle broken into roughly
   3-inch pieces

≈ Rinse the soaked beans well, drain and set aside.

≈ Warm the olive oil in a large soup pot over a gentle flame. Add the onion, carrot, and celery, and cook, stirring from time to time until the vegetables begin to soften (about 10 minutes). Add a tablespoon or two of water if the vegetables are sticking to the pan. Add the tomato paste and cook over a low flame for 3 to 4 more minutes.

≈ Add the beans, potatoes, sage leaves, and prosciutto and cover with 4 inches of water. Simmer over low heat for 1½ hours, using a slotted skimmer to remove any foam from the top of the soup. Season to taste with salt and freshly ground black pepper toward the end of the beans' cooking time. When the beans are tender to the bite, add the shrimp and simmer for 3 to 4 minutes, then add the pasta and cook 5 to 7 minutes more until the pasta is al dente.

≈ Ladle into individual soup bowls, drizzle with olive oil, and serve.

Winter Squash and Wild Mushroom Soup
Zuppa di Zucca e Funghi di Bosco
SERVES 4

This comforting winter soup pairs the subtle sweetness of orange winter squash with the full, dense flavor of wild mushrooms. The mushrooms are sautéed separately, which retains their flavor and texture best, then they are added to the soup toward the end of the cooking time.

For the Mushrooms

1 pound wild mushrooms, such as porcini, oyster, stemmed shiitake, or chanterelle

3 tablespoons extra-virgin olive oil

1 teaspoon finely chopped garlic

1 teaspoon finely chopped Italian parsley

Salt

Freshly ground black pepper

For the Base

    3 tablespoons extra-virgin olive oil

    1 onion, finely chopped

    1 carrot, finely chopped

    2 cups diced winter squash, preferably kabocha

    2 potatoes, peeled, quartered, and thinly sliced

    6 cups cold water

    1 tablespoon tomato paste

    Salt

    Freshly ground black pepper

∽ *The mushrooms:* Wipe the mushrooms clean with a damp cloth, or, if they are very dirty, run them under cold water and pat dry. Trim the stems (discard the entire stem of the shiitake mushrooms), then slice the stems and heads to a ¼-inch thickness. Warm the olive oil over a medium flame in a large skillet, add the garlic, and sauté it briefly until it is lightly golden. Add the mushrooms and parsley, stirring well to coat them with the oil. When the mushrooms begin to soften (3 to 4 minutes), reduce the heat to low, add salt and freshly ground pepper to taste, and continue cooking for another 15 minutes, stirring frequently.

∽ *The base:* Heat the olive oil in a soup pot, then add the onion and carrot and sauté, stirring often, until the vegetables soften (about 10 minutes). Add a touch of water if the vegetables are drying out.

∽ Add the squash, potatoes, and 6 cups of cold water. Bring to a boil, stir in the tomato paste, then simmer slowly for 25 minutes, stirring occasionally. Add the cooked mushrooms to the pot, stir well, and season to taste with salt and freshly ground black pepper. Cover and simmer very gently for 15 minutes. Allow the soup to sit for 5 minutes before serving.

Venetian Fish Soup
Zuppa di Pesce
SERVES 6

For all its splendor, this wonderfully aromatic and flavorful soup is surprisingly easy to make. Serve it either as a first course or main course. Have your fishmonger clean the fish for you, removing the heads, tails, bones, and skin. Smaller, tender fish should be cut into 1½-inch strips, while the thicker slabs of fish can be cut into large chunks. We like to bring the soup to the table in a terra-cotta pot and serve it with toasted country bread rubbed with garlic and drizzled with good olive oil.

1 pound fresh manila or littleneck clams
Salt
½ cup extra-virgin olive oil
½ cup finely chopped garlic
2 cups fresh tomato puree (about 1½ pounds fresh tomatoes, skins and seeds removed, pulp pureed) or 2 cups pureed canned Italian plum tomatoes
2 pounds mixed, cleaned fish (use any combination of scorpion fish, monkfish, grouper, halibut, sea bass, or red snapper; do not use salmon or swordfish)
½ cup finely chopped Italian parsley
12 medium shrimp in their shells (you may substitute shelled, deveined shrimp)
½ pound fresh mussels, scrubbed and debearded
½ cup dry white wine
2 bay leaves
Freshly ground black pepper

ᗧ Soak the clams in several changes of lightly salted cold water for 1½ to 2 hours.
ᗧ Warm the olive oil with the garlic in a stockpot. When the garlic is fragrant and lightly golden, remove it from the pot with a small slotted spoon and set it aside, leaving just a touch of garlic in the pot with the oil.

∾ Coat the bottom of the pot with a couple of tablespoons of tomato puree. Begin to layer the fish, placing the toughest fish on the bottom and the most tender on top and interspersing each layer of fish with a sprinkle of parsley and salt and a couple of tablespoons of tomato puree. We would layer the fish we have listed in the following order: scorpion fish on the bottom, followed by monkfish, grouper, halibut, sea bass, then red snapper.

∾ Cover the fish with the shrimp, clams, and mussels. Sprinkle with the remaining garlic, parsley, and tomato puree. Pour the white wine over the top, then cover the contents of the pot with 2 to 3 inches of water, depending on whether you prefer a thicker or thinner broth. Add the bay leaves and a grinding of black pepper, bring to a boil, then reduce to a simmer. Cover and cook for 15 to 20 minutes without stirring until the fish is tender and cooked through.

∾ Serve immediately.

GNOCCHI

Gnocchi means "dumplings" in Italian. Primarily a northern Italian invention (although you will find them made with coarse-ground semolina in Rome), they originated in the poorest households, where there wasn't enough flour to make pasta. By bringing together a bit of flour with potatoes or winter squash, something resembling pasta could be formed. Many variations exist that add spinach, rice, Parmesan, or even fillings to the basic combination of flour, starch, egg yolk, nutmeg, and cinnamon.

"People have the wrong idea about gnocchi," says Antonio, defending one of his favorite *primi*. "I've heard them called 'heavy,' 'gummy,' and 'eraserlike' . . . and I've been asked to prepare them 'al dente,' which is like asking for your ice cream at room temperature—the term just doesn't apply to the dish. If someone tries a poorly prepared plate of gnocchi, they conclude that they just don't like the beast, and that the only people who would are those who grew up on the leaden weights and didn't know any better."

I think that what Antonio likes best about gnocchi (besides their taste) is the challenge involved in taking the most humble ingredients and turning them into something that completely transcends its modest origins. After all, it's one thing to throw a filet mignon in a pan with some herbs and butter, it's entirely another to take potatoes and flour and transform them into tender, light little dumplings.

Antonio is resolute about getting his point across: "In America, and even in parts of Italy where gnocchi are not a big part of the local culinary tradition, people don't really know what gnocchi are supposed to taste like . . . how light and delicate they are meant to be, how *totally delicious* they are when they are properly prepared—which isn't easy, but isn't even all that hard once you learn a few *trucchi*."

The *trucchi* he's talking about are culinary tricks. Every chef's bag is full of them. In this case, call them "tricks" or "techniques," but they make all the difference between light little pillows that melt in your mouth and chewy, sodden weights that stick to your gut.

The Principles of Gnocchi-Making

- The less flour you use, the lighter your gnocchi will be.
- The less moisture in your ingredients, the less flour you will need.
- Boiling the potatoes in their skins and slipping off the skins while they're *hot*, then passing the potatoes through a ricer and gently spreading them out on a flat work surface to cool, is the *best* way to coax the moisture out of potatoes. This allows you to use less flour. Less flour → lighter gnocchi.
- Floury potatoes, such as large baking potatoes, have the perfect high-starch/low-moisture combination for making gnocchi. New potatoes are too waxy and high in moisture to use.
- The exact amount of flour you'll use is going to vary depending upon the moisture in your ingredients and the humidity in the air. The rule of thumb is to use only as much flour as is necessary for the dough to lose most of its stickiness and become soft and pliant, but never dry. Be miserly with the flour, adding only small amounts at a time.
- Gnocchi dough does not need to be energetically kneaded, like bread. Five minutes of gentle folding and kneading is all you need.

- Let the dough rest for 5 minutes before shaping the gnocchi.
- Gnocchi can be rolled into 1-inch little logs or shaped with the tines of a fork or the back of a cheese grater. The fork and grater method isn't just for decorative effect—it helps the gnocchi hold their sauce. It takes a bit of practice to get the rolling down just right, but after a couple of batches you'll be up there with the best Venetian *casalinga.*

Fork shaping: Roll each "gnocco" (the singular of "gnocchi") along the tines of a fork (the curved outside bottom of the fork works best) and onto a floured work surface, pressing firmly at the beginning and then more or less flicking the gnocco onto the work surface. The gnocchi will be slightly flattened, with a dimple on one side (where your finger was pressing) and the ridged imprint of the tines on the other.

Grater shaping: Using the dull inside of a rectangular handheld cheese grater, press each gnocco firmly on the inside of the grater and then, with one quick flick, down the grater and onto your floured work surface. Your gnocchi will be marked with small craters rather than ridges, but the result is the same: better rapport between gnocco and sauce.

Gnocchi shaper: If you do happen to develop a passion for gnocchi making, then the next time you're in Italy, go into a kitchenware shop or any farmers' market that sells kitchen gadgets and ask for a gnocchi shaper, *"una tavoletta per fare gnocchi."* You will be given a 4-inch-long rectangular piece of ridged wood attached to a thin wooden handle. Roll the gnocchi diagonally across the ridges using the same pressure/flick motion you'd use with a fork or grater. Splurge—this nifty device will cost you all of $1.50 and takes up very little space in the suitcase. Besides, it makes an interesting little culinary conversation piece . . . or gift for one of those food-loving friends who thinks he or she has every kitchen gadget known to man. And it might be just the thing to inspire you to make gnocchi as often as Antonio would have you make them—which is *often.*

- Gnocchi should be cooked within a few hours of when they are made, any longer and they begin to release their moisture and become sticky.

- When choosing a pot to cook gnocchi, opt for width over depth. Gnocchi sink to the bottom of the pot when they begin cooking and rise to the top about half a minute before they're ready. Ideally, they should rise in one even layer, so that there's no risk of their sticking to each other. Don't throw all the gnocchi in the pot at once. Cook them 2 or 3 portions at a time, dropping them one by one (but quickly) into the pot so as to form only 1 layer of gnocchi on the bottom of the pot. Since they only take a few minutes to cook, boiling them in batches isn't really a problem. You may choose to put 2 large pots of water to boil on the stove if you want to cook all the gnocchi at once.

- Gnocchi are relatively delicate creatures and should be handled as little as possible once they are cooked. For this reason, it's really best to use a slotted skimmer to take them straight from the pot to individual bowls. Spoon some sauce over the top and a generous grating of Parmesan cheese and serve.

- Don't expect to make perfect gnocchi the first time. Too little flour will make your gnocchi fall apart in the water, too much flour makes the gnocchi heavy and chewy. Antonio suggests boiling a small saucepan of water and testing a couple of gnocchi before cooking a whole batch so that you can adjust the flour if necessary.

- It takes a bit of practice to get the feel for when the gnocchi dough has reached the right consistency. Don't just follow the recipe—engage your senses and pay attention so that when you do end up with a batch of exquisitely light gnocchi, you'll know just how to make them the next time . . . and the next.

Potato Gnocchi
Gnocchi di Patate
SERVES 6

The classic gnocchi. We like them best tossed with melted butter and freshly grated Parmesan, or in a savory tomato sauce or meat ragù. Since gnocchi take only minutes to cook, have whatever sauce you choose ready before setting the gnocchi to boil.

For the Gnocchi

3 pounds baking potatoes, scrubbed

Pinch of salt

Pinch of nutmeg

Pinch of ground cinnamon

3 egg yolks

2½ cups all-purpose flour (approximately)

For the Sauce

⅓ cup melted butter or

2 cups Locanda Veneta tomato sauce (page 99) or

2 cups meat ragù (page 102)

½ cup freshly grated Parmesan cheese

⌀ Place the unpeeled potatoes in a pot with ample cold water and bring to a boil. Reduce the flame and cook the potatoes at a low boil until a toothpick inserts easily into the center. (Don't test too often or you will let too much liquid into the potato.) Drain the potatoes in a colander and peel away skins while the potatoes are still hot.

⌀ Pass the potatoes through a ricer or food mill onto a flat work surface. Handling them as little as possible (you don't want to compress the potatoes and seal in their moisture), spread the potatoes evenly over the work surface in a 1-inch thickness. Leave them to cool completely.

∽ Put a large, wide pot of water on the stove to boil. Add salt when the water reaches boiling.

∽ Sprinkle the potatoes with salt, nutmeg, and cinnamon. Beat the yolks lightly and spread them over the surface. Use your hands to combine the potatoes, spices, and egg. Form a large ball with the mixture, then wash your hands and wipe down your work surface. Pour 1 cup of flour onto the work surface and place the potato ball on top. Press it down into a thick tablet, then turn it over in the flour. Fold the tablet in half, then in half again. Keep folding it gently over and over for 3 or 4 minutes, until the dough becomes smooth. You will need to dust the dough with small amounts of flour as you work until the mixture loses most of its stickiness and becomes soft and pliant, but don't use any more flour than is absolutely necessary. Let the dough rest for 5 minutes.

∽ Form a loaf with the dough, then cut it into four sections. Wipe your work surface clean and lightly flour your hands. Take one of the sections of dough and roll it lightly back and forth on the work surface into a snake of about the thickness of your index finger.

∽ Cut the snake into 1-inch sections, roll into little logs, and shape with the tines of a fork or the back of a cheese grater (page 196). Place the gnocchi on a lightly floured platter or baking sheet. Dust them very lightly with additional flour. Continue rolling out the dough and shaping the gnocchi until all the dough has been used.

∽ Boil the gnocchi in 2 or 3 batches in salted water. They are ready about half a minute after they float to the top. Scoop them out with a slotted skimmer and place in individual serving bowls. Spoon over butter or sauce and grated Parmesan and serve immediately.

Polpettine in Tomato Sauce
Polpettine in Salsa di Pomodoro
SERVES 8

This is one of Antonio's favorite sauces for potato gnocchi

½ recipe meatballs (page 88)
½ cup red wine
2½ cups tomato sauce (page 99)
Freshly grated Parmesan cheese for the table

Prepare one half of the master recipe for meatballs. Dip your hands in wine and roll the meat into small balls ½ inch in diameter. Do not cover with bread crumbs. Gently heat the tomato sauce in a large skillet. Distribute the meatballs evenly over the top, cover and simmer very gently for 20 minutes, stirring the sauce and turning the meatballs occasionally. Spoon over gnocchi. Offer grated Parmesan.

Pumpkin Gnocchi with Butter and Sage
Gnocchi di Zucca con Burro e Salvia
SERVES 4 TO 6

The area around Venice abounds with squash. Antonio tells me that as a child, his favorite was known colloquially as *"zucca santa"* or "holy squash." His mother would let one dry and take it to the beach for him to use as a float when he was learning how to swim. You can go ahead and use the pagan but ever so delicious kabocha squash if you can find it, otherwise butternut squash works well. Other types of squash are overly watery or stringy. The flesh of the squash must be very firm and dry—November through January is the best time of the year for squash that has been off the vine long enough to dry out a bit.

Nothing complements the soft sweetness of winter squash better than a simple sauce of butter and fresh sage.

For the Gnocchi

2 to 3 pounds kabocha or butternut squash (to yield 2 cups cooked squash)
3 medium floury potatoes, boiled in their skins
1 egg yolk
⅓ cup grated Parmesan cheese
Pinch of cinnamon
Pinch of nutmeg
Pinch of salt
Pinch of white pepper
1¾ cups all-purpose white flour (approximately)

For the Sauce

⅓ cup salted butter
20 whole fresh sage leaves

~ *The gnocchi:* Preheat oven to 350°.

~ Cut the squash into 1-inch slices, remove the seeds and strings and bake in a shallow baking dish, covered with aluminum foil until tender. When a fork easily pierces the skin, they are ready. This can take anywhere from 1 hour and 15 minutes to longer, depending on the size of the squash.

~ In the meantime, boil the potatoes until a toothpick inserts easily into the center. Drain, then place them in the oven with the squash for 5 minutes. Peel the potatoes, then pass them through a ricer onto a flat work surface or baking sheet. Leave to cool.

~ Remove the squash from the oven and spoon it hot out of the shell into a ricer.

Pass the squash through the ricer onto a flat work surface or baking sheet. Do not blend or mash—the ricer allows the squash to cool and release its moisture. Leave to cool. (Don't refrigerate.)

∾ Fill a large pot with water and start it boiling.

∾ Using your fingers, combine the squash, potato, and egg yolk, then add the grated Parmesan, cinnamon, nutmeg, and a pinch each of salt and white pepper. Form a ball with the resulting mixture.

∾ Pour ½ cup of flour onto your work surface and place the squash/potato mixture on top. Sprinkle another ½ cup of flour over the squash mixture. Begin to knead the dough gently, rolling it back and forth, flattening and folding, slowly incorporating just enough flour into the dough so that you are able to push your finger down into the dough and it will leave an imprint but not be sticky. Let the dough rest for 5 minutes.

∾ Redust your work surface lightly with flour. Roll the dough into long, thin snakes about ½ inch in diameter. Shape according to the instructions on page 196. Salt the water when it begins to boil.

∾ *The sauce:* Heat the butter over a low flame in a skillet large enough to hold the gnocchi once they have cooked. When the butter has partially melted, add the sage leaves. The sauce is ready when the leaves begin to become crisp and the butter just barely begins to brown.

∾ Gently place the gnocchi in the boiling water. They are ready when they rise to the top (1 to 2 minutes). Drain them with a slotted skimmer and transfer to the skillet with the butter. Toss gently and serve.

Spinach and Bread Dumplings with Fresh Tomatoes, Garlic, and Basil

Strangolapreti al Pomodoro, Aglio, e Basilico

SERVES 6

Literally called "priest-stranglers," legend has it that gluttonous priests were so fond of these little dumplings made from spinach and day-old bread that more than one met his early demise when a gnocchetto lodged in his throat. You may prepare the dough the same day and cover it tightly with plastic wrap until you are ready to roll out the individual dumplings. The sauce is quick and easy to make.

For the Dumplings

1 pound day-old country white bread, crusts removed

1¼ cups milk

1 pound spinach, leaves only

¼ cup freshly grated Parmesan cheese

4 tablespoons all-purpose flour, plus flour for dusting

Salt

Pinch of nutmeg

Pinch of cinnamon

2 eggs, lightly beaten

2 tablespoons finely ground bread crumbs, optional

For the Sauce

3 tablespoons extra-virgin olive oil

3 whole cloves garlic, peeled and crushed

2 pounds ripe plum tomatoes, peeled, seeded, and crushed

Handful of fresh basil leaves

Salt

Pepper

The dumplings: Break the bread into small pieces and place in a mixing bowl with the milk. Push the bread down into the milk with your fingertips and let it rest for at least 1 hour, breaking the bread up with your fingers every so often. The bread and milk mixture will turn into a heavy paste. If it is at all watery, form a ball with the paste and squeeze out as much liquid as you can. Divide the bread and milk mixture into 4 balls.

In the meantime, wash the spinach under running water, then cook it in the water that clings to its leaves. When the spinach is tender, allow it to cool, then form it into a ball and squeeze out as much liquid as possible. Chop the spinach very fine by hand or by pulse blending in a food processor. Once again, squeeze out as much liquid as you can.

Add the bread, 1 ball at a time, to the spinach, combining it well with your fingers until it forms an even paste. Lightly flour your work surface and lay the spinach/bread mixture on top. Press the mixture down with your hands to make a thick tablet. Sprinkle with the Parmesan flour, salt, and spices, then spread the beaten eggs over the top.

Using a firm motion, fold the tablet in half, then in half again. Continue doing this for a couple of minutes, until the ingredients are well combined. If the dough feels very wet to the touch, knead in 2 tablespoons of bread crumbs. Allow the dough to rest for at least 30 minutes.

Heat a large, wide pot of water, adding salt when it reaches a boil. Allow the water to boil steadily but not violently. Strangolapreti are more delicate than potato gnocchi and will break apart if the water boils too strongly.

Dust the dough lightly with flour and roll into snakes, as you would gnocchi. Cut the dumplings into 1-inch lengths and roll between your palms to form small logs.

The sauce: Warm the oil and garlic in a large skillet. After 1 minute, add the crushed tomatoes and simmer over low heat for about 20 minutes, stirring frequently. Add the basil leaves during the last few minutes of cooking. Season to taste with salt and pepper.

Cook the dumplings in batches as you would potato gnocchi, removing them from the boiling water just after they float to the surface (they will take a couple of minutes longer than gnocchi to cook). Use a slotted spoon to drain the dumplings, transfer to individual bowls, spoon sauce over, and serve.

POLENTA

There are few images more distinctly northern Italian than that of a woman standing before a steaming copper cauldron stirring polenta with a long wooden spoon. Certainly there are other foods such as risotto or borlotti beans that are associated primarily with the cuisine of the north, but even they cannot compare with the breadth of use to which northerners (dubbed "polentoni" by their southern neighbors) put the coarse yellow maize meal.

Making polenta the traditional way is a time-honored rite, almost medieval in its stark simplicity and deliberateness. A roaring fire is lit in the hearth. Hours later, a large copper pot (or "*paiolo*") is hung over the fire's glowing embers and filled with fresh water. When the water begins to simmer gently, handfuls of the golden maize are poured into the pot in a thin, steady stream. For the next thirty to forty minutes the pot is stirred with a long wooden spoon while the polenta bubbles and spits. When it is thick and soft, the steaming polenta is scooped into a bowl or poured onto a large cutting board where it will be left to cool until it can be cut with a string held taut between two hands.

There are less arduous ways of making traditional polenta but all require constant stirring and a watchful eye. There is even quick-cooking polenta, which requires less time and stirring and produces a suitably palatable substitute for the real thing.

However you make your polenta, once made it can be consumed in one of any number of ways. It is wonderful served soft and tender with a thick savory stew or hearty sauce. When left to cool it becomes firm and solid and can be cut into slices and grilled or lightly fried until its outer crust is crisp and golden. It can be made with water or milk, and flavored with mushrooms, herbs, butter, or cheese. Sweetened, it can be eaten at breakfast or incorporated into cakes or cookies.

That such a huge variety of delicious dishes can be made from one humble ingredient is yet another example of the seemingly endless creativity and industriousness of the Italian home cook.

Serving Polenta

Soft
Spoon the polenta straight out of the pot onto dinner plates
or
Place a tablespoon of olive oil in a serving bowl, fill with freshly cooked polenta, and serve immediately.

Firm
Pour the steaming polenta onto a large wooden cutting board and spread it into a mound with a wet spatula. Bring the polenta to the table after 10 to 15 minutes. It will still be quite warm but will have become firm enough to slice with a knife or, in the traditional style, with a length of kitchen twine held taut between two hands.

Grilled, Broiled, or Panfried
Lightly oil a loaf pan and fill with soft polenta (this can be done the day ahead). When the polenta has cooled completely, slice it like bread to a ½-inch thickness. Leave each slice whole or cut into two triangles or rectangles.

Grilling:
Set the slices over a medium-hot outdoor or stovetop grill and cook until the polenta is hot and shows grill marks on both sides.

Broiling:
Lay the polenta slices on a wire oven rack and heat under a hot broiler, turning once until the polenta has formed a thin golden crust.

Panfrying:
Heat a couple of tablespoons of olive oil in a large, preferably nonstick pan. Fry on both sides until the surface of the slices are golden and crispy.

Traditional Polenta
Polenta Tradizionale
SERVES 4 TO 6

Jean-Louis's mother, like many northern Italian women, has a special *paiolo* for making polenta—a copper pot with an electric rotating arm that stirs the polenta as it cooks. For the rest of us, making polenta involves serious culinary calisthenics, in the form of 30 to 40 minutes of near-constant stirring. Make it one day when you have lots of hands in the kitchen—open a bottle of wine, set out a wedge of cheese and some olives, and give everyone a turn with the spoon.

6 cups water
2 teaspoons salt
1¼ cups imported coarse-ground cornmeal

↝ Bring the water to a gentle boil in a heavy-bottomed pot. Add the salt. When the water returns to a boil, pour the polenta into the pot in a fine, steady stream, stirring continuously with a wire whisk so that no lumps form. Reduce the heat to medium. After a few minutes, when the polenta begins to thicken, lower the flame to a minimum and stir continuously with a wooden spoon. The polenta will bubble and spit as the cornmeal thickens.

↝ Continue stirring more or less continuously, for 30 to 40 minutes. The polenta is ready when it comes away easily from the sides of the pot.

↝ Serve in any of the ways described on page 206.

Veal Stew with Soft Polenta
Polenta e Tocio

SERVES 4

Unlike the French, who have a penchant for christening every recipe in their vast culinary repertoire with its own elegant name, in the Veneto, a single word can easily refer to a whole host of recipes that all share one common characteristic. For years, though I'd skip happily to my mother-in-law's table whenever she announced she had made *polenta e tocio,* I was never entirely sure what *tocio* was. In a general sense, I knew to expect some kind of rich meat-based stew that we would eat with soft, golden polenta. The meat was usually veal, but occasionally beef or lamb. The sauce tended to be tomato-based but was sometimes embellished with peas, mushrooms, potatoes, artichokes, or peppers. Eventually I assumed without asking that *tocio* meant "stew." I was wrong. In Venetian dialect, *tociare* means "to dip, to soak up." *Il tocio* actually refers to the stew's thick, savory sauce, a wonderfully rich (ever-changing) blend of flavors for the polenta to mop up.

2 tablespoons butter

2 tablespoons olive oil

1 onion, finely chopped

1 carrot, finely chopped

1 celery stalk, finely chopped

1 clove garlic, minced

1½ pound veal shank or shoulder, cut into medium cubes

½ cup dry white wine

1 teaspoon white wine vinegar

One 14½-ounce can Italian plum tomatoes

Small handful of fresh sage leaves

1 teaspoon fresh thyme

1 bay leaf

Salt

Freshly ground black pepper

1 cup beef broth (page 174), or high quality bouillon or water

⌒ Warm the butter and oil in a large, heavy-bottomed skillet over a medium flame. Add the onion, carrot, celery, and garlic and cook, stirring often, until the vegetables are tender (about 15 minutes).

⌒ Turn the flame to high, then add the meat, turning it in the pan until it is well browned on all sides. Pour in the wine and wine vinegar and stir the meat to coat with the liquid, scraping the bottom with a wooden spoon. Let the wine bubble away for a minute then reduce the flame to medium-low and stir in the tomatoes, herbs, salt, and a generous grinding of black pepper. Use a wooden spoon to break up the tomatoes in the pot.

⌒ Cook uncovered until the pot begins to simmer, then reduce the flame to a minimum, cover and cook very gently for 1½ to 2 hours, or until the meat is tender. Stir the pot every so often, adding a bit of broth or bouillon to the meat if the sauce is too dry.

⌒ Ladle over individual servings of soft polenta.

Grilled Polenta and Seafood
Polenta e Mare
SERVES 6

This recipe pairs a thick, flavorful seafood stew with crisp slices of grilled polenta. Many northern Italian restaurants grill polenta right in the dining room fireplace or *focolare*, along with meats and local cheeses. For a summertime meal, we grill the polenta on an outdoor barbecue. We like to serve the stew right at the table out of an earthenware bowl.

1 recipe traditional polenta (page 207) or 1 box fast-cooking polenta made
    according to package instructions

½ cup extra-virgin olive oil

2 cloves garlic, crushed

2 salt-cured anchovy fillets

1 pound ripe plum tomatoes, cut into large dice

1 tablespoon capers

2 bay leaves

1 small red chili pepper, crumbled

½ pound monkfish tail, meat only, cut into large chunks

½ pound sea bream, filleted, then cut into chunks

1 pound fresh mussels, scrubbed and debearded

1 pound clams, soaked for 2 hours in several changes of lightly salted water

½ pound medium shrimp, shelled and deveined

½ pound small cleaned squid, tentacles whole, pouch cut into ½-inch rings

1 teaspoon finely chopped Italian parsley

Salt

Pinch of crushed red pepper, optional

The polenta: Make the polenta the day before or several hours earlier the same day you will be eating it and pour the hot polenta into a lightly oiled loaf pan to cool.

The stew: Warm the olive oil and garlic in a large heavy-bottomed casserole over a medium flame. When the garlic is lightly golden and fragrant, add the anchovies, stirring them in the pan until they begin to break apart. Stir in the tomatoes, capers, chili pepper, and bay leaves and simmer the mixture lightly for 3 minutes.

Add the monkfish and sea bream, stirring them well in the pan to coat with the tomato sauce. When they have cooked for 5 minutes, reduce the flame to low and add the remaining seafood. Cook partially covered, for 15 minutes. After the first 10 minutes, sprinkle in the chopped parsley and season to taste with salt (keeping in mind that both the anchovies and capers are quite salty in their own right) and a pinch of crushed red pepper if desired.

In the meantime, cut the cooled polenta into ½-inch-thick slices and lay them on a lightly oiled outdoor or stovetop grill, or in the oven under a hot broiler. Grill the polenta on both sides until the polenta is hot and the grill marks are imprinted on the surface. If broiling, heat for a few minutes on each side until the polenta has formed a thin golden crust. Transfer to a platter and bring to the table with the stew.

～ To serve, ladle the stew into shallow bowls next to slices of grilled polenta.

Pork Ribs in a Savory Sauce with Soft Polenta
Costicine al Sugo Casareccio con Polenta
SERVES 4

This is the sort of dish for a cold winter night, best eaten near a roaring fire. The ribs simmer for hours in a rich tomato sauce until they are so tender the meat falls from the bone. This was a favorite dish of Antonio's father, who always browned the ribs in a bit of lard. Although we've altered the recipe in deference to the current aversion to cooking with animal fat, if you are feeling on the adventurous side, substitute ¼ cup of lard for the olive oil and enjoy the rich flavor it imparts to the dish. Serve with soft polenta (page 207).

2 slabs baby back ribs
3 tablespoons olive oil or ¼ cup lard
1 onion, finely chopped
2 cloves garlic, finely chopped
1 cup dry white wine
1½ cups tomato sauce (page 99)
Salt
Dash of crushed red pepper, optional
½ cup freshly grated Parmesan cheese

～ If your butcher hasn't already done so, use your fingers to pull away the thin membrane covering the inside of the ribs. Use a cleaver or sharp meat knife to divide each slab into 3 pieces, cutting between the ribs.

Heat the oil or lard, onions, and garlic in a large, heavy-bottomed skillet and sauté over a medium flame until the onions are golden. Add the ribs to the pan and brown them for a couple of minutes on each side. Pour the wine over the ribs and cook down the alcohol for 5 minutes, stirring occasionally and turning the ribs in the pan to coat them in the pan juices.

Stir in the tomato sauce, salt, and, if you wish, a pinch of crushed red pepper. Cover the pan and cook over a low flame for 2 to 2½ hours, adding ½ cup of water at a time to the sauce if it becomes too dry—it should maintain the consistency of a thick tomato sauce. The ribs are ready when the meat is moist and tender and falls away from the bone.

During the final hour that the ribs are cooking, prepare 1 recipe of soft polenta (page 207).

Pour the soft polenta onto a large serving plate. Spoon the ribs and sauce over the polenta, scatter with Parmesan, and serve.

A SKILLET AND A BOX OF RICE

Just as our kids would never dream of asking Jean-Louis to make them pancakes, they never, ever ask me to make them crepes. And why would they, when the can sit at the kitchen counter, watching their father, with a touching mixture of awe and astonishment, as he effortlessly flips a succession of perfectly round, parchment-thin crepes in the pan? His crepes are like Olympic divers—one little flick of the wrist sends each one in the air to perform a perfect half turn and land gracefully back in the pan. Without a splash. Without a wrinkle.

I've always been intimidated by Jean-Louis's crepe-flipping prowess. Every now and then, when no one was looking, I'd make a feeble attempt at trying it myself. The poor crepe would either land halfway off the pan (doing irrevocable damage to itself in the process), or fall back into the skillet in such a bunched-up heap that it could no longer be called a crepe.

Savory cornmeal crepes were on the testing menu this morning, and I thought it perfectly logical that I make the batter and leave the actual crepe making to Jean-Louis. I measured our flour and cornmeal, then whisked in the eggs and milk. I was happily absorbed in these simple tasks, letting my mind wander as I mixed the batter smooth.

Somewhere in the course of my efforts, it dawned on me that in delegating the crepe-making task to Jean-Louis, I was breaking my own loose code of culinary ethics. I could hear my own voice echoing in my ears, "Be bold and brave in the kitchen. Don't be overly attached to the outcome. Experiment. Have fun. Let yourself enjoy the art of cooking." Hmm. Maybe it was time for me to put recipe testing on hold for a moment and try to follow my own advice.

I went to our resident master crepe flipper and asked for instruction. He sent me outside with a skillet and a box of rice.

"Scatter a handful of rice in the pan, then hold it out in front of you, about waist-high," he explained. "Bring the pan toward you, then down, then back up again in a circular motion—the rice will fly up in the air. When it starts landing in the pan instead of on the grass, come back into the house."

I did as I was told and it wasn't too long before I was flipping first the rice and then the crepes. Of course, I wasn't able to make it look as totally effortless as Jean-Louis did, but considering I had secretly feared myself incapable of mastering such culinary acrobatics no matter how many boxes of rice I scattered to the winds, I was pleased with myself.

Of course, you can grab a crepe with the tips of your tender fingers and turn it over in the pan. You can even slip a spatula and a knife under the crepe for a more-awkward and dangerous (to the crepe) flip. But it isn't half the fun . . . and it's sure not the Olympics.

Savory Cornmeal Crepes
Crespelle di Farina di Polenta
MAKES APPROXIMATELY 20 7½-INCH CREPES

Cornmeal crepes are just the sort of thing you'd expect from a food lover whose parents are northern Italian but who himself grew up in France. They are a perfect vehicle for leftover pasta sauces and cooked vegetables. We eat then in several ways: straight from the pan, either plain or spread with soft robiola or goat cheese; stacked one over the other between thin layers of meat ragù, finely chopped sautéed spinach, and/or béchamel, then baked in a 375° oven for 30 minutes; or lightly filled, then gently folded into quarters in the shape of a fan, and baked as described in the recipes on the following pages.

TIPS

- *The batter can be made the night before and stored covered in the refrigerator for a couple of days, although it should be beaten well before using.*
- *The first 1 or 2 crepes are often "throw-aways." It usually seems to take a few tries to get all the elements to come together properly—but they almost always do.*
- *You can wrap the cooked crepes in plastic and store in the refrigerator overnight or in the freezer for up to 3 weeks. Thaw in the refrigerator overnight.*

1 cup fine-ground cornmeal

1 cup pastry flour

1 teaspoon salt

4 large eggs

2 tablespoons olive oil

2 cups whole milk

Butter for greasing the pan

⌒ To mix by hand, combine the dry ingredients in a medium mixing bowl and make a well in the center. Break the eggs into the center of the well, add the olive oil, and lightly beat with a fork. Use a wire whisk to swirl the egg mixture in a circular motion so that the flour is incorporated from the sides of the well. When about half the flour has been incorporated, slowly pour in the milk and continue to mix the batter gently until it is smooth. Allow the batter to rest for 1 hour before using.

⌒ Alternatively, mix all the ingredients in a food processor or blender at a medium speed until smooth. Stop the mixing to scrape down the sides of the container with a spatula or wooden spoon. Continue blending for 10 to 15 seconds, then pour the batter into a mixing bowl and leave to rest for 1 hour.

⌒ If you will be stuffing the crepes, then prepare the filling while the batter is resting and preheat the oven to 425°.

⌒ To make the crepes, heat a 7-inch nonstick skillet or crepe pan over a medium flame. Add a tablespoon of butter to the pan and spread it evenly around the cooking surface with a folded paper towel. Using a small ladle, pour 2 to 3 tablespoons of batter into the center of the pan. Tilt and turn the pan to swirl the batter until it lightly coats the entire flat surface of the pan, adding additional batter if needed.

⌒ Cook the crepe for a couple of minutes until the bottom is lightly browned and the top is beginning to dry out. Flip the crepe over (page 212) or run a knife around the edges of the crepe, and using a knife, spatula, or your own tender fingers turn the crepe over. Cook the second side for 30 seconds to 1 minute. It will not brown as much as the first and will be the inside of the crepe if you are going to fill it. Slip the crepe off the pan onto a round plate.

⌒ Continue making the crepes in the same manner and stacking them one on top of the other until no batter remains. You may want to add a bit of additional butter to the pan every few crepes, but if they are not sticking, there is no reason to do so.

Cornmeal Crepes with Asparagus and Béchamel
Crespelle con Asparagi e Besciamelle
SERVES 4 TO 6

1 pound fresh asparagus

Salt

2 cups béchamel sauce (page 150)

Freshly ground black pepper

20 cornmeal crepes (page 214)

2 tablespoons butter for greasing the pan

5 tablespoons freshly grated Parmesan cheese

9 by 13-inch ovenproof baking dish

∾ Preheat the oven to 425°.

∾ Trim away the white fibrous ends of the asparagus spears. Use a potato peeler to pare away any of the remaining tough outer stalk. Place the asparagus, tips up, in lightly salted boiling water and cook until tender for 6 to 8 minutes. Drain and blend in a food processor until smooth.

∾ In the meantime, prepare the béchamel. It can be used right away. There is no need to set it aside to cool.

With a wooden spoon, stir together the pureed asparagus and béchamel. Correct seasonings, adding salt and pepper to taste.

Stack the crepes one on top of the other with their darker side (the side that was cooked first in the pan) down. Place a heaping tablespoon of the asparagus mixture in the center of each crepe, then create a fan shape by folding the crepe in half, and then in half again. Lightly butter the casserole.

Layer the crepes in 2 rows down the length of the pan as follows: lay 1 filled and folded crepe in the upper corner of the pan with its pointed edge down and curved edge up. Lay another crepe so that it partially covers the first, with its pointed edge an inch or two below the first crepe's pointed edge. Continue layering the crepes until an entire row is complete. Lay another row of crepes alongside the first row until the casserole is filled. Sprinkle grated Parmesan over the crepes and bake in the oven for 15 minutes or until the cheese is golden. Serve immediately.

Cornmeal Crepes Filled with Mushrooms or Ragù

SERVES 4 TO 6

20 cornmeal crepes (page 214)
1 recipe *funghi trifolati* (page 281) or 1 recipe meat ragù (page 102)
1 cup tomato sauce (page 99)
4 tablespoons freshly grated Parmesan cheese

Preheat oven to 425°.

Stack the crepes dark side down and place a heaping tablespoon of mushrooms or meat sauce in the center of each crepe. Fold the crepes into fans and layer as described in the preceding recipe.

Spoon the tomato sauce over the layered crepes. Scatter Parmesan over the top and bake for 15 minutes or until the cheese is golden.

Serve immediately.

Secondi

A CULINARY QUANDARY

Jean-Louis, the kids, and I spent last spring vacation in Portugal with a group of friends. We were six adults and five children in all—one huge "family" sharing a house and a kitchen, doing our best to parcel out the tasks inherent in keeping a band of travelers happily fed.

We attempted to divide our labors so as to take into account the individual habits and eccentricities of each member of the group. This explains, for example, how it happened that I did not do the marketing the day it was my turn to make lunch. That responsibility went to Jean-Louis and Robbie Leone, the only two in our group for whom the word "vacation" was not synonymous with "sleeping in." Grabbing a couple of straw baskets and a wad of foreign currency, they set off for the seaside farmers' market while the rest of us were still in our pajamas, idly making our way through a pot of English tea and thick slices of toast dripping butter and honey.

I've had almost twenty years to adjust to the marketing habits of my husband. This made me fairly certain that my designated shoppers would have no agenda, no shopping list, nothing but their senses to guide them through the labyrinth of stalls heaped with local delectables. They would whir around the marketplace like bees hunting for nectar in the succulent hearts of flowers—and I would be completely at the mercy of their gastronomic whims.

Sure enough, like wanderers from a far-off land, they returned home to draw their treasures out of overladen baskets: a necklace of dried peppers, thick braids of garlic, a bouquet of laurel branches, lemons with bright leaves still attached to their stems, dusky green olives in a vinegary brine, several pounds of monkfish caught early that morning, a jug of local wine, and a fat loaf of crusty bread.

Faced with the raw ingredients with which to craft our meal, I foresaw only one problem—I had absolutely no idea what to do with monkfish, and could barely stand to look at the eel-like tail covered with slick gray skin. I reminded myself that some of the best recipes are born of invention and necessity, two factors that I knew would weigh heavily on the outcome of the meal—invention, because I had never cooked monkfish before (and had no cookbooks in my temporary kitchen), necessity because a hungry crew of eleven was counting on me to satisfy their bellies.

I couldn't fail to note the touch of mischief in Jean-Louis's eyes as he pulled the fish out of the bag and set it on the wooden worktable. He gave me his most beguiling look and a bit of advice: "Cut it up," he said, "and peel the thin gray membrane off. . . . You might try to make a stew," were his final words as he plunged out of the kitchen and into the swimming pool.

Left to my own devices with two girlfriends and an unattractive lump of fish flesh, I began to chop up a couple of onions and sauté them in olive oil (which is what I usually do when I'm in a culinary quandary). When the onions had softened, I added the chunks of monkfish and gave them a quick go-around in the pot to give them some color. By now the fish looked a bit less daunting and I was ready to switch to a more creative cooking mode. "Potatoes," I thought. "I'll add some potatoes, some plum tomatoes, and a handful of those green olives that the Portuguese seem to love as much as the Italians."

I let it all simmer awhile, then dipped a spoon into the pot to see how things were progressing. Something was missing. As I added some salt, my eye fell upon a bowlful of lemons. "Lemon peel," I thought, "lots of it." I added two lemons' worth of fragrant yellow lemon zest cut into great, wide pieces and waited a few minutes to see their effect in the pot. Alas, something was still missing, so I plucked a dried pepper from the ruby strand and added a dash more salt.

Things were starting to look, and smell, pretty good, when Jean-Louis peeked into the kitchen and asked me, oh so sweetly, why I was sugaring the stew. Terra-cotta "salt" shaker still in hand, I stared at him blankly, until it dawned on me that my "salt" shaker was, in fact, a "sugar" shaker.

As luck would have it, sugar sugars less than salt salts. If anything, the sweet granules only thickened the broth and gave it a wonderful softness. What's more, I'm convinced that it was the lack of salt that kept me searching for other flavors—I doubt I would have kept adding a dash of this or that if I had put the salt in at the beginning. My experiment was so successful that this dish has actually become one of our current repertoire of favorites.

Braised Monkfish with Olives and Lemon Peel
Stufatino di Coda di Rospo
SERVES 6

Although you'll almost never see them in all their brutish glory in American markets, whole monkfish are decidedly unattractive—they have two long filaments extending from the tops of their heads, and lower jaws that thrust menacingly forward. Only their tails are edible, and the meat is sweet and mild with a texture reminiscent of lobster (hence their nickname, "poor-man's lobster"). Once the thick center cartilage is removed, the fillets are truly boneless. The only remaining prep work (if your fishmonger has not already done so) is to use a paring knife to remove the thin gray membrane that covers the fillets.

1 pound new potatoes

2 lemons

¾ cup large Italian or Spanish green brine-cured olives, with stones

¼ cup olive oil

2 medium onions, chopped

3 cloves garlic, peeled and crushed

2 pounds monkfish tail fillets, cleaned of cartilage and membrane and cut into 3-inch chunks

One 28-ounce can Italian plum tomatoes

Pinch of crushed red pepper

Salt

∼ Scrub the potatoes under running water. Without removing their skins cut them into bite-sized chunks and set aside.

∼ Use a sharp paring knife or potato peeler to shave large, wide strips of zest from the lemons. (Take care to remove only the fragrant yellow skin and not the bitter white pith underneath.)

∼ Cut and remove the stones from the olives.

∼ Warm the olive oil in a large, heavy-bottomed casserole, add the onions and garlic and cook over a medium-low flame, stirring frequently, until the onions are soft and golden and the garlic fragrant.

∼ Increase the flame to medium, add the monkfish, and stir continuously until the fish is lightly browned. Add the potatoes, plum tomatoes, olives, lemon zest, red pepper, and salt to taste. Bring to a simmer, then reduce the heat to low and cook, partially covered, for 40 minutes, stirring regularly.

∼ Serve with crusty country bread.

Red Snapper Stewed in a Vegetable Medley
Gallinella in Guazzetto di Verdure

SERVES 4

Many things in the Veneto are cooked *in guazzetto,* which, literally translated, means "stewed." The English word brings to mind things like prunes and other unappetizing morsels of food cooked until unrecognizable. That's anything but the case here where saffron works its subtle magic on tender fillets of fish cooked gently in the aromatic juices of a colorful medley of vegetables.

The recipe calls for a small amount of flageolet beans, tender immature kidney beans very popular in France but available in many markets canned, frozen, and, more rarely, fresh. Substitute any very tender white bean if necessary.

4 tablespoons extra-virgin olive oil

4 cloves garlic, chopped

1 carrot, peeled and cut into small dice

1 medium celery stalk with leaves, finely chopped

1 medium new potato, cut into cubes

½ cup fresh, frozen, or canned flageolet beans

10 cherry tomatoes, halved

Salt

2 medium Japanese eggplants, unpeeled, cut into small cubes

1 medium zucchini, cut into small cubes

1 medium yellow onion, chopped

4 fillets red snapper (striped bass or halibut can be substituted)

Freshly ground black pepper

10 saffron threads, crushed, or 1$\frac{1}{20}$-ounce (sometimes sold as $\frac{3}{64}$-ounce) vial of saffron

ﾟ Preheat oven to 450°.

ﾟ Heat 1 tablespoon of olive oil in a medium saucepan, add the chopped garlic, and sauté for a few seconds. Add carrots and celery, and sauté for another minute, then add the potatoes, beans, tomatoes, 2 cups of water, and a pinch of salt and cook covered over a low flame for 25 minutes, stirring occasionally.

ﾟ In the meantime, sauté the eggplant, zucchini, and onion in 3 tablespoons of olive oil over a medium flame until cooked but still firm (about 7 minutes).

Spread the eggplant, zucchini, and onion mixture on the bottom of a medium casserole dish. Cover with the fish fillets, salt, pepper, and saffron threads. Spoon the *guazzetto* of vegetables over the top (it should be relatively liquid) and bake uncovered until the fish is cooked through (15 to 20 minutes depending on the thickness of the fillets). Serve immediately.

Fillet of Striped Bass with Rosemary and Lentils

Filetto di Branzino al Rosmarino con le Lenticchie

SERVES 4

Striped bass is a wonderful fish with firm, white flesh and a delicate flavor. The savory lentils make a perfect companion and you will have more than enough of them to serve with the fish. We've done this on purpose—there is simply no reason to make only a small amount of lentils. They will keep well in the refrigerator for several days and can be enjoyed in countless ways.

For the Lentils

2 cups lentils
1 small onion, papery skin removed
1 small carrot, peeled
1 small celery stalk
3 ripe tomatoes
Sprig of Italian flat-leaf parsley
4 fresh sage leaves
1 bay leaf
Salt
Freshly ground black pepper
2 tablespoons extra-virgin olive oil
1 tablespoon red wine vinegar
1 clove garlic, minced

For the Fish

4 small sprigs of fresh rosemary

4 fillets of striped bass, 6 to 8 ounces per portion (scales removed but skin intact)

2 tablespoons extra-virgin olive oil

1 clove garlic, peeled and thinly sliced

Salt

Freshly ground white or black pepper

The lentils: Rinse the lentils well, then soak them in abundant cold water for 30 minutes. Drain, then place in a soup pot with 8 cups of water, the onion, carrot, celery, tomatoes, and herbs and heat over a high flame until the water begins to boil. Skim any foam off the surface, then reduce the flame to achieve a gentle simmer and cook, stirring occasionally, until the lentils are tender (about 45 minutes). Three quarters of the way through the cooking time, season to taste with salt and freshly ground black pepper.

In a small bowl, mix together 2 tablespoons of olive oil with the vinegar and minced garlic. Set aside.

The fish: Insert 1 sprig of rosemary at a 45-degree angle into the flesh of each fillet. Warm 2 tablespoons of olive oil in a large skillet. Add the sliced garlic and sauté until it is golden and fragrant. Increase the flame to high and place the fillets in the pan, skin side up. After 3 or 4 minutes, when the fish is lightly golden, turn the fillets and continue cooking until they are pale white in the center (about 3 minutes). Sprinkle with salt and freshly ground white or black pepper.

Quickly drain the lentils and stir in the oil, vinegar, and garlic mixture. Arrange the fillets on individual plates next to a portion of lentils. Serve immediately.

Grilled Tuna with Pureed Sweet Yellow Peppers
Tonno con Purè di Peperoni Gialli
SERVES 4

Nothing surpasses the flavor of fish cooked over the fragrant embers of mesquite or other aromatic hardwoods. Tuna holds up especially well on the grill and although not all fish could stand up to the flavor of yellow peppers, tuna, with its solid, sturdy texture and taste, most certainly can. This particular recipe is the result of Jean-Louis's creative efforts to deal with our vegetable garden's abundance of potatoes and peppers. The pureed vegetables could almost masquerade as polenta made from coarsely ground cornmeal.

6 tablespoons extra-virgin olive oil
1 medium onion, finely chopped
3 sweet yellow peppers, seeded and chopped
2 large potatoes, peeled, halved, and cut into paper-thin slices
Salt
2 pounds tuna fillet, skinned and cut into 4 steaks at least 1 inch thick
Freshly ground black pepper
12 leaves fresh green or purple sage

↝ Prepare a charcoal or wood fire for grilling, or preheat the oven grill or broiler.
↝ Heat 2 tablespoons of olive oil over a medium flame in a large, heavy-bottomed skillet. Sauté the onions gently until they begin to soften, then add the peppers and potatoes and cook for about 10 minutes, stirring often. Add ⅓ cup of water and salt to taste. Continue cooking until all the vegetables are soft and cooked through (another 10 to 15 minutes). Add 2 tablespoons of olive oil, then puree the mixture until smooth with a hand or stationary blender.
↝ Brush the tuna steaks with the remaining olive oil and sprinkle with salt and freshly ground black pepper. Place them on the grill or under the broiler for 3 to 5 minutes on

each side. Check for doneness by inserting a knife in the center of one of the steaks. We prefer our tuna steaks still pink in the center but not seared on the outside and raw inside, which is the current fashion.

〜 Spoon the pureed vegetables into large pools on individual serving plates. Place the tuna steak in the center over the puree and garnish around the edges with the sage leaves.

Giant Grilled Prawns with Garlic and Parsley
Scampi Giganti alla Griglia con Aglio e Prezzemolo

SERVES 4

We first served grilled Blue Hawaiian prawns at an open-air food fair in Santa Monica. Our mobile "kitchen" was a three-foot-long fire-engine red barbecue and the line for the garlicky shrimp seemed to snake halfway around the fair. We've since offered them on the menu at Locanda Veneta whenever we can find them. Blue Hawaiian prawns have very sweet meat and can weigh over half a pound each. If you can't find them, buy the largest shrimp that are available.

6 tablespoons extra-virgin olive oil	Salt
Juice of 1 lemon	Pepper
8 garlic cloves, finely chopped	3 pounds extra-large shrimp, in their shells
1 hot red chili pepper, crushed into flakes	1 tablespoon finely chopped Italian parsley

〜 Prepare a medium-hot wood, gas, or charcoal barbecue.

〜 In a small bowl, whisk together the oil, lemon juice, garlic, and chili pepper. Season to taste with salt and pepper and leave the mixture to sit for 20 minutes.

◠ In the meantime, pull the front legs and feelers off the shrimp. Butterfly the shrimp by laying them on their sides and cutting along the inside curl of the shrimp, starting just above the tail and continuing along the length of the body. Cut almost, but not completely, through the meat, then open the shrimp and use the palms of your hands to press them flat. The inside of the shrimp may contain orangy-red coral as well as a pale yellow or green cream. Rub the coral and cream into the meat of the shrimp, then brush each shrimp with the olive oil marinade and sear over a hot grill, shell sides up for 1 to 1½ minutes. Turn the shrimp onto their shells and grill for another 2 to 4 minutes depending upon their size. The meat will be opaque all the way through when cooked. Cut through one of the shrimp to test for doneness.

◠ Transfer the shrimp to a serving platter, drizzle with any remaining marinade, sprinkle with parsley, and serve immediately.

River Shrimp Sautéed in a Spicy Tomato Sauce
Gamberi di Fiume al Pomodoro e Peperoncino

SERVES 4

Antonio likes the flavor of this recipe best when the shrimp are cooked and served in their shells. Jean-Louis likes nothing better than to forgo a knife and fork and peel away the shells with his hands, dipping the heads in the garlicky sauce and sucking out the juices. You may substitute with peeled shrimp if you wish—but you'll be missing out on half the fun. Be sure to make the sauce first, since the shrimp cook very quickly, and, like all shellfish, should not be overcooked.

4 tablespoons extra-virgin olive oil
1 small onion, finely chopped
1 tablespoon finely chopped celery
1 tablespoon finely chopped carrots

1 pound very ripe plum tomatoes, quartered lengthwise and seeds removed

Salt

1 small, hot red chili pepper or pinch of crushed red pepper

24 large shrimp in their shells (approximately 1 pound)

8 cloves garlic, thinly sliced

1 glass dry white wine

*Heat 2 tablespoons of olive oil in a medium, heavy-bottomed pan. Add the chopped onions, celery, and carrots and sauté until tender (about 10 minutes).

*In the meantime, chop the seeded tomatoes into large cubes without removing their skins (although you may if you wish). Add the tomatoes to the sautéed vegetables and cook uncovered over a medium flame until they form a thick, chunky sauce (about 15 minutes). Add salt and crushed chili pepper to taste and remove from heat.

*Rinse the shrimp in cold water and, if you are leaving the heads on, pull off the long feelers attached to the heads. Put the sliced garlic and 2 tablespoons of olive oil in a large skillet and sauté over low heat until the garlic is golden. Lay the shrimp flat in the pan over the garlic, raise the heat to high, and sear the shrimp for 30 seconds on each side, turning once. Pour in the wine and continue cooking over a high flame for 2 or 3 minutes while the alcohol evaporates. Reduce the heat to medium, add the tomato sauce, and cook for 2 or 3 minutes, stirring frequently. Serve immediately.

WHY WE INVITE

If you happen to be in the business of feeding people, it sometimes feels as if the likelihood you'll be invited to someone's house for dinner is inversely proportional to how well the hosts like your restaurant's food. The lighter your gnocchi, the more savory your ossobuco, the smaller the chance that someone who might otherwise delight in your company is going to want you at their table when they are doing the cooking.

When an invitation is finally extended, then along with an otherwise perfectly wonderful meal, you may find yourself being served a variety of apologies, excuses, and self-critical observations dissecting the failings of every dish. It's a bit like the observation

Woody Allen once made about women—that they'll point out their most loathed physical imperfections to a man before he's even noticed them, just so he'll know they are already well aware of their every flaw.

Who needs enemies when we do such a good job of sabotaging ourselves all on our own? And why the fixation with perfection? Could it be that we've forgotten why we invite in the first place? *A dinner party isn't a performance. It's a gift.* To invite someone into the little space in the world you've carved out for yourself—your own kingdom, however grand or small—is an act of generosity. It has everything to do with the pleasure of breaking bread with friends, and nothing at all to do with impressing our guests with our lifestyle or wowing them with our culinary prowess.

In a perfect world, we'd like our homes (and ourselves) to look splendid, the meal to be exceptional, and our kids to be paragons of good behavior. Jean-Louis and I are able to pull off the fiction of the "perfect life" about once a year—the other 364 days *something* happens: we get into a little spat as our guests are walking up the drive, a cake that's supposed to take 30 minutes to cook takes an hour and a half, the sink stops up, the kids behave like *real* kids (being alternately charming and annoying, refusing at all costs to go to bed at a reasonable hour). Not a perfect life, but a *real* one.

If your goal is perfection, then chances are that for at least part of the evening, you'll find yourself inwardly hysterical and outwardly ever so slightly uptight. Your guests will sense this. Their natural instinct will be to help, but they'll be paralyzed into inaction by their desire to maintain the fiction that everything is going just splendidly, even though there's a mysteriously acrid smell coming from the kitchen, the dog has just piddled on the dining room rug, and it's 10:30 P.M. and dinner is showing no signs of arrival.

If you can keep your cool in the midst of whatever calamities have assaulted you, your guests will be happy—they will love you, your home, and your meal regardless of how well they conform to your own standards of perfection. There is no single more important thing you can do to assure the success of a dinner party than to be relaxed and at ease no matter how well (or not) your plans are going. Your guests will happily forgo the fallen soufflé for a glass of wine and a wedge of cheese if the company is relaxed and the mood is right.

If you're having trouble believing me, think about the memorable dinner parties you've attended. What made them so special? Could it be that it had more to do with the people and the atmosphere their combined presence created than with the hosts' seamless execution of a meal?

Of course, it doesn't help one bit that we're constantly bombarded with media images of beautiful people in spectacular homes, leading perfect lives with their perfectly functional families. But, really, whose life even remotely resembles a magazine's glossy pages for any longer than it takes the photographer to shoot the pictures? For that matter, I'm not sure I'd even want to know anyone whose life was that perfect. Would you?

Sautéed Scallops with Lemony Mushrooms
Canestrelli con Funghi al Limone
SERVES 4

Scallops have the sweetest meat of all shellfish. While the beautiful, fanlike shells are found in great abundance in Venice's Rialto fish market, in America, scallops are almost always sold shucked and cleaned—a pity, since the shells are spectacular on the plate and the cleaning takes away some of the scallops' most flavorful parts.

This recipe combines the mild earthiness of cultivated mushrooms with the scallops' tender sweetness. Use the small delicate bay scallops if you can find them where you live. Otherwise, the larger sea scallops will work fine.

For the Mushrooms
   3 tablespoons olive oil
   2 cloves garlic, sliced
   1 pound button or cremini mushrooms, brushed and wiped clean, then thinly
      sliced

1 teaspoon finely chopped parsley

1 tablespoon lemon juice

1 bay leaf

Salt

Freshly ground pepper

For the Scallops

3 tablespoons olive oil

4 cloves garlic, thinly sliced

1½ pounds shelled bay or sea scallops

1 cup white wine

༆ *The mushrooms:* Gently warm the olive oil and garlic in a skillet. When the garlic is fragrant, add the sliced mushrooms and parsley. Mix everything well for a minute, then increase the flame to high, add the lemon juice and bay leaf, and sauté, stirring regularly, until the mushrooms have released their moisture and are cooked through (8 to 10 minutes). Season to taste with salt and freshly ground pepper.

༆ *The sauce:* In the meantime, prepare the scallops by heating the olive oil and 4 thinly sliced cloves of garlic in a large skillet over a medium flame. When the garlic turns pale gold and fragrant, increase the heat to high and place the scallops in the skillet so that they do not overlap. Sauté the scallops until they color pale white on the outside, then cover with the wine and continue cooking until the scallops are colored a flat white all the way through. (This will only take a few minutes. Obviously, the smaller the scallop the shorter the cooking time.)

༆ Use a slotted spoon to remove the scallops from the skillet, then reduce the pan juices to a thin sauce over a strong flame. Add the reduced juices to the mushrooms, and cook the mixture over a medium flame for 1 minute.

༆ Remove the bay leaf, then spoon the mushrooms onto individual plates, scatter the scallops over the top, and serve immediately.

Octopus with Swiss Chard and Braised Onions
Polpo con Bietola e Cipollotte all'Agrodolce
SERVES 6

On the off chance that you have yet to discover the delicious flavor of octopus, look at the Italians—they virtually swoon over the eight-armed creatures. Your palate is sure to appreciate them more than your eyes, for they are as sweet a gift from the sea as anything you could imagine. Trust us on this one. Octopus come in all sizes, but the smallest will be the most tender. Old Italian cookbooks recommend tenderizing the meat by pounding it. Our fishmonger advises us to freeze it overnight, or even buy it frozen. The extreme cold has the same effect as pounding, only it's easier on all the participants. Almost all octopus available in the United States is predressed (i.e., cleaned of its eyes, mouth, and viscera). Ask your fishmonger to clean it for you if it is fresh off the boat and still fully intact.

When we're in Italy, instead of Swiss chard, we use agretti, *an early spring vegetable that looks something like clumps of deep green sea grass. It has a slightly mouth-puckering sourness appropriate for its name, which stems from* agro, *Italian for "sour." If you ever have the good fortune to come across* agretti, *take home a couple of pounds, boil them for 10 minutes in salted water, and dress them with olive oil and lemon juice.*

For the Octopus
¼ cup olive oil

4 cloves garlic, minced

2 shallots, finely chopped

2 pounds octopus, cleaned and cut into bite-sized pieces

1 cup white wine

Salt

Freshly ground black pepper

For the Chard

¼ cup olive oil

3 tablespoons lemon juice

Salt

Freshly ground black pepper

3 pounds Swiss chard, carefully washed, thick stems removed

The Rest

1 recipe braised onions (page 292)

⌒ *The octopus:* Heat ¼ cup olive oil in a heavy-bottomed casserole over a medium flame. Add the garlic and shallots, stirring frequently until the shallots soften and the garlic is fragrant. Add the octopus and white wine to the pot and stir for a minute or two while the alcohol evaporates. Then add 2 cups of water, ½ teaspoon of salt, and freshly ground black pepper to taste. Reduce the heat to low, cover the pot, and simmer for 1 hour without lifting the lid.

⌒ In the meantime, whisk together ¼ cup of olive oil with 3 tablespoons of lemon juice. Season with salt and pepper and set aside. Wash the chard thoroughly, but do not dry it; it will cook in the water that clings to its leaves. Remove and discard any tough, thick stems but leave the smaller, thin ones. Place the chard leaves in a large pot over a medium flame, sprinkle them with salt, and cook them, stirring frequently, until the leaves and thin stems are soft and wilted (5 to 7 minutes). Drain and dress with the olive oil and lemon dressing.

⌒ Prepare the braised onions.

⌒ Transfer the cooked octopus to the center of a large serving platter and surround it with the chard. Scatter the onions evenly over the chard and serve immediately.

Venetian-Style Mussels and Potatoes
Peoci e Patate
SERVES 4

Peoci is the Venetian word for "mussels." You'll see them in large clusters hugging the rocks off the shore of the Lido, attached to the edges of the canals leading out to the lagoon, in mesh sacks for sale at the Rialto market, and on almost every menu in town.

1½ pounds fresh live mussels, scrubbed and debearded

Salt

1½ pounds boiling potatoes

3 tablespoons extra-virgin olive oil, plus oil for drizzling

1 large white onion, minced

3 cloves garlic, 2 minced, 1 peeled

1½ cups vegetable broth (made from good-quality bouillon)

Freshly ground black pepper

¾ cup dry white wine

3 tablespoons finely chopped Italian parsley

꙳ Soak the mussels in several changes of lightly salted cold water for 2 hours. Drain. Throw away any mussels that do not close when tapped on.

꙳ Peel the potatoes and cut them into small chunks.

꙳ Place the olive oil, onion, minced garlic, and ½ cup of vegetable broth in a large shallow-sided casserole and stew very gently, taking care that the onion and garlic cook without coloring (about 10 minutes). Add the potatoes and a touch of broth and cook, covered, over a low flame until the potatoes are soft but not mushy (about 15 minutes). Add additional broth in small quantities as it is absorbed by the potatoes. Season to taste with salt and a generous grinding of black pepper.

In the meantime, place the mussels in a stockpot with the white wine, garlic clove, and parsley. Cover and cook over a high flame until the shells open (5 to 6 minutes). Use a slotted spoon to ladle the mussels into a bowl. Set aside 4 large or 8 small shells and remove the remaining mussels from their shells. Strain the juices from the pot through a cheesecloth or chinois. Add the shelled mussels and strained juices to the cooked potatoes, and stir everything together for a couple of minutes over a low flame while the flavors meld. Remove the garlic clove, then ladle the mussels and potatoes onto a shallow serving dish. Scatter the unshelled mussels over the top, drizzle with olive oil and serve immediately.

"Stuffed" Soft-Shell Crab
Moleche con Pien
SERVES 4

Antonio is a huge fan of Venetian-style soft-shell crabs. Like most Italians, he seems to appreciate them all the more because of the brevity of their season—the crabs molt only during the months of April, May, September, and October, although lagoon hatcheries are able to coax them into shedding their shells all summer long. The classic Venetian method of preparing them is not for the squeamish—the live crabs are placed in a bowl of beaten eggs for 2 to 3 hours, during which time they eat the eggs and then expire—whether by gluttony or drowning no one knows. The results are crabs that fry up light and fluffy—the "stuffing" being the egg itself.

8 live soft-shell crabs
Salt
3 eggs, beaten
Flour for dredging
Pepper
Corn or safflower oil for frying

∽ Wash the crabs in abundant salted water, then place them in a bowl with the beaten eggs. Cover with a dish and set aside for 2 to 3 hours. Remove the crabs from the eggs and use kitchen shears to clip off the eyes and mouth. Dredge the crabs lightly in flour.

∽ Heat ¼ inch of oil in a medium skillet. When the oil is hot but not smoking, place the crabs in the pan and fry them until golden brown, 2 to 3 minutes per side. Blot between paper towels, sprinkle with salt, and serve.

Variation: Soak the crabs in eggs as above, then dredge with flour. Heat 2 tablespoons of olive oil in a pan with 4 to 5 cloves of crushed garlic. When the garlic is golden and fragrant, add the crabs and a small handful of basil leaves. Lightly fry the crabs for 2 minutes on each side, then add a splash of white wine to the pan. Allow a minute for the alcohol to evaporate, then serve.

VINEGAR RINSING CHICKEN

Antonio always rinses raw chicken with a cup of white wine vinegar before cooking it. He places the meat in a bowl, douses the body and cavity with vinegar, turns the meat over a few times to coat it with the liquid, and leaves it to sit for about 10 minutes. Then he rinses the poultry well under running water and pats it dry with paper towels.

He told me he does this for two reasons: first, because his father always did it—whether at home or in any one of the famed kitchens in which he worked; second, because he claims the vinegar not only cleans poultry of any surface bacteria it contains, but also gives the meat a sweeter, cleaner flavor.

Antonio's Favorite Roasted Chicken
Il Pollo Arrosto Preferito di Antonio

SERVES 4

What does a chef cook when he's cooking for himself? In Antonio's case, a farm-raised chicken roasted with aromatic vegetables, herbs, and lemon. The frequent turning of the bird helps to make the meat especially moist and flavorful.

One 3½-pound roasting chicken,
    neck and giblets removed
1 cup white wine vinegar
Salt
Freshly ground black pepper
3 tablespoons extra-virgin olive oil
1 cup dry white wine
1 tablespoon Dijon mustard

6 cloves garlic, peeled
2 sprigs of fresh rosemary
Generous handful of fresh sage leaves
1 small lemon, cut into wedges
4 carrots, coarsely chopped
3 onions, cut in half lengthwise
    and then sliced
1 stalk celery, broken in half

∽ Preheat the oven to 375°.

∽ Rinse the chicken with the vinegar as described opposite. Pat the chicken dry with paper towels, then sprinkle the skin and cavity with salt and black pepper.

∽ Lightly oil a shallow rectangular baking pan large enough to comfortably hold the chicken. Place the chicken breast side up in the pan and roast until the skin browns (10 to 15 minutes). Turn the chicken over and lightly brown the back for 5 to 10 minutes.

∽ Remove the pan from the oven, turn the chicken breast side up and pour the wine over the top. Stir the mustard into the pan juices, then baste the chicken with the juices. Place 2 cloves of garlic, a sprig of rosemary, a few sage leaves, and a wedge of lemon in the cavity of the chicken, then sprinkle the remaining vegetables, herbs, and lemon wedges over and around the bird. Return the chicken to the oven for 10 minutes, then remove the pan from the oven, turn the meat over, stir the vegetables and return the pan to the oven. After another 10 minutes, turn the chicken breast side up for the duration of the cooking, and stir the vegetables once again. The total cooking time will be 1 hour, more or less, depending on the size of the bird and the particularities of your oven. The chicken is ready when the juices run clear from the thigh when pricked with a fork.

∽ Discard the rosemary sprigs and celery. Transfer the chicken to a larger serving platter, cover with a loose tent of aluminum foil, and let cool for 10 minutes. Turn the oven off and set the pan with the vegetables in the oven, leaving the door ajar while the chicken cools.

∽ Spoon the vegetables around the chicken, pour the pan juices over and around it, and serve. Carve at the table.

Flattened Chicken Marinated in Herbs, Mustard, and Vinegar
Battuta di Pollo Ruspante Marinato all'Aceto, Erbe, e Senape
SERVES 4

This is a favorite at Ca' Brea. The chicken marinates overnight in an herb and oil mixture and is cooked on the stove with a weighted object on top. Chickens cooked this way are sometimes called *"pollo al mattone,"* the *mattone* referring to the bricks used to keep the chickens flat while cooking. We use a cast-iron kitchen weight at the restaurants—a large pot filled with water will work fine at home. You can cook the chickens either in a heavy-bottomed skillet or over a medium-low barbecue or stovetop grill. Ask your butcher to bone the chickens for you. Keep in mind that the chickens are marinated for a day before cooking.

2 whole boneless, preferably free-range chickens with skin
   (approximately 2½ pounds each once boned)
1 cup white wine vinegar

For the Marinade

    1 cup extra-virgin olive oil
    1½ tablespoons finely chopped fresh sage leaves
    1½ tablespoons finely chopped fresh rosemary
    1½ tablespoons finely chopped fresh thyme
    1½ tablespoons finely chopped fresh marjoram
    1 bay leaf, finely chopped
    Zest of ½ lemon
    2 cloves garlic, finely chopped

For the Spray

    ½ cup white wine
    ⅓ cup white wine vinegar
    1 tablespoon honey

∽ Place the chickens in a large bowl with 1 cup of wine vinegar and 2 cups of water. Soak the meat in the mixture for 1 hour, then drain and pat the chickens dry with paper towels. In the meantime, mix together the marinade ingredients.

∽ Paint both sides of the chickens with the herb marinade. Place the chickens in a shallow glass or ceramic baking dish, cover with plastic wrap, and refrigerate for 24 hours.

∽ When you are ready to cook the chickens, whisk together the wine, vinegar, and honey and transfer to a spray bottle. In the meantime, heat an outdoor barbecue or stovetop grill to medium-low, or heat a skillet large enough to accommodate both chickens lying flat (or else 1 skillet per chicken).

∽ Lay the chickens skin side down in the pan or on the grill and lightly brown for 5 minutes. Turn the chickens over, spray with the wine and vinegar mixture, then weight the chickens down with a pot filled with water or other kitchen weight. Turn the chickens every 3 or 4 minutes, spraying them each time with the wine and vinegar mixture. You can remove the weight after the chickens have cooked for 15 to 18 minutes. Continue cooking, turning the chickens every few minutes, and spraying with the wine and vinegar mixture until the juices of the thigh run clear when pricked with a fork (25 to 30 minutes total cooking time). Serve a half chicken per person.

Spicy Flattened Chicken
Pollo Piccante Schiacciato

SERVES 4

For this version of flattened chicken, the bird is oven-roasted on the bone and seasoned with a spicy mixture of cayenne powder, herbs, olives, and sweet chilies.

1 whole roasting chicken
1 cup white wine vinegar
2 tablespoons extra-virgin olive oil
Salt
Black pepper
Generous pinch cayenne chili powder
1 cup kalamata olives,
Small handful of fresh sage leaves,
    very finely chopped

1 small sprig fresh rosemary,
    very finely chopped
5 cloves garlic, very finely chopped
½ teaspoon lemon zest
½ cup dry white wine
1 tablespoon whole grain mustard
4 shallots, thinly sliced
10 sweet chili peppers

↝ Preheat oven to 450°.

↝ Soak the chicken in the vinegar as described on page 236. Pat dry with paper towels.

↝ Lay the chicken breast side down and cut it open along both sides of its backbone. Discard the backbone, turn the chicken over, and flatten it down with your hands. Make a couple of incisions into the skin around the meaty part of the legs to help the chicken remain flat while cooking.

↝ Pour the olive oil into a rectangular baking pan large enough to accommodate the chicken lying flat. Lay the chicken, skin side down, in the oil, then turn it over to lightly cover both sides in the oil. Use your hands to massage the oil evenly over the chicken. Sprinkle the entire chicken with salt, pepper, and ground cayenne chili pepper.

↝ Slice around the perimeter of the olives, then squeeze them to remove their stones. Set aside.

In a small bowl, combine the chopped sage, rosemary, garlic, and lemon zest. Set aside.

Place the chicken skin side up in the oven until the skin has browned (about 10 minutes). Turn it over to brown the other side for another 10 minutes, then remove the pan from the oven, quickly turn the chicken skin side up and douse with the wine. (Expect a great sizzle and clouds of vapor when the wine hits the chicken.) Give the pan a shake to mix the juices and keep the chicken from sticking, then use a wooden spoon to rub both sides of the chicken with the herb and garlic mixture. Stir the mustard into the pan liquid and sprinkle the shallots, peppers, and olives around the chicken.

Return the pan to the oven, and baste the chicken with its juices every 5 minutes. When the vegetables begin to darken, hide them under the body of the chicken for the duration of the cooking time. Total cooking time will be around 45 minutes, but will vary according to the size of the chicken and your particular oven. The juices of the thigh will run clear when pricked with a fork when the meat is done.

Remove the pan from the oven, cover with a loose tent of foil for about 10 minutes, then cut the chicken into pieces and serve on a large platter covered with the olives, peppers, and shallots.

Pan-Roasted Chicken with Mixed Forest Mushrooms

Pollo in Padella con Funghi di Bosco

SERVES 4

There is no better way to cook chicken pieces than to pan-roast them over the stovetop. Here the meat is browned on all sides in olive oil, then cooked with a mixture of aromatic vegetables and woodland mushrooms. The result is neither stew nor meat smothered in a heavy sauce—but something in between. The chicken, although browned on the outside, is moist and fork-tender inside. The mushrooms add a variety of textures as well as a complex earthy flavor.

One 3½-pound chicken, cut into 8 pieces

1 cup white wine vinegar

1 pound any combination mixed wild mushrooms,
 such as porcini, stemmed shiitake, chanterelle, or oyster

3 tablespoons extra-virgin olive oil

2 carrots, finely chopped

2 stalks celery, finely chopped

1 onion, finely chopped

Small handful of fresh sage leaves

1 cup dry white wine

Salt

Freshly ground black pepper

∽ Place the chicken parts in a large mixing bowl. Pour in the vinegar and swish the pieces around to cover with the liquid. Let the liquid rest on the chicken for 10 minutes, then rinse the pieces under running water and pat dry with paper towels.

∽ Wipe the mushrooms clean with a damp cloth. If they are very dirty, rinse them under running water and dry them well. Unless the mushrooms are quite large, leave them whole. Otherwise, cut the larger mushrooms into chunks.

∽ Heat the olive oil in a large, heavy-bottomed skillet over a medium-high flame. Lay the chicken skin side down in the hot oil and brown for 3 to 4 minutes, making sure not to let the chicken stick to the pan. Turn the pieces over and let them brown on the other side.

∽ When the chicken has become browned all over, add the carrots, celery, onion, and sage leaves and sauté, stirring regularly, for 5 minutes. When almost all the liquid in the pan has evaporated, pour in the wine. Let it bubble and steam for a minute, then add the mushrooms and salt and pepper to taste. Stir the pot well for a couple of minutes and then rest the chicken pieces on top of the mushrooms and cook, turning over the chicken pieces from time to time until the mushrooms are soft and the meat feels very tender when prodded with a fork (about 35 more minutes).

∽ Transfer the chicken and mushrooms to a warmed platter and serve immediately.

CHEF WATCHING

Until embarking on this project, I had always paid much more attention to the results of Antonio's culinary efforts than to the efforts themselves. At most, I mentally jotted down a recipe's ingredients and threw together some reasonable facsimile sometime later. During the past year, I have spent many, many days in the kitchen observing Antonio's every gastronomic move with brain-numbing concentration. Most of what I've garnered has made it into individual recipes, but there were some things in Antonio's general approach to *la cucina* that deserve to be singled out and highlighted.

- Antonio cooks with *all* his senses. He uses his hands whenever he can to mix ingredients. He knows when a dough has reached the proper consistency by its texture and touch, rather than by some scientific flour-to-moisture ratio. Often he stands over a bubbling saucepan using his hands to wave the fragrant vapors toward his nose. This is how he knows just when the alcohol has evaporated from a splash of wine he's added to a risotto, or when the roux for a béchamel has that biscuity smell that tells him it's time to whisk in the hot milk. Whenever he can, he tastes things along the way to see if the flavors are right.

  "Unlike French cuisine, Italian cooking doesn't require absolute precision. Whether you dress sautéed spinach with three rather than four tablespoons of olive oil, or simmer your pasta sauce ten minutes longer than a recipe suggests, will rarely make much difference," he explained to me. "It's more important that you learn to recognize the flavor of wonderfully fruity extra-virgin olive oil, than that you practice diligently measuring it out by the teaspoonful. Written instructions are just a *starting place*. It's only when the words are filtered through your senses that you begin to learn to really cook well."

- He always takes a moment to organize himself mentally before beginning to cook. He'll think through a recipe, get out all the ingredients he needs, and prepare as many of them as he can before any olive oil hits the saucepan.

- Antonio manages to keep his kitchen in scrupulous order, without ever seeming fastidious about it. He simply cleans up after himself as he goes along, wiping the counters clean, rinsing and reusing knives, mixing bowls, measuring cups, and spoons, rather than grabbing something new from the cupboard every time.

- "The single most common thing lacking in home kitchens is a set of good, sharp knives," Antonio told me one day when it seemed as if we had spent most of the morning wielding our blades. "The problem is less that people don't have the knives than that they go for years without sharpening them," he added. In many ways, dull knives are more dangerous than sharp ones. You must exert much greater pressure on the object to be cut than you do with a sharp, clean edge that slices easily on contact.

- He cooks much more aggressively than most home cooks I know. Where we would tentatively brown a piece of meat in a skillet, he cranks the fire up and lets things sizzle, as he does with vegetables he's sautéing or anything else that requires a bold, strong flame. The difference is that he watches over it all with the eye of a hawk, giving the pans a quick shake now and then, the vegetables a good go-around with a spoon, and providing any other immediate intervention he sees fit. (This is not to say that Antonio cannot be a gentle cook. My observation here is limited to those times that the kitchen is awash in the crackle and sputter of serious, high-powered heat.)

- He scolded me the first ten times I tried to "help out" by stirring the pot while he was busy doing something else. It wasn't that he didn't want the help. The problem was in my stirring *technique*—my stirs tended to leave the sautéing onions, mushrooms, meat, or whatever was cooking clumped up at the bottom of the pan. Or else I would forget to sweep the spoon around the edges of the pan where food is most likely to stick and burn. Not a trifling matter. "Can't you see that things won't cook evenly this way?" he reprimanded me . . . constantly. I knew he was right, but it took me a couple of days to get into the habit of making sure that whatever I had simmering or sautéing in the pan was stirred *thoroughly* and spread *evenly* over the surface.

- What makes Antonio a *chef* rather than just a fabulous cook is his inexhaustible curiosity about culinary matters. He'll spend a day pruning rosemary bushes and burning the trimmings outside in the garden because he heard somewhere that centuries ago rosemary ashes were added to the brine in which olives were cured. He'll dig his father's ancient alembic out of the attic and try his hand at making grappa and fruit liqueurs. He'll try cooking pasta by adding only small amounts of broth at a time the way you would cook a risotto—just to see what happens. Sometimes his experiments are successful. Sometimes they're not. During these little forays, it never seems to matter to him much one way or the other—he is clearly more intent on satisfying his curiosity than his belly.

Pan-Roasted Chicken with Sweet Peppers, Olives, and Capers

Pollo in Padella con Peperoni, Olive, e Capperi

SERVES 4 TO 6

This savory dish is just as good the second day, when the flavors have had a chance to mingle. Add a touch of liquid (broth or water) to the pot if you are reheating.

One 3½-pound chicken, cut into 8 pieces

1¼ cups white wine vinegar

3 tablespoons extra-virgin olive oil

3 ounces Italian pancetta,
  chopped into small dice

Handful of whole fresh sage leaves

3 onions, halved lengthwise, then sliced

2 red or yellow peppers,
  seeded and cut into large dice

3 cloves garlic, peeled

4 plum tomatoes, quartered

Salt

Freshly ground black pepper

⅓ cup black kalamata, Gaeta,
  or niçoise olives, with stones

¼ cup capers

❧ Place the chicken parts in a large mixing bowl. Pour in 1 cup of vinegar and swish the pieces around to cover with the liquid. Leave to rest for 10 minutes, then rinse the chicken with fresh water and pat dry with paper towels.

❧ Heat the olive oil in a large, heavy-bottomed skillet over a medium-high flame. Lay the chicken pieces skin side down in the pan and brown for 3 to 4 minutes. Turn the pieces over, lower the flame, and pour in ¼ cup of vinegar. (The vapors are acrid and sharp—they won't hurt you, but I prefer to keep my distance from them for the first couple of minutes after the vinegar hits the hot pan.) After a couple of minutes, add the pancetta. When it begins to brown, add the sage and stir the contents of the pot well for 1 minute.

❧ Scatter the onions, peppers, and garlic into the pan and set the chicken pieces on top of the vegetables. Raise the flame to medium and cover the pot for 10 minutes, stirring occasionally. Add the tomato, and salt and pepper to taste. Cook uncovered for another 10 minutes, turning the meat every few minutes. Add a couple of tablespoons of water if the pan liquid is very dry.

❧ Cut along the length of the olives and squeeze out the stones. Add the olives and capers to the pan and stir well for a couple of minutes to blend the flavors. Transfer to a large platter and serve.

Hunter's-Style Rabbit
Coniglio alla Cacciatora
SERVES 4

Fall mornings will find two sorts of people scouring the woods—hunters and mushroom gatherers. The latter are armed only with baskets and long sticks, which are used to upturn damp leaves in the hopes of finding an edible mushroom underneath; the hunters sling long shotguns over their shoulders and traipse through the woods, pairs of hounds trotting alongside, on the lookout for thrush, pheasant, wild hare, or boar.

Food cooked *"alla cacciatora"* means hunter's style, and usually refers to rabbit or chicken. Of course, like most Italian recipes, there seem to be as many styles as there are hunters (or hunters' wives, as is more probably the case). Most commonly, the meat is slowly cooked with some combination of onions, tomato, wine, and herbs. Here is our version, which combines aromatic vegetables, spices, herbs, and tomato.

One 3½-pound rabbit, cut into 8 pieces
1 cup white wine vinegar

For the Marinade

1 cup red wine
3 crushed juniper berries
3 bay leaves
1 cinnamon stick

Cooking the Rabbit

¼ cup extra-virgin olive oil
2 tablespoons butter
3 ounces Italian pancetta,
   cut into thick 3 by 1-inch slices
2 carrots, finely chopped
1 onion, halved and thinly sliced
1 celery stalk, chopped
1 small sprig of fresh rosemary,
   leaves finely chopped
Small handful of fresh sage leaves,
   finely chopped

1 clove
1-inch piece of cinnamon
1 sprig of fresh marjoram
Freshly ground black pepper
1 cup red wine
2 cups fresh tomato puree
   (about 1½ pounds fresh tomatoes,
   skins and seeds removed, pulp
   pureed)
Salt

↝ *The night before:* Place the rabbit pieces in a medium bowl with the vinegar and enough water to cover. Refrigerate overnight.

🌿 *The marinade:* The following day, drain the pieces and rinse them well in cold water. Return them to a medium bowl with 1 quart of water and the marinade ingredients. Marinate for 3 hours, then drain the pieces and pat them dry.

🌿 *Cooking the rabbit:* Heat the olive oil and butter in a large, heavy-bottomed skillet. Distribute the rabbit pieces in a single layer, set the slices of pancetta on top, and brown the meat on all sides over a medium flame. Scatter the remaining vegetables and herbs and spices (except for the tomato puree) over the rabbit, grind liberally with black pepper, and continue cooking for 10 minutes, turning the pieces over occasionally and stirring the vegetables so that they cook evenly.

🌿 Pour in the red wine and stir the pot gently for 5 minutes while the alcohol bubbles away. Stir in the tomato puree and 2 cups of water. Bring to a simmer and partially cover. Salt to taste after 20 minutes.

🌿 Continue simmering gently at low heat until the rabbit has cooked for about 1½ hours and the meat is very tender when prodded with a fork. Remove the cinnamon stick and clove. Transfer to a large platter and serve.

Herbed Rabbit
Coniglio alle Erbe
SERVES 4

Soaking the rabbit in vinegar for a couple of hours removes any gamy flavor. The white meat cooks tender and juicy, while the mixture of herbs, lemon, pancetta, and wine creates a bold and savory palate of flavors. Serve with polenta or boiled new potatoes.

One 3½-pound rabbit, cut into 8 pieces
1 cup plus 2 tablespoons white wine vinegar
⅓ cup extra-virgin olive oil

2 tablespoons butter

2 small sprigs of fresh rosemary, finely chopped

Generous handful of fresh sage leaves, finely chopped

⅓ cup Italian prosciutto, cut into small dice

6 large shavings of lemon zest

1 cup dry white wine

Salt

Freshly ground black pepper

ᴄᴏ Place the rabbit pieces in a medium bowl. Pour in 1 cup of vinegar and enough water to cover and soak for 2 hours. Drain, then rinse the pieces in cold water. Pat dry with paper towels.

ᴄᴏ Heat the olive oil and butter in a large, heavy-bottomed skillet over a medium flame. Set the pieces in a single layer in the pan, sprinkle with the chopped herbs and prosciutto, and brown the rabbit on all sides. Add the lemon zest and continue browning the meat for a couple of minutes, turning the pieces over in the pan with tongs.

ᴄᴏ Pour the remaining 2 tablespoons of vinegar over the rabbit and stir until the liquid evaporates. Pour in the white wine, lower the flame, and gently cook for about 1 hour, occasionally turning the pieces and stirring the pot. After the first half hour of cooking, season to taste with a generous pinch of salt and grinding of black pepper. When most of the pan juices have been absorbed (after about 45 minutes), add ½ cup of water and stir the pot well. Continue cooking until the rabbit has soaked up most of the herbed juices and is tender when tested with a fork.

OUR BUTCHER

Il Nostro Macellaio

Jean-Louis and I took Antonio on a "field trip" one drizzly spring morning, the kind of day everyone here complains about, but no one will admit is responsible for the lushly verdant, almost Irish look of the countryside.

We grabbed a sheaf of recipes-in-progress and headed off to Panzano-in-Chianti, a charming hillside town, home to several good wine shops, a rare Sunday farmers' market, and Dario Cecchini, the legendary Tuscan butcher whom we wanted to give Antonio the pleasure, or should I say experience, of meeting. A foray into Dario's world is a quintessentially Italian experience, carrying with it all the elements that have lent fame to Italy's reputation as a country where life still moves at a livable pace, and beauty, hospitality, and wondrous food take precedence over almost everything else.

The tiny jewel of a shop is perched halfway up a narrow road running off the main square. When the front door is open, you actually *hear* the place before you *see* it. Today, gentle strains of Mozart drift out into the street, on another day, an impassioned aria might have trumpeted our arrival. The inviting storefront is a collage of milky white tiled walls, well-worn wooden butcher blocks, and wicker baskets brimming with rare varieties of heirloom dried beans and pistachios handpicked in Israel (by Dario himself). Braids of garlic, dried red peppers, and legions of cured meats hang decorously from the ceiling.

We said our hellos, made our introductions, and settled in to watch . . . and wait as Dario held court before the handful of customers gathered around the wide glass display counter laden with hand-cured and aged meats, heavy strands of sausages, delicately flavored pâtés, roasted turkey laced with pistachios, orange zest, and peppercorns, and Dario's famous *tonno del Chianti,* which is really pork that has simmered overnight in white wine and taken on the texture of a fine tuna fillet and a flavor that's hard to forget.

Although it was scarcely past breakfast-time, and the taste of our morning's cappuccinos was still imprinted on our palates, we soon found ourselves with glasses of local Chianti in one hand and slivers of piquant salami in the other, listening to tales of Dario's latest culinary escapades and sampling a seventeenth-century recipe for hot fruit mustard.

What so strikes me about Dario is the passion and enthusiasm that he has brought to what many would consider to be the most humble of callings. Though he could easily move to a much grander location and hire a bevy of assistants to help him behind the counter, he won't. It's simply not his style. In an age where everyone else seems to be striving for more and more, Dario appears perfectly contented right where he is—in his tiny shop in the middle of the Tuscan countryside, doing what he does best.

It was noon before we made out way home, bags filled with everything but what was on our shopping list—but, then, how could we resist the chicken and ginger sausages we watched Dario make using century-old equipment handed down to him from his grandfather? Or the lamb stuffed with aged pecorino cheese and rosemary?

Exhibiting uncharacteristic decisiveness, we unanimously decided to abandon our own culinary plans for the chance to play with the delicacies good fortune had strewn in our path. Our own recipes could wait for another day.

Ossobuco with Polenta Fritters
Ossobuco con Frittelle di Polenta

SERVES 4

Ossobuco is one of those wonderfully descriptive Italian words that has become part of the American vocabulary. The "osso" refers to the cross-section of bone at the center of a horizontally cut veal shank. The treasure is in the heart of the "buco," the hole inside the bone containing the richly flavorful marrow. Our recipe differs from the traditional Milanese ossobuco in two respects: we serve it at Ca' Brea garnished with polenta fritters rather than saffron rice; and our *gremolata* is made with sage, lemon zest, and garlic, rather than the more traditional parsley, lemon, garlic mixture.

Although ossobuco can be served right out of the oven, Antonio likes the flavor best when the cooked shanks are allowed to sit for a couple of hours before being warmed in a hot oven and served. You can also cook the ossobuco the night before as follows: reduce the cooking time by ½ hour, allow the meat to cool and then refrigerate overnight. The following day, add ½ cup water to the pan, stir the contents gently, and finish cooking the meat in a 425° oven for 40 minutes.

For the Ossobucco

4 carrots, finely chopped

3 stalks celery, finely chopped

2 onions, very finely chopped

7 tablespoons extra-virgin olive oil

2 cups crushed Italian plum tomatoes

4 veal shanks, cut to a thickness of
  1½ to 2 inches, with bone and marrow

Flour for dredging

4 cups beef broth (see page 174) or
  high quality bouillon

Salt

Freshly ground black pepper

½ cup red wine

1 teaspoon lemon zest

5 sage leaves, chopped

1 clove garlic, minced

For the Polenta Fritters

½ recipe traditional polenta (page 207) or ½ box fast-cooking polenta made
  according to the package instructions, cooled in an oiled loaf pan

3 tablespoons olive oil

Salt

∽ *The ossobuco:* Preheat the oven to 425°.

∽ Sauté the carrots, celery, and onions with 3 tablespoons of olive oil in a medium saucepan. When the vegetables are soft (about 15 minutes), stir in the plum tomatoes and cook over a medium flame until they form a juicy sauce (about 10 minutes). Set aside.

∽ In the meantime, make 2 small cuts (a couple of inches from each other) into the outer edge of the veal at the meaty side of the shank opposite the bone. This will help the meat remain flat during cooking. Heat 4 tablespoons of olive oil over a high flame in a heavy-bottomed skillet large enough to accommodate the meat in a single layer. When the oil is hot but not smoking, quickly dredge the shanks in flour, lay them in the pan, and brown well on both sides, turning once.

✑ Heat the stock or bouillon to a low simmer.

✑ Transfer the veal shanks to a rectangular roasting pan and season both sides well with salt and freshly ground pepper. Deglaze the skillet by discarding the oil used for browning the meat, but not the small darkened bits of meat and flour resting at the bottom. Place the skillet over a high flame and add the wine, lemon zest, sage, and garlic, stirring continuously for 1 minute and scraping the bottom and sides of the skillet with a flat-bottomed wooden spoon. Stir ¼ cup of water into the pan, then pour the contents over the veal shanks.

✑ Spoon the tomato and vegetable mixture evenly over the meat, then gently pour the broth over the shanks to just barely cover the meat. Cover the pan with a lid or heavy aluminum foil and braise in the oven until the meat is fork-tender (about 2 hours). Carefully baste the meat with the stock from time to time, and gently lift the shanks off the bottom of the pan to allow some liquid to circulate underneath and keep the meat from sticking to the pan.

✑ Transfer the shanks to individual plates and spoon sauce and juices over the top.

✑ *The polenta fritters:* Slip the cooled polenta out of the loaf pan and cut into ¼-inch slices. Cut the slices diagonally through the center to form 2 triangles from each slice.

✑ Heat the olive oil in a heavy-bottomed nonstick skillet. Lay the polenta in an even, nonoverlapping layer in the pan and fry until lightly crispy on both sides, turning once. Sprinkle with salt and arrange several fritters per serving on each dinner plate with the ossobuco.

Pan-Roasted Veal Chops with Radicchio
Lombatina di Vitello alla Rustica con Radicchio

SERVES 4

The radicchio and pancetta give the veal a subtle richness that pairs up well with the soft mellow flavor of an Italian Merlot. Use the long-leafed radicchio di Treviso if you can find it, otherwise round heads of radicchio will work fine. Veal chops have a thin layer of fat around the edges. You may trim away a portion of it, but we like to leave at least ¼ inch around the meat for added flavor and moisture.

For the Meat
4 veal chops, cut to 1½-inch thickness
Freshly ground black pepper
4 tablespoons extra-virgin olive oil
Generous handful of fresh sage leaves

4 sprigs of rosemary
3 cloves garlic, crushed
1 cup dry white wine

For the Radicchio
2 tablespoons diced Italian pancetta
2 tablespoons extra-virgin olive oil
1 shallot, finely chopped
2 small heads radicchio, cored and sliced
1 tablespoon vinegar
Salt

∽ Sprinkle the veal chops with freshly ground black pepper.

∽ Warm the olive oil over a medium flame in a large skillet, then lay the herbs and garlic in the pan and place the chops on top. Brown the meat for a couple of minutes on each side, then cover with the herbs from the pan and continue cooking for 5 minutes, turning once.

∽ When the meat has cooked for 10 minutes, remove the skillet from the flame and pour in the wine. When the cloud of alcohol vapor dissipates, return the pan to the fire and let the wine bubble away for another minute before reducing the flame to low and covering the pan. Continue cooking for a few minutes over a gentle heat while the wine reduces, turning the meat once.

∽ In the meantime, place the pancetta and olive oil in a separate skillet and sauté the pancetta over a medium flame until the fat begins to melt. Add the shallot and sauté for a couple more minutes, then stir in the radicchio, mixing the pan well to coat it with the seasoned oil. When the radicchio has wilted, add the vinegar and a pinch of salt and continue cooking for another couple of minutes.

Transfer the radicchio to the pan with the chops, cover and cook over a gentle heat for a couple of minutes. Arrange the meat on individual dinner plates, spoon the radicchio over the top, pour on the pan juices, and serve.

Breaded Veal Scaloppine with Asparagus Tips and Fontina

Scaloppine Dorate con le Punte d'Asparagi e Fontina

SERVES 4

There are a few easier pieces of meat to work with than veal scaloppine. They literally take less than 3 minutes to cook—a fraction longer here because the meat makes a brief stop under a hot broiler before hitting the table. Make sure to use boned top round, cut against the grain—this way the veal cooks flat in the pan and will never have the stringiness of improperly cut scaloppine.

1 pound veal scaloppine, sliced to about ¼-inch thickness, lightly pounded
All-purpose flour for dredging
2 eggs, lightly beaten
1½ cups bread crumbs
1 pound fresh asparagus (you will only be using the tips)
2 tablespoons butter
4 shallots, finely chopped
¼ cup beef broth (page 174) or chicken broth (page 173) or high quality bouillon
Salt
¼ cup corn oil
4 ounces thinly sliced Fontina cheese

⌒ Preheat broiler to high.

⌒ Coat the scaloppine lightly with flour, then dip each scaloppina first in the beaten eggs, then in the bread crumbs. Set aside.

⌒ Trim the asparagus to the top 2 inches of the stalk and tip (use the remaining stalks for a soup or risotto). Melt the butter over a low flame in a small skillet, add the shallots, and sauté very gently until they become soft and translucent. Add the asparagus tips, broth, and a pinch of salt and cook until the broth reduces to a thin sauce and the asparagus tips are cooked but still firm (4 to 5 minutes).

⌒ In a separate heavy-bottomed skillet, heat the corn oil over a medium flame. When the oil is hot but not smoking, arrange as many scaloppine as will fit comfortably in the pan without overlapping (you may have to work in batches). Turn the meat after 30 seconds, then turn once again after the same amount of time. Use tongs to drain the meat over the pan, then blot between several layers of paper towels. Spread the scaloppine over a large baking dish, then cover each piece with a layer of cheese. Spoon the asparagus sauce over the top and place the meat under the broiler until the cheese begins to melt and soften. Serve immediately.

Rack of Veal
Costola di Vitella al Latte
SERVES 6

This is certainly not an economical dish, but it is both delicious and beautiful—the sort of thing to make for a Christmas or New Year's celebration. There is simply no better way to highlight the meat's tender succulence than by roasting a whole rack. It has all the festive grandeur of a roasted turkey yet cooks in less than half the time, and without the endless basting, turning, and fiddling that the giant birds demand. We serve the meat with a generous ladling of herbed brown milk sauce, sautéed spinach or Swiss chard, and mashed potatoes laced with butter and Parmesan.

One 6-rib rack of veal (about 6 pounds)

3 tablespoons extra-virgin olive oil

1½ tablespoons fresh rosemary,
   finely chopped

3 garlic cloves, finely chopped

Salt

Freshly ground black pepper

1 red onion, cut into small dice

1 carrot, cut into small dice

1 celery stalk, strings removed,
   cut into small dice

1½ cups white wine

2 tablespoons all-purpose flour

¾ cup whole milk

2½ cups chicken broth (page 173)

∽ Preheat oven to 450°.

∽ If your butcher has not already done so, use a well-sharpened knife to scrape the exposed portion of the bones free of all fat or meat. Discard the fat and set aside the meat. Rub the rack first with the olive oil, then with the rosemary and garlic. Sprinkle with salt and freshly ground black pepper.

∽ Spread the diced onion, carrot, and celery onto a shallow roasting pan along with any pieces of meat you have trimmed off the bone. Place the rack, meat side up, on top of the diced vegetables and roast for 20 minutes before lowering the heat to 400°.

∽ When the exposed bones begin to darken (this will happen anywhere from the first 40 to 60 minutes of roasting), wrap them in aluminum foil. After the rack has cooked a total of 45 minutes, pour the white wine over the meat and continue roasting for another 30 to 45 minutes, depending on how well cooked you like your meat. Generally, the meat is considered ready when a meat thermometer inserted into the thickest part of the rack reads 145°, or when the center of the rack is pink and juicy even though the outer crust has thoroughly browned (you will have to cut in between the bones to check this). Keep in mind that the exterior pieces of rack will be slightly more well done than the meat in the center and the rack will continue cooking while it cools on a cutting board and you prepare the sauce.

∽ Remove the rack from the oven, place the meat on a cutting board, and cover with aluminum foil. Set the roasting pan over a medium flame with the vegetables, pan juices, and scraps of meat and bring to a low simmer. Sprinkle the flour into the pan, whisking constantly, then add the milk and chicken broth, mix well, and transfer to a saucepan over a low flame. Simmer, uncovered, for about 15 minutes, skim off any fat that rises to the surface and pass the sauce through a chinois or a colander lined with cheesecloth. Season to taste with salt and freshly ground black pepper. The sauce will be quite fluid, rather than a thick gravy. Carve 1 bone per person, ladle sauce over veal, and serve. Pour the remaining sauce into a pitcher or gravy tureen, and set on the table.

Beef "Rags" with Basil and Garlic
Straccetti al Basilico e Aglio
SERVES 4

❧

If ever there was a case of rags to riches, this is it—tender pieces of filet cut to a ½-inch thickness and cooked in olive oil seasoned with garlic, basil, salt, and pepper. The meat is not fried—its juices emulsify with the oil so that each ingredient retains its fresh flavor, lending a subtle perfume to the meat. These "little rags" cook in a flash—make sure everyone is already at the table when you start the meat cooking.

1 pound beef filet, trimmed
6 tablespoons extra-virgin olive oil
6 cloves garlic, cut into thirds
Generous handful of fresh basil leaves
Freshly ground black pepper
Salt

∾ Cut the filet into ½-inch slices.

∾ Gently heat the olive oil in a large frying pan, sprinkle in the garlic, basil, and a generous grinding of black pepper. When the oil has warmed, lay the meat on top of the basil, sprinkle lightly with salt and 2 tablespoons of water. Cook the meat for 1 minute on each side, then transfer to a warmed serving dish and cover with the garlic, basil, and pan juices. Serve immediately.

Filet Mignon with Creamy Gorgonzola
Filetto al Gorgonzola

SERVES 4

We like to pair this most tender cut of beef with the ripe, rich flavor of creamy Italian Gorgonzola cheese. The filets are brown and flavorful on the outside while still mild and meltingly tender inside. Antonio likes the sauce to be relatively abundant—his pet peeve is to run out of sauce when he's only made it through half the filet. He "stretches" a sauce that has become too thick or dry in the cooking with a bit of broth.

3 tablespoons extra-virgin olive oil

4 pieces filet mignon, approximately 7 ounces each

Freshly ground black pepper

4 small sprigs of fresh rosemary

2 small shallots, minced

1 tablespoon mild Dijon mustard

⅓ cup dry white wine

6 tablespoons soft Italian *dolcelatte* Gorgonzola

2 tablespoons fresh cream

1 tablespoon butter

⅓ cup beef (page 174) or chicken broth (page 173) or high quality bouillon, optional

෴ Heat 2 tablespoons of olive oil in a heavy-bottomed skillet over a medium flame. Lay the filets in the pan and brown each side for a couple of minutes without moving them so that they form a thin, brown crust. Sprinkle both sides of the filets with a generous grinding of black pepper and place 1 sprig of rosemary under each filet. Continue cooking for 1 minute, then discard the rosemary and transfer the meat to a plate.

෴ Add the remaining tablespoon of olive oil along with the mixed shallots to the pan in which the meat was browned. Sauté lightly for 1 minute, then use a wooden spoon to blend the mustard in with oil and pan juices. Reduce the mustard and pan juices, stirring constantly, then return the filets to the pan. Move the filets around, turning them over once to coat in the mustard-shallot mixture. Pour in the wine and let it bubble away until the liquid has almost evaporated, then spoon in the Gorgonzola and blend it into the pan liquid with a spoon. When the cheese has dissolved into the pan juices, pour in the cream, turn the meat over, and move it around in the pan to help combine the sauce ingredients.

∽ Transfer the filets to dinner plates, then add the butter to the Gorgonzola sauce (and a bit of broth if the sauce looks too dry). As soon as the butter melts, pour the sauce over the meat and serve.

Sliced Entrecôte with Arugula and Shaved Parmesan

Tagliata con Rucola

SERVES 4

Tuscany is famous for the dwindling herds of Chianina cattle that populate the Val di Chiana area outside of Florence. Their meat is the preferred choice for the classic *bistecca alla fiorentina*—gargantuan beefsteaks that serve at least two people each. When we are lucky enough to find Chianina beef at home in Italy, we use it to prepare the relatively smaller *tagliata*—pan-sautéed entrecôtes or New York steaks cut into ½-inch strips and sprinkled with chopped arugula and slivers of Parmesan cheese. Antonio prefers cooking the meat at a high heat over the stove because of the pan juices this method of cooking creates. "The juice is like gold," he says. Our customers at Il Moro seem to agree—the *tagliata* has been a hit there since the restaurant first opened.

4 entrecôte or New York steaks, 10 to 12 ounces each

1 clove garlic, peeled

1½ tablespoons cracked black peppercorns

2 tablespoons plus ⅓ cup extra-virgin olive oil

Salt

4 handfuls of tender young arugula, coarsely chopped

2 ounces parmesan cheese, cut into thin shavings

⌒ Rub the steaks with the garlic clove and sprinkle a pinch of cracked pepper on both sides of each steak.

⌒ Heat 2 tablespoons of olive oil in a large, heavy-bottomed skillet over a strong flame. Lay the meat down in the pan and brown both sides for a couple of minutes each for steaks that are medium-rare (best for this dish).

⌒ Turn off the flame, transfer the meat to a cutting board, and return the pan with its juices to the stovetop. Cut the meat against the grain into ½-inch strips. Pour any juices released from the meat back into the pan in which it cooked. Add ⅓ cup warm water to the pan and scrape the sides and bottom well, then use a fork to whisk the ⅓ cup olive oil together with the pan juices.

⌒ Layer the meat on a large serving platter and sprinkle with salt. Pour the liquid from the pan over the meat. Scatter with chopped arugula and Parmesan shavings and serve.

Pork Medallions with Mushrooms and Peppers
Medaglioni di Maiale con Funghi e Peperoni

SERVES 4

These pork tenderloin medallions are succulent and tender and have no more fat than a boneless chicken breast.

4 tablespoons extra-virgin olive oil

1 clove garlic, thinly sliced

1 shallot, finely chopped

1 pound button or cremini mushrooms, sliced

1 small yellow pepper, ribs and seeds removed, cut into thin strips

Salt

½ cup dry white wine

1 pound pork tenderloin, cut crosswise into ½-inch slices

Flour for dredging

Freshly ground black pepper

1 sprig of rosemary, leaves only

Small handful of fresh sage leaves

1 tablespoon Dijon mustard

~ Warm 2 tablespoons of olive oil with the sliced garlic and shallot in a shallow pan. When they are fragrant but not browned, stir in first the mushrooms, then the pepper. Sauté for a couple of minutes over a medium flame, then season to taste with salt. Continue cooking the vegetables until they have softened and released much of their moisture but are still firm, then splash in a couple of tablespoons of white wine and stir for a minute while the liquids reduce.

~ Dredge the medallions lightly in flour and sprinkle with a grinding of black pepper. In a separate skillet, heat the remaining olive oil, add the rosemary and sage, then lay the meat in 1 layer on top of the herbs. Turn the medallions over after 1 minute and set the herbs on top. When both sides of the meat are browned, add the mustard to the pan along with the remaining wine. Stir in the mustard and allow the wine to bubble away for a couple of minutes until the liquid reduces to a light sauce. Sprinkle the meat with salt and add in the sautéed vegetables. Turn the meat and vegetables around in the pan for a minute, then layer the medallions on a serving plate, cover with the vegetables in their sauce, and serve.

Baby Back Ribs with
Italian Beans and Sage
Fagioli Conzi alla Salvia con Costicine
4 AS A MAIN COURSE OR 6 AS AN APPETIZER

These baby back ribs, cooked with a heady mixture of herbs and served with a medley of Italian beans, were awarded Dish of the Year by *Esquire* magazine. Although baby back ribs are more expensive than other pork ribs, they are easier to cook and have the most meat.

For the ribs

3 slabs baby back ribs, 1½ to 2 pounds each
Salt
Freshly ground black pepper

8 large sprigs of fresh rosemary
8 branches of fresh thyme
4 handfuls of fresh sage leaves

For the Beans

1 cup dried cannellini beans, soaked overnight in abundant lukewarm water
Salt
1 cup dried borlotti or cranberry beans, soaked overnight in abundant lukewarm water
2 tablespoons extra-virgin olive oil
1 small onion, chopped
1 tablespoon finely chopped Italian pancetta
2 teaspoons minced garlic
1 cup tomato sauce (page 99)
1 teaspoon each finely chopped fresh rosemary, sage, and thyme
1½ cups chicken broth, hot (page 173)

⌒ *The ribs:* Preheat the oven to 350°.

⌒ If your butcher has not already done so, pull away the thin opaque membrane that covers the underside of the ribs. Sprinkle both sides of each slab with salt and a generous grinding of black pepper.

⌒ Place a wire rack inside a large baking or roasting pan. Fill the pan with 1½ inches of water. (If the water rises above the wire rack, place 4 overturned espresso cups in the corners of the pan and set the rack on top.) Lay half of the herbs on the rack, then place the ribs, meaty side up, on top (you may have to cut the slabs in half to get them to fit into your pan). Cover with the remaining herbs, then tent the pan with aluminum foil so that no steam will escape during cooking.

⌒ Cook the ribs in the oven for about 2 hours. They are ready when the meat is tender and moist. Let the meat cool for 5 minutes before cutting the ribs into 2 or 3 rib sections.

⌒ *The beans:* Rinse the beans well—do not mix them, as they will cook separately. Place the cannellini in a medium saucepan, cover the beans with 3 inches of cold water, cover, and simmer gently until the beans are soft and creamy (40 to 50 minutes). Salt to taste after the beans have cooked for ½ hour. Cook the borlotti or cranberry beans exactly as the cannellini, increasing the cooking time by 10 minutes. These beans should be soft when fully cooked, but are not as creamy as cannellini. Leave both beans to steep in their cooking water until you are ready to use them.

⌒ In the meantime, heat the olive oil in a medium saucepan over low heat, add the onion, pancetta, and garlic and sauté until the onion and garlic are golden and the pancetta has sweat most of its fat (about 8 minutes). Stir in the tomato sauce. When it begins to bubble, add the chopped herbs, then the cooked beans drained of any liquid, and the chicken broth. Simmer the mixture together for a couple of minutes, then ladle the beans onto individual plates, place a portion of ribs on top, and serve.

THE HEARTH
Il Camino

Most Italian country houses are dominated by great, open fireplaces—giant caverns with heavy mantels made from rough-hewn beams or pale gray stone, and hearths so spacious a family of six could sit comfortably inside. Beautiful as they may be, they are anything *but* decorative—in winter, they become the soul of the house, serving a variety of functions, the most obvious of which is to heat but, since this is Italy, also to cook.

The fireplace that fills an entire wall of our Tuscan farmhouse has a raised floor of worn terra-cotta and a mantel of soft local stone called *pietra serena*. It's beautiful, though I quickly learned how ill prepared I was for the rigors of "operating" it. My first attempts at building a fire in Italy were fruitless—or rather fireless. I'd wad up a week's worth of newspapers, pile a couple of thick logs on top, light a match to the whole thing and watch in dismay as the brilliant burst of flames reduced itself to a ribbon of smoke while my logs, although lightly scorched, remained intact. Like a rat in a maze, I employed this technique regularly without success until finally Jean-Louis sat me down and explained the primordial art of making fire.

I'm a regular Boy Scout now, foraging in the woods for pinecones and small scraps of wood to use for kindling, building my fires slowly and deliberately, tending them with care. I've had several years to adjust to the rhythm and flow of the seasons—a rhythm to which our hearth is inextricably linked. Toward the end of September, when the summer's unrelenting heat shows the first signs of waning, we call the *spazzacamino,* or chimneysweep. He gives the great beast a thorough cleaning to prepare it for the *many* cords of wood it will consume in the coming months. Then we call the *boscaioli*, who drop an *enormous* truckload of wood somewhere on the property (where it sits for weeks before getting properly stacked and piled). We can never imagine going through such a mountain of wood, but somehow, every year we do—because if we spend any amount of time at home, the hearth is perpetually lit, each morning's fire built upon the previous night's embers.

We cook at the fireplace whenever and whatever we can, and have accumulated a collection of "fireside cooking" paraphernalia to help satisfy our pyroculinary whims:

- A gleaming, albeit somewhat battered copper pot for making polenta, suspended a safe distance above the flames by a thick chain of iron rings.
- A rectangular grill with two long handles and four short legs. We lay any combination of meats, sausages, cheese, vegetables, and bread over the metal slats, and set the grill atop a bed of glowing embers.
- A two-sided copper pot for roasting chestnuts—really two pots hinged together, one of solid copper, the other perforated to allow for an exchange of air as the chestnuts roast.
- Massive wrought-iron andirons whose front legs are topped with cupped iron baskets once used for holding wine flasks filled with white beans left to cook all day near the flames.
- Pokers, tongs, and legions of long-armed tools for tending the flames, the embers, and the tender morsels cooking by the fire's bright heat.

When the days become long and warm, and winter is just a faded memory, we sweep away the ashes, make some room between the andirons for a vase of wildflowers, and hang bunches of lavender and herbs from the gray stone mantel. Our *camino* gets a well-deserved rest—until the first wintry chill.

Pork Sausage with Cabbage
Salsicciotti alla Verza
SERVES 4

This sort of food makes one think of wool sweaters, damp winter nights, and a fire roaring away at the hearth. This simple, hearty dish can be prepared with a minimum of effort and goes wonderfully with a full-bodied Cabernet.

2 pounds cabbage, preferably Savoy

2 tablespoons olive oil

8 links good-quality Italian pork sausage or pork and chicken sausage

1 onion, finely chopped

1 clove garlic, sliced

1 bay leaf

1 cup vegetable broth or high quality bouillon

Freshly ground black pepper

Salt

½ cup red wine vinegar

∽ Core the cabbage, slice thin, then wash and drain well.

∽ Heat the olive oil in a large, heavy-bottomed skillet over a high flame and brown the sausage on all sides (2 to 3 minutes). Drain off most of the fat, then add the onion, garlic, cabbage, and bay leaf. Ladle the broth over the cabbage and cook for 15 minutes over a high flame, turning the cabbage over in the pan while it softens and cooks down. Season with a grinding of black pepper. Add salt with moderation since both the sausage and the broth are salty in their own right.

∽ Reduce the flames to medium, pour the vinegar over the sausage and cabbage, and simmer for 20 minutes, stirring occasionally.

∽ Arrange the cabbage in a bed on a serving platter, set the sausages on top and serve.

I come from a long line of women who make no excuses for the delight they take in making a meal for themselves. As long as I can remember, a phone call from my mother or grandmother always included some mouthwatering tale of what they had just eaten for dinner or were about to eat—especially if they were cooking for one.

My mother seems to use such occasions to make for herself what she couldn't get the rest of the family, especially my father, to eat. Grilled lamb chops with garlic and rosemary; a baked yam (she is the only person I know who eats them other than at Thanksgiving); sliced tomatoes with olive oil and salt. These little feasts are unapologetically eaten at the dining room table. My grandmother's meals tended more toward tamale pie and potato salad. But the basic philosophy was shared: Eating alone is no excuse for culinary asceticism.

I would have thought these female role models were entirely unremarkable (in this respect only) if I didn't know for a fact that there are huge numbers of people for whom a solitary meal consists of un-warmed-up leftovers eaten standing up in front of an open refrigerator. And they are the "lucky" ones—half my single friends seem to have little else in their refrigerators besides a jar of olives (to go with the vodka in the freezer), a greasy carton of half-eaten Chinese take-out, and a selection of dubious-looking condiments living out their shelf lives in some sort of arctic limbo.

Why is it that we generally delight in cooking for others and disdain doing the same for ourselves? What *is* your excuse for not taking the time to make a delicious meal when you're all alone?

For those of you who have not yet delighted in the pleasure of your own company, consider this advice:

Basic Instructions for a Dinner for One

- Set the table for yourself—the kitchen table, the dining room table, wherever it feels warm and inviting. This is where you are going to eat. Not at the kitchen counter, not in front of the television, and *not* standing up in front of the open refrigerator. You don't have to drag out Granny's silver and the crystal goblets. On the other hand, if it wouldn't kill you to add one tiny cloth napkin to the rest of your laundry, then get one out.

- Go into the kitchen and make yourself something to eat. You don't need to spend hours slaving over a five-course meal unless that's what you feel like doing. Be creative and free—leave your inner critic locked in a closet somewhere—you only have yourself to please. You can selfishly indulge your tastebuds' most bizarre proclivities. Eat those smoked herrings, that outrageously spicy pasta. This is the time for those things that would  cause a mutiny at the family dinner table. Eat leftovers, or a simple salad with a wedge of cheese, a pear, and a couple of walnuts. Whatever it is, put it on a plate with the same care that you would use if you were making it for someone else.

- *Don't* eat anything until you sit down.

- Open a bottle of wine. Cut some bread.

- Bring everything to the table before you sit down, so you won't have to get up even once during your meal.

- Put on some music you like.

- Light a couple of candles (this is a tried-and-true seduction technique—use it to seduce yourself).

- If you must (and I admit I can hardly ever resist), get something to read. Something beautiful or thought-provoking—not the newspaper, not the stack of bills sitting by the telephone.

- Sit down at the table and pour yourself a glass of wine. Take a minute before you start eating to give yourself a chance to slow down, to shake off the rest of your day. The dentist appointment you have to make, the phone calls to return, your mother-in-law's birthday—it can all wait for another time. Your list of things-to-do is *not* invited to this little party.

- Taste. Savor. Linger over your meal. The usual distractions—the chatter, the getting up from the table to get more of this or that, the taking care of everyone's needs—are for another day. You'll be surprised at the force of your senses. How clearly the flavors sing, how utterly relaxed you are, how well you can enjoy your own quiet company. It's like a warm, slow soak in the tub. Only it tastes better.

Grilled Lamb Loin Chops
Costolette d'Agnello
SERVES 4

All over Italy, lamb is served as part of the traditional Easter meal. The preparation varies throughout the country, but one factor remains constant—lamb is eaten only in season, during the spring when the animals are still quite young and their meat most tender and delicately flavorful. These loin chops marinate for 1 day in a fragrant vegetable, herb, and spice mixture and then are grilled over an outdoor barbecue or oven grill.

8 lamb loin chops, ¾ to 1 inch thick

Marinade
1 cup full-bodied red wine such as Cabernet or Merlot
½ cup extra-virgin olive oil
1 onion, minced
1 carrot, minced
1 celery stalk, minced
3 cloves garlic, minced
Small bouquet of fresh sage, thyme, rosemary, and marjoram

3 bay leaves

2 sprigs of Italian parsley

2 cloves

4 juniper berries, crushed

1-inch stick cinnamon

Additional Ingredients

2 tablespoons extra-virgin olive oil

1 tablespoon Dijon mustard

Freshly ground black pepper

Salt

⤳ *The marinade:* Whisk together the wine and olive oil, then add the remaining marinade ingredients. Spoon a bit of the marinade into a glass or ceramic baking dish, then lay the lamb chops in 1 or 2 layers in the dish and cover with the remaining marinade. Cover the dish with foil and refrigerate for 24 hours, turning the meat over in the marinade two or three times during this period.

⤳ *The chops:* When you are ready to cook the meat, prepare a medium-hot outdoor barbecue or stovetop grill. Remove the lamb from the herb marinade, discard the cloves and cinnamon stick, and strain the remaining marinade, placing the liquid mixture to one side and the herbs and minced vegetables to another.

⤳ Heat 2 tablespoons of olive oil in a pan over a medium flame. Add the strained herbs and vegetables from the marinade and sauté for 4 to 5 minutes until lightly roasted. Discard the herb bouquet, bay leaves, and parsley, then add the mustard to the pan, stirring constantly for 2 minutes. Pour in the wine and oil mixture reserved from the marinade and let the sauce simmer for about 4 minutes while much of the wine evaporates.

⤳ Sprinkle the chops with freshly ground pepper, and grill for 3 to 5 minutes on each side (3 minutes for rare, 5 for medium-rare), then season to taste with salt. Spoon the sauce over the meat and serve.

Pan-Roasted Lamb Loin with Black Olives
Agnello alle Olive Nere

SERVES 4

Once the ingredients are prepared, this recipe takes just over 5 minutes to cook. The lamb makes a thick savory sauce that goes well with peperonata (page 283) for an interesting contrast of flavors.

3 cloves garlic, crushed

3 tablespoons extra-virgin olive oil

⅓ cup diced Italian pancetta

4 to 5 sprigs of fresh thyme

1 small sprig of rosemary

1 teaspoon capers

1½ pounds lamb loin, trimmed and cut into chunks

Freshly ground black pepper

1 cup Italian or Spanish black olives, pits removed

2 tablespoons dry white wine

2 medium very ripe tomatoes, skins and seeds removed, crushed

Salt

Warm the garlic and oil in a large, heavy-bottomed pan over a medium flame. When the garlic begins to color, add the pancetta and herbs, stir for a couple of minutes, then sprinkle in the capers. Stir the ingredients well, then add in the lamb chunks and a generous grinding of black pepper. Sauté for 2 minutes, then stir in the olives.

When the meat has browned lightly on all sides, add the wine, then stir the pan well while the wine reduces. Add the tomatoes, simmer gently for a couple of minutes, salt to taste, and serve.

Rack of Lamb with Walnuts and Whole Grain Mustard

Carré d'Agnello in Salsa di Noci e Senape

SERVES 4

Whole grain mustard, honey, and walnuts combine to make a dark, lightly peppery sauce that complements the rich flavor of the meat. We use the small New Zealand lamb at the restaurants, with 1 rack providing 2 generous servings. You may use domestic lamb if you wish, keeping in mind that one 8-rib rack will weigh almost as much as 2 of the New Zealand racks and will be enough for 4 slightly smaller servings.

Two 8-rib racks New Zealand lamb (approximately 1 pound each) or one 8-rib rack
  domestic lamb (approximately 2 pounds), trimmed of all but a thin layer of
  surface fat
Salt
Freshly ground black pepper
3 tablespoons extra-virgin olive oil
3 shallots, chopped
½ cup white wine
⅓ cup coarsely chopped walnuts
2 tablespoons honey
2 tablespoons whole grain Dijon mustard
½ cup meat broth (page 174) or high quality bouillon

↬ Preheat oven to 450°.

↬ Sprinkle the meat with salt and pepper, then heat 2 tablespoons of olive oil in a large, heavy-bottomed skillet. Hold the rack by the ribs and lay the fat-lined exterior in the pan, rotating it until it is evenly browned. Transfer the meat to a roasting pan and set aside.

⚬ Pour off the oil and fat from the skillet used to brown the meat, and return the skillet to the stove. Add 1 tablespoon olive oil and the chopped shallots and gently sauté over a medium-low flame until the shallots begin to soften, stirring often. Remove the skillet from the flame, pour in the wine and allow the alcohol to bubble away and reduce. Without returning the skillet to the fire, add the walnuts and honey, stirring until the ingredients are well blended. Return the pan to a low flame, stir in the mustard, and simmer for 1 minute, stirring constantly.

⚬ Coat the lamb with the mustard-honey sauce, then roast, bone side down, for 7 to 10 minutes (7 minutes for rare and 10 for medium-rare). Transfer the meat to a cutting board, cover with aluminum foil, and allow to stand 5 to 10 minutes before cutting.

⚬ Add the pan juices to the skillet with the mustard sauce. Stir in the broth and simmer the sauce gently over a medium-low flame for 2 minutes, stirring at all times.

⚬ Cut the meat between every second bone if you are using New Zealand lamb and between each bone if using larger domestic lamb. Transfer to individual dinner plates, spoon some sauce over the meat, and serve.

Contorni

CHASING AFTER NATURE

My writing desk sits angled between two windows and two different views of the country-side—one wild and unruly, the other, equally beautiful, but tamer, sweeter. The windows are open to let in the morning air, still tinged with nighttime dew and smelling of cut grass and wildflowers.

Despite the early hour, the countryside is wide awake. Swallows dart in and out of the little mud huts they've made under the eves, popping insects into the straining beaks of their little chicks; bees take a noisy buzz around the room, then, satisfied that there are no spring flowers to sip from, they depart. An old tractor chugs up and down between the rows of grapevines, covering them with fine mist of blue-green copper or *ramato* (pronounced "ramaho" around these parts). The birds are engaged in their daily conversations and, as usual, I wish I knew their names and spoke their language.

Silvano, our gardener, has been here since dawn. He seems slightly overwhelmed, as we all are, with all there is to do. The story repeats itself every year. We champ at the bit, ready to cast off winter and plant the garden with spring peas, onions, fava beans, and baby lettuces. Nature plays into our overeagerness by giving the season a brief, false start. Inevitably, the round of early vegetables we plant perishes the moment winter heaves its last frosty breath, and Silvano chastises us all (himself included) for our lack of patience. We clean up our mess and wait for "true" spring to arrive. When finally it does, we find our-

selves in a frenzy of tilling and planting and watering. Breathlessly chasing after nature, which we know will outrun us every time.

Nonetheless, our garden gets more ambitious every year. Three and a half acres of fertile soil can sound like a lot or a little, depending on what you're used to. In farming terms, it's not much at all. Certainly not enough to justify buying tractors and tillers and the panoply of heavy machinery that it takes to keep a "real" farm in action. On the other hand, it's way too much earth to tend by hand, unless you have lots of hands willing to do lots of work—and we don't.

Our solution was to divide and conquer. We attacked small pieces of the property at a time. First we took care of the immediate area around the house—ours was being consumed by brambles and thorny vines. We systematically mowed a large patch of weeds until we tamed them into something resembling a lawn. We planted two dozen fruit trees—far more twiglike than treelike—and a small vegetable garden.

A year ago, we decided that it was finally time to attack the last wild acre of land. It was covered with gnarled old grapevines that rambled over rows of slack rusted wires attached to slanting cement posts. Not the picturesque vineyard of anybody's dreams—although it must have been, years before, when the posts stood like sentries at the ends of each row, and the wires were pulled taut so that the new shoots could climb and twist around them.

A friend told us of someone who could bring a tractor and a tiller up to the house. His name was Valerio, a gray-haired, blue-eyed Tuscan with the perpetual tan of someone who spends his life outdoors. He lived just over the hill, and like most people around here knew just where our little house and its few wild acres sat.

It was only barely light out the October morning when the two tractors rumbled up the dirt road leading to the house. The kids bolted out of bed and threw on their clothes so they could go outside and have a look. This was a big event—especially for Julien, who's had something of a tractor fetish since he was nine months old.

For the next two weeks, we had our fill of the giant yellow beasts. They sputtered to life at daybreak and lumbered about the yard all day like a pair of foraging dinosaurs, uprooting everything in their path, turning the landscape inside out. It was noisy, destructive work. Disconcerting, in a way. For better or worse, our eyes had grown accustomed to the tangle of vines and posts and wires and we asked ourselves whether we were doing the right thing.

Finally, the remains of the vines were carted away and the tractors set off to forage somewhere else. In their place was a gently sloping plot of rich, tilled earth. A horticultural tabula rasa of burnt-sienna-hued soil dotted with stones.

Jean-Louis and I were ready to plant. Actually, we had been ready to plant from the beginning. It was the rest of the work we were never really prepared for. The whole process reminded me of junior high school sewing class—all that pinning, basting, cutting, and ironing before getting the satisfaction of pushing my foot down on the sewing pedal.

But it still wasn't time. "The soil's not ready yet. We've got to let it sit for a while," Silvano advised us. We had found a wonderful nursery that specialized in heirloom plants that were resistant to garden pests and we were eager to rush off and pick out saplings and berry bushes and vines. *"Ancora no,"* our patient gardener repeated. "This garden is going to be as good as the prep work is. There's just no way around the working and the waiting."

So instead we cleared the soil of the pale white rocks as best we could, loading them onto wheelbarrows and wagons and piling them in a heap by the toolshed. Over the coming months, Silvano would use them to build a low stone ledge off the front of the house and a fountain in the corner of the garden. In the meantime, we let the soil rest until the thick clumps of earth crumbled into a fine loam.

We decided to have Ugo from the nursery come out to see us so he could have a look at the land, see how it was situated and advise us on the best varietals to plant. Based on past history, it seemed like the wisest course of action. We had learned a thing or two since first buying the property and planting it (against wise advice to the contrary) with a score of olive trees. All but one of them succumbed to the bitter winter *tramontana* that blows down from the north and whips through our hill like an icy torch. The lone survivor looks more like a bonsai than a full-fledged *olivo* and bears no more than a dozen fruits a year.

We spent hours with Ugo designing our little orchard and a berry-strewn pathway around its perimeter. We wanted lush red pears like something out of a still life; pomegranates and persimmons; peaches, white and yellow; plums both for eating and pies—

and that was only the *P*'s. We ordered an entire alphabet of fruit. The saplings arrived bare-root and leafless, lower-case letters whose apricots were indistinguishable from apples but for the tags looped around their slim trunks. An anticlimax after all the waiting.

Six months have passed. Except for some exceptionally sweet raspberries, we've had no fruit. But we have had leaves, and blossoms. Buttercups, wild poppies, and purple anemones have grown along with wild grasses among the young trees. The orchard is still in its infancy. And we are learning how to wait.

Braised Artichokes
Carciofi Brasati
SERVES 4 TO 6

At Locanda Veneta, we serve these artichokes stems up in a shallow pool of *porcini ragù* (page 103). But they are just as delicious served simply as a side dish. The prosciutto, garlic, and herbs are used only for flavoring and don't make the trip from pan to plate.

12 medium artichokes
Juice of 2 lemons
⅓ cup extra-virgin olive oil
⅓ cup Italian prosciutto, cut into small dice
6 whole cloves garlic, peeled and crushed
Handful of fresh basil leaves
Salt
Freshly ground black pepper

꙳ Discard all but the top inch of the artichoke stems. Peel the outer leaves off each artichoke until you reach the tender yellow-and-purple-tinged inner leaves. Turn each artichoke on its side and cut off the tough tips of the leaves, leaving only the tender pale edible portion. Pare away the tough green outer skin from the base and remaining stem. Place the artichokes to soak in a large bowl of water with lemon juice until you are ready to use them.

⌒ Pour the olive oil into a large skillet, then place the artichokes, stems up, in the pan with the prosciutto, garlic, and basil. Sprinkle with salt and grind generously with black pepper.

⌒ Cook over a high flame for 2 minutes, then add 1 cup of water to the pan. Reduce the heat to low, cover the pan, and cook until the artichokes are tender (15 to 20 minutes depending on the size of the hearts). Check the artichokes while they cook to make sure the pan liquids have not been completely absorbed. You may add an additional ½ cup of water to the pan if it is dry. The artichokes are cooked when the tip of a sharp knife inserts easily where the stem meets the base.

⌒ Serve the artichokes stems up on a serving dish.

Variation: Make a pasta sauce by cutting the cooked artichokes in half, slicing thinly, and tossing with the prosciutto, garlic, and herbs from the pan. You can add a tablespoon or two of butter to the sauce for a richer flavor. Serve with 1 pound cooked penne and offer grated Parmesan cheese. Makes 4 servings.

Spring Peas with Pancetta
Piselli Freschi con Pancetta
SERVES 4

How many people (yourself included?) do you know who think they can't stand peas? I say "think" because the thing they really—rightfully—have an aversion to is as far a cry from the real thing as a shriveled, mealy apple is from a tart, crunchy one right off the tree.

If you've never had a bowl of freshly shucked spring peas gently cooked until tender, then you've never really tasted peas. In Italy, spring peas are considered something of a delicacy—both because of their relatively short season and because of the time involved in reducing a huge pile of pea pods into a much smaller bowl of peas. You'll pay for the delight of eating them this way—but the price is small for something so delicious.

4 pounds fresh green peas in their pods (about 4 cups shucked peas)
4 ounces Italian pancetta, cut into small dice
3 cloves garlic, finely chopped
Freshly ground black pepper

∽ Shuck the peas and set them aside in a bowl.
∽ Heat the pancetta in a medium, heavy-bottomed pan over a low flame. When the fat begins to melt in the pan, add the garlic and stir frequently until the garlic is lightly golden and fragrant.
∽ Add the peas and stir well. If your pancetta is salted, you probably won't need to add additional salt. Add 1 cup of water, cover the pot, and cook over a low flame until the peas are tender but not mushy, 5 to 10 minutes stirring occasionally. Season to taste with freshly ground black pepper.

Variation: You can easily convert this recipe into a pasta sauce by replacing the cup of water with 1½ cups of chicken broth (page 173) and stirring in a tablespoon of butter when the peas are cooked. We like the sauce over thin egg noodles such as tagliolini. Sprinkle the pasta liberally with freshly grated Parmesan cheese.

Sautéed Mushrooms with Parsley and Garlic
Funghi Trifolati
SERVES 4

"Trifolato" is an adjective that means that the vegetable in question (particularly mushrooms, eggplant, or zucchini) has been cooked in a fragrant mixture of olive oil, garlic, and parsley, a combination that works magic on anything it touches. The venerable porcini is the mushroom of choice for *funghi trifolati* if you can find it. But any mushroom, wild or cultivated, can be cooked this way with delicious results.

2 pounds fresh wild or
    cultivated mushrooms
⅓ cup extra-virgin olive oil
2 garlic cloves, finely chopped

2 tablespoons finely chopped
    Italian flat-leaf parsley
Salt
Freshly ground black pepper

∽ Trim off and discard the tips of the mushroom stems (for shiitake mushrooms, discard the entire stem). Wipe the mushrooms clean with a damp cloth or paper towel. If they are very dirty, run them under cold water in a colander, wipe them clean, and dry. Slice the mushrooms thinly.

∽ Heat the olive oil, garlic, and parsley in a large, heavy-bottomed skillet over a medium flame, stirring frequently. When the garlic is golden and fragrant, add the mushrooms. They will quickly absorb the oil and may stick to the pan for a moment before they begin to release their moisture. Use a flat-bottomed wooden spoon to stir the mushrooms until they begin to wilt. It is not necessary to add additional oil.

∽ When the mushrooms begin to soften (3 to 4 minutes), reduce the heat to low, add salt and freshly ground pepper to taste and continue to gently sauté for another 15 minutes, stirring frequently.

🍂 *Variation: When the mushrooms have finished cooking, stir in 1 tablespoon of aged balsamic vinegar and serve immediately.*

Green Beans and Plum Tomatoes
Fagiolini Verdi con Perini
SERVES 4

❧

Tender fresh vegetables are like young children—they need very little in the way of adornment to show off their natural beauty. When green beans are thin, crisp, and stringless, we like them best steamed and dressed simply with olive oil, lemon juice, and salt. When we do feel like dressing them up a bit here's what we do.

1 pound ripe plum tomatoes
2 tablespoons extra-virgin olive oil
1 onion, coarsely chopped
1 pound fresh green beans, strings, and ends removed
Handful of whole fresh basil leaves
Salt
Freshly ground black pepper

〜 Plunge the tomatoes in a pot of boiling water for a minute. Remove them with a slotted spoon, leave to cool for a minute and slip off their skins.

〜 Heat the olive oil in a medium, heavy-bottomed pot. Add the onion and sauté over a medium flame until the onions are lightly golden (about 5 minutes).

〜 Add the green beans and stir them around the pot for a couple of minutes to coat them with the onions and oil. Reduce the heat to low and crush the tomatoes with your hands over the beans. Add the basil leaves, and salt and pepper to taste. Cover the pot and cook for about 20 minutes, stirring occasionally (and adding a bit of water if necessary) until the beans have lost their crunch but are still firm.

Peperonata
Pevaronada
SERVES 4 TO 6

The Italian equivalent of the French ratatouille, peperonata (or "pevaronada," as it is called in the Veneto) takes its name from peperoni (which is Italian for bell peppers, *not* for the spicy sausage found on American pepperoni pizzas). There are many variations of this summer vegetable stew, the one constant, of course, being peppers, and usually some mixture of onions and tomatoes.

Jean-Louis is the peperonata maker at our house, and his version always contains a couple of zucchini and occasionally a few new potatoes. When Antonio gave me his recipe for this Italian standard, I asked him why he left out zucchini. He laughed: "Didn't you know you married a Frenchman, not an Italian? The French always add zucchini—*real* Italians usually don't." No doubt eighteen years in Paris, even with two native Italian parents, made a huge culinary impact on my husband. Nonetheless, I think both versions are delicious and can be served warm (never boiling hot) or cold, or used as a flavorful sauce on thick, tube-shaped pasta.

2 medium Japanese eggplants, unpeeled
Salt
5 tablespoons olive oil
1 pound white onions, quartered, then thinly sliced
1 celery heart, chopped
1 pound mixed red and yellow peppers, seeded, quartered, then sliced in strips
1 pound fresh plum tomatoes, peeled and seeded
3 small zucchini, halved lengthwise, then cut into half circles, optional
½ cup black olives, with stones
1 tablespoon capers

⟳ Cut the eggplant into bite-sized chunks, sprinkle with salt, and leave them to rest in a colander for 20 minutes. Rinse and pat dry.

⟳ Warm the olive oil in a large soup pot. Layer the pot with the onions on the bottom, then the chopped celery, peppers, tomatoes, eggplant, and, if you are using them, zucchini. Turn the heat to high and cover for 15 minutes. Every so often poke into the pot with a wooden spoon and, without stirring, shift the vegetables to keep them from sticking to the pan. Don't fully stir the vegetables during this initial cooking period but try to maintain them in loose layers. After 15 minutes, the vegetables will begin to release much of their moisture and can be stirred. Lower the flame to medium, and cover the pot once again, stirring occasionally.

⟳ In the meantime, make a slit in each olive and squeeze gently to remove the stones. When the vegetables have cooked a total of 40 minutes, stir in the olives and capers, and simmer uncovered for 5 minutes. Remove the pot from the heat and allow the peperonata to sit for at least 15 minutes before serving.

Braised Fennel with Parmesan
Finocchio al Burro e Parmigiano

SERVES 4

Fennel is one of those much-loved Italian vegetables that have yet to receive the recognition they deserve at the American table. Raw, it is crisp and aromatic, perfect for salads or cut into wedges to dip into ramekins of olive oil seasoned with lemon, salt, and pepper. Cooked, its flavor is warm and subtle—perfect for a cool fall evening. I first ate fennel twenty years ago at the small pensione in Florence where I spent the summer studying Italian. It was served braised in butter and scattered with Parmesan. I had no idea what it was . . . but I never forgot the flavor.

4 fennel bulbs, trimmed

Salt

⅓ cup butter

Freshly ground black pepper

⅓ cup freshly grated Parmesan cheese

꠸ Peel away the tough outer layers of the fennel. Wash the bulbs and cut them into medium wedges. Boil in abundant salted water for 5 minutes. Drain well.

꠸ Warm the butter in a skillet, add the fennel, sprinkle with salt and freshly ground black pepper, and sauté over a medium flame until the fennel is tender (5 to 8 minutes). Arrange on a serving dish, sprinkle with grated Parmesan, and serve.

Fennel with Balsamic Vinegar and Chestnut Honey
Finocchio all'Aceto Balsamico e Miele di Castagne

SERVES 4

Fennel is beautiful prepared this way—the balsamic vinegar and rich chestnut honey color it a warm brown. On the plate it looks like something out of a Renaissance still life.

4 medium fennel bulbs, tops and root ends trimmed

2 tablespoons butter

1 tablespoon extra-virgin olive oil

1 bay leaf

Salt

Freshly ground black pepper

¼ cup balsamic vinegar

2 tablespoons chestnut honey

∼ Remove the tough outer leaves of the fennel. Rinse the bulbs and then quarter them lengthwise.

∼ Warm the butter and olive oil in a medium, heavy-bottomed saucepan. Add the fennel and bay leaf to the pan and sauté over medium heat until the fennel begins to color on all sides (about 5 minutes). Sprinkle with salt and a generous grinding of black pepper.

∼ Remove the saucepan from the flame and pour on the balsamic vinegar. Turn the fennel over a few times to coat it well, then return the pot to the burner. Drizzle the honey over the top of the fennel and reduce the heat to low. Cover the pan and cook, stirring from time to time, until the fennel has absorbed most of the pan juices (about 25 minutes). Stir in ¼ cup of water, cover, and continue cooking until the fennel is tender when prodded with a fork (about 10 minutes).

NEW POTATOES
Patate Novelle

The humble potato. Cheap and plentiful at the market. Modestly growing underground in the dark, tilled earth, they can hardly compete with the beauty queens of the garden—summer's heavy red tomatoes, frilly lettuces, and bright bouquets of basil and other fragrant herbs. For years, we never even considered planting potatoes in our kitchen garden.

"Ma perchè!" Antonio scolded us when he realized what feeble recognition we gave one of his favorite vegetables. He had grown up in the Veneto making gnocchi from garden-grown potatoes stored all winter in a dim, cool cellar. But he was especially partial to late spring's new potatoes, gently steamed and doused with melted butter, salt, and pepper. These, he convinced us, were as fine a delicacy as anything our tastebuds could fantasticate—and he was right.

To our surprise, the potato plant was not quite as lackluster as we had imagined—and far less work to grow than its showier garden mates. Potatoes go into the ground months before the annual spring planting frenzy and grow into innocuous, but not unattractive,

1½-foot green leafy shrubs that produce pale blue flowers in the spring—a sign that means that after a week or so, you can begin to unearth the tender new potatoes.

Perhaps because the entire show goes on unseen, there is something magical about the idea of planting a potato in the ground and virtually forgetting about it for several months until that day you dig into the soft, crumbly soil and find that for every tuber you've planted, you have an armload of delicate new potatoes with barely a trace of soil clinging to their wispy skins.

Steamed New Potatoes with Butter, Salt, and Pepper
Patate Novelle con Burro, Sale, e Pepe

SERVES 4

1 pound small new potatoes
4 tablespoons butter, softened to room temperature
Salt
Freshly ground black pepper

 Wash the potatoes in cold water, taking care to leave their skins intact.
 Place them in a steamer basket over 1 inch of water. Bring the water to a gentle simmer, then cover the pot and steam until the potatoes are tender (15 to 25 minutes).
 Transfer the potatoes to a medium serving bowl, add the butter, salt, and a generous grinding of freshly ground pepper. Gently stir to coat the potatoes with the butter and seasonings and serve.

Jean-Louis's Mashed Potatoes
Purè di Patate

SERVES 4

Even Italians use the French word for mashed potatoes: *purè*. Whether or not this is a tacit acknowledgment of French superiority on such an important culinary matter, at our house and in the restaurants, Jean-Louis has the last word on the making of *"purè."* This is his Italian take on a French classic.

Boiling the potatoes in their skins allows them to retain the most flavor, using hot milk and softened butter helps the puree remain light, fluffy, and free of lumps.

2 pounds russet or Idaho potatoes, washed, then boiled in their skins
Pinch of nutmeg
Salt
1 cup hot milk
6 tablespoons butter, softened to room temperature
¾ cup grated Parmesan cheese

Peel the potatoes as soon as they are cool enough to handle. Pass them through a ricer or mash with a potato masher in a medium saucepan over a very low flame. Grate with a pinch of nutmeg and sprinkle with salt.

Slowly whisk in ¾ cup of milk and then the butter. Continue whipping with a fork or whisk until the mixture is smooth and fluffy.

Remove from the heat and slowly incorporate the Parmesan and as much of the remaining milk as necessary to make the texture soft but not runny.

Crispy Fried New Potatoes with Sage

Patatine Croccanti con la Salvia

SERVES 4

These golden, crispy potatoes are as addictive as potato chips and unless we are vigilant, they never make it from the kitchen to the dining table. Don't worry if some of the potatoes stick to each other in small clumps. They're delicious anyway.

1 pound medium new potatoes, in their skins
½ cup olive oil
2 handfuls of whole fresh sage leaves
Salt

Wash the potatoes in cold water without removing their skins. Using a mandoline or sharp paring knife, slice the potatoes as thinly as possible.

Heat the oil in a large, heavy-bottomed skillet over a medium flame until it is quite hot but not smoking. Scatter the potatoes evenly over the surface of the pan. Cover with the sage leaves. Cook them for a few minutes until they begin to brown, then turn them over with a slotted skimmer and fork, taking care not to spatter the oil. When the potatoes are lightly browned and crispy on both sides, lift them out of the pan with a slotted skimmer and lay them on several layers of paper towels. Blot off excess oil, sprinkle with salt, and serve.

Garlic-Roasted Eggplant, Potatoes, and Tomatoes
Melanzane, Patate, e Pomodori Arrostiti all'Aglio

SERVES 4

Summertime at our house is also the time for unexpected guests, mostly friends from Florence escaping the city's heat and humidity with a trip to the country. A *teglia* or baking pan of roasted vegetables—usually containing whatever we have on hand—has become one of the mainstays of our improvised meals. Here's one of Jean-Louis's favorite versions, using Japanese eggplant, yellow-fleshed potatoes, and plum tomatoes.

2 Japanese eggplants, unpeeled, cut into medium chunks

1 pound yellow-fleshed potatoes, unpeeled and cut into chunks

4 tablespoons extra-virgin olive oil

Salt

4 plum tomatoes, seeded and quartered

Freshly ground black pepper

Preheat the oven to 475°.

Place the eggplants, potatoes, olive oil, and garlic in a large roasting pan. Toss the vegetables well to coat them with the oil, sprinkle with salt, and roast in the oven for 20 minutes.

Use a metal spatula to gently turn the vegetables in the pan. Scatter the tomatoes over the top, grind with black pepper, and return to the oven until the potatoes are golden and cooked through and the eggplant is soft (about 20 more minutes).

Venetian-Style Swiss Chard
Coste di Bietole alla Veneziana
SERVES 6

Much as Italians prefer their pasta al dente, they like their vegetables *cotte bene,* that is, cooked well, especially things like chard, which can have a strong, grassy taste if under-cooked.

3 pounds Swiss chard	1 tablespoon finely chopped parsley
⅓ cup extra-virgin olive oil	Salt
1 clove garlic, minced	2 tablespoons white wine vinegar

∽ Wash the chard several times in cold water to remove any soil clinging to its leaves or stalks. Separate the stalks from the leaves. Coarsely chop the green leaves and set them aside. Chop the stalks into small dice, place them in a large pot barely covered with water, and simmer, uncovered, for 8 minutes.

∽ Drain most of the water from the pot, then add the olive oil, garlic, parsley, and salt to taste. Simmer, covered, over a medium-low flame for 5 minutes. Add the chard leaves and stir the pot well. Cook the greens, uncovered, until there is barely a trace of water in the pot (3 to 5 minutes), then stir in the wine vinegar and cook for 3 minutes more, stirring regularly.

Braised Onions
Cipollotte in Agrodolce
SERVES 6

❧

Small onions cooked this way taste both tart and slightly sweet. This is a perfect accompaniment for roasted meats or fish.

2 tablespoons extra-virgin olive oil
12 small boiling onions, 1 to 2 inches in diameter, outer skins removed
¾ cup dry white wine
Salt

꙳ Over a medium flame, heat the olive oil in a short-sided, heavy-bottomed pan. Add the onions and sauté them, rolling them around in the pan until they brown thoroughly (about 15 minutes). Pour the wine into the pan and mix well with the onions and oil. After the wine reduces, add a cup of water to the pan, reduce the heat to the lowest flame, and cover. Cook for 45 minutes, stirring occasionally and adding water, if necessary, ½ cup at a time as the liquid evaporates in the pan.

SWEETS AND SWEETNESS
Dolci e Dolcezze

Four women enter a restaurant at lunchtime. They order sparkling water, iced tea, or Diet Cokes and peruse the menu for a moment. "I'm not that hungry," says one of the women, "I think I'll just have a salad." "Me too," the other three respond in chorus, and so two salads ("Dressing on the side, please") are ordered to be divided among the four.

Sometime later, the waiter clears away the salad plates and the nearly full breadbasket and hands the ladies dessert menus. They order coffee, tea, and four rich and luscious desserts, which they consume with much gaiety and sensual abandon.

This scene is played out daily in restaurants all over America, and it is one that Jean-Louis and Antonio cannot help but watch with a mixture of morbid fascination and amusement. For though many cultures share a fixation for sweet things, nowhere is the national sweet tooth as insatiable as in America, where for many dessert is considered the highlight of a meal (if not the meal itself).

In Italy, *il dolce* is not so much an afterthought as one of the many harmonious components of a fine meal. The most common and frequently eaten dessert is fruit—especially in warm weather or at the end of a simple lunch or dinner with friends or family. In spring and early summer, there will be bowls of cherries, or sliced strawberries tossed with sugar and lemon. Summer brings peaches (sometimes sliced into a carafe of wine), plums, and apricots as well as thick, juicy slices of watermelon. Cantaloupe is served at the beginning of a meal with slices of cured prosciutto, rather than as dessert. Late summer there is a brief but glorious moment when sweet, soft figs abound (and are eaten either at the end of a meal, or at the beginning with slices of mild salami). In fall, there are grapes, the intensely perfumed *uva Italia* being just about everyone's favorite, despite their tart seeds. Winter brings chestnuts, glossy orange persimmons, and juicy tangerines.

Cookies, especially in the Veneto, are another favorite end to a meal. Italians are particularly fond of dipping their biscotti—into steaming bowls of caffè latte or milk in the morning, or into tiny glasses filled with sweet wine such as *vin santo* or *moscato* at the end of a meal. We've always offered a variety of homemade cookies at our restaurants—although recently we've had to resort to storing them in a locked bin inside the kitchen (there were never enough cookies for our customers after our waiters and kitchen staff had finished snacking on them).

Certain desserts are synonymous with specific times of the year or holidays, such as the soft and golden *fritole* eaten around Carnival time in Venice. Other moist, wholesome cakes like *pinza* are more likely eaten as an afternoon snack or *merenda* than served at the end of a meal.

Though fruit, cookies, and homey simple cakes are the sweets for everyday, we would never end this book without including some of the tried and true favorites from our restaurants' kitchens—*dolci* like soft vanilla cream custard with homemade caramel sauce, ricotta cheesecake with strawberry compote, cinnamon-laced country apple tart, and chocolate almond torte.

Summer Peaches in Prosecco with Mint

Pesche al Prosecco con Profumo di Menta

SERVES 6

Next to the manicured public gardens of the small town of Vittorio Veneto, where Jean-Louis's parents live, is the main café, Bar Lux. Take a seat there at any time of day and you will likely find a group of men engaged in an animated conversation, *ombretta* in hand. An *ombretta* is dialect for a small glass of wine. Very often that wine is a sparkling Prosecco made from the northern Italian grape of the same name. Wonderfully light and fragrant, it is characterized by its drinkability—and by the faintest trace of apple, peach, and almond it leaves on the palate. While Prosecco is delicious on its own, the combination of ripe summer peaches, fresh mint, and this lovely sparkling wine makes this a perfect midsummer dessert.

6 ripe but firm peaches

1 bottle Italian Prosecco Brut, chilled

⅓ cup sugar

12 whole mint leaves, gently crushed between your fingers,
  plus mint leaves for garnish

∾ Peel away the peach skin using a paring knife. Cut the peaches around the pit into thin half-moon-shaped slivers. Place in a medium bowl, cover with the Prosecco, sugar, and mint, gently stir, then cover and refrigerate for 2 hours.

∾ Ladle the peaches and Prosecco into small, shallow bowls. Garnish with fresh mint and serve.

Winter Pears Poached in Spiced Red Wine
Pere al Vino Aromatizzato
SERVES 6

It is impossible to exaggerate the simple beauty of pears cooked this way. The spiced wine combines with the juices from the fruit to form a deep red sauce. We use Bosc or Barlett pears, which hold up well to poaching. Choose pears that are still crisp and firm, rather than overly ripe.

12 small or 6 large pears
½ cup granulated sugar
3 cups red wine
2-inch stick of cinnamon
2 bay leaves
1 clove
Peeled zest of 1 lemon

꙰ Peel the pears without removing the stems. Place them in the smallest pot in which they are able to fit in 1 layer. Sprinkle with sugar, then cover with the red wine, spices, and lemon zest. Fold a piece of aluminum foil into a circle just small enough to fit inside the pot. Lay the foil over the pears—do not use a lid.

꙰ Heat the fruit over a low flame to a gentle simmer. After 20 minutes, carefully turn the pears over, then poach for another 20 minutes over the lowest possible flame so that while the pears finish cooking, the wine thickens without evaporating completely.

꙰ Transfer the pears to a serving dish, spoon sauce over them, and serve warm or at room temperature.

Italian-Style Hot Chocolate
Cioccolato in Tazza all'Italiana
SERVES 6

Sometime toward the end of November, Christmas decorations are festooned along the streets of Italian cities, and in the windows of many bars and cafés signs offering *"Cioccolato in Tazza"* or *"Cioccolata Calda con Panna Fresca"* beckon you in from the cold. Italian hot chocolate is a chocolate lover's dream—thick, bittersweet, and served with sugar and freshly whipped unsweetened cream.

3 cups milk

1 cup heavy cream

One vanilla bean, split along its length

7 ounces dark or bittersweet chocolate, cut into small pieces

1 tablespoon unsweetened cocoa

✎ Fill your sink with 3 to 4 inches of cold water.

✎ Stir the milk and cream together in a medium, heavy-bottomed saucepan. Add the vanilla bean and heat the mixture to just below boiling, stirring occasionally. Remove the saucepan from the heat and set it to cool in the cold water. After 2 minutes, stir in the chocolate pieces and cocoa. Return the pan to the stove over a low flame, stirring continuously as the chocolate melts. When the chocolate has melted completely, continue cooking the mixture, without boiling, over a low flame for 5 minutes. Remove the vanilla bean and serve with sugar, unsweetened whipped cream, and cookies.

Polenta Fritters with Berries and Grand Marnier
Polenta al Latte con Frutti di Bosco e Grand Marnier

SERVES 4

This dessert combines the rustic wholesomeness of polenta with the sophistication of fresh berries and Grand Marnier or port wine. We like the sauce best with fresh ripe blackberries, but you may also use blueberries, raspberries, sliced fresh peaches, or strawberries. For a winter breakfast, you might want to try one of our favorites: Cook the polenta in the hot spice milk according to the directions below, but eat it warm and creamy as you would oatmeal or other porridge.

For the Polenta

3 cups whole milk

1 tablespoon butter,
   plus butter for greasing

2 teaspoons sugar

1 teaspoon salt

1 clove

Pinch of ground nutmeg

2-inch cinnamon stick

¾ cup quick-cooking
   imported Italian polenta

The Rest

3 tablespoons butter

¼ cup granulated sugar (approximately)

1⅓ cups Grand Marnier or port wine

1⅓ cup fresh blackberries

∽ Bring the milk, butter, sugar, salt, and spices to a low boil over a medium flame. Pour the polenta into the pot in a fine, thin stream with one hand, while using the other to vigorously whisk the mixture to keep any lumps from forming. Reduce the flame to the lowest heat and stir the polenta with a wooden spoon for 8 minutes, taking care not to let it stick to the bottom or sides of the pot. Remove the cinnamon and clove.

⌒ Pour the polenta into a lightly buttered loaf pan and set it aside to cool and solidify. When you are ready to make the fritters, unmold the polenta and cut it into ½-inch-thick slices.

⌒ Melt 2 tablespoons of butter in a nonstick skillet. Sprinkle both sides of the sliced polenta with sugar, then lay the slices out in the skillet so that they do not overlap. Lay the polenta slices in the butter, turning once or twice until they are golden and crisp on both sides. Portion them onto individual serving plates.

⌒ Pour the Grand Marnier or port wine into the pan and let it bubble for a minute before adding the berries, a tablespoon of sugar, and a last tablespoon of butter. Stir well for just a minute, then pour the berries in their sauce over the polenta and serve.

Victoria's Chocolate Almond Torte
Dolce di Cioccolato e Mandorle "Victoria"

1 TORTE

Every so often, Antonio astonishes us with some surprising gesture of sentimentality or affection. Last week, he came to the house bearing an off-season "birthday gift" for Jean-Louis—a beautiful red enamel kitchen scale he had seen Jean-Louis coveting the week before at an antique fair near Venice.

Yet another bout of sentimentality recently found Antonio in the kitchen creating a new torte to bring to the house of a close friend who had just had a beautiful baby daughter named Victoria. Both the *bambina* and the torte are lovely . . . and delicious!

For the Cake

   3½ cups cake flour

   ¾ cup plus 1 tablespoon butter, at room temperature

   1¼ cups granulated sugar

¼ cup unsweetened cocoa powder

1½ teaspoons vanilla extract

5 eggs

⅓ cup blanched almonds, ground in a food processor to a coarse powder

⅔ cup blanched almonds, finely chopped

Parchment paper

For the Filling

4 egg yolks

½ cup granulated sugar

½ teaspoon vanilla

½ cup cake flour

2 cups whole milk

3-inch strip of orange zest

1 ounce unsweetened dark chocolate, coarsely chopped

3 tablespoons plus 1 teaspoon butter

1 tablespoon Grand Marnier

Powdered sugar for dusting

∽ *The cake:* Pour the flour in a mound onto a flat work surface. Use a pastry blender or 2 knives to cut in the butter. When the mixture resembles coarse meal, transfer it to a large mixing bowl and use a fork to work in the sugar, the cocoa powder, vanilla extract, 4 eggs, and the almond powder. Work the dough with your hands until it forms a ball, cover with plastic wrap, and refrigerate for at least 1 hour.

∽ Preheat the oven to 350°.

∽ Cut the dough ball into 4 equal pieces. Work 1 piece at a time, returning the other pieces to the refrigerator until you are ready to work with them.

∽ Place a piece of dough on a length of parchment paper. Use a rolling pin to roll the dough into a circle roughly ¼ inch high. (Dust the rolling pin with flour if the dough sticks.) Roll out the remaining pieces of dough in the same manner.

⌒ Lay the parchment paper with the rolled-out dough on 2 baker's sheets. Paint the surface of the dough with a beaten egg, sprinkle with the chopped almonds, and bake for 10 minutes (turning the baking sheets around once if your oven bakes unevenly). If your oven will not accommodate all the dough at once, cook the layers in 2 batches.

⌒ Turn the oven off and let the torte layers rest in the oven while you prepare the filling.

⌒ *The filling:* Whisk together the egg yolks, sugar, and vanilla for a couple of minutes until well blended. Slowly incorporate the flour and 2 tablespoons of cold milk. Set aside.

⌒ Place the strip of orange zest in a saucepan with the remaining milk and bring to a boil. (Use a potato peeler to peel away a strip of zest only—do not include the bitter white pith.) Remove the saucepan from the stove, take out the orange zest, and slowly beat in the egg yolk mixture. Return the saucepan to a low flame and cook for 2 minutes, then add the chocolate pieces and cook for 1 minute more. Remove the saucepan from the flame and beat in the butter and Grand Marnier.

⌒ Allow the mixture to cool.

⌒ *Assembling the torte:* Remove torte layers from the oven and spread each layer with a thin covering of filling. Set the layers one atop the other. Cut around the outside of the assembled torte if necessary to even out the edges. Use the remaining filling to cover the sides of the torte. Sprinkle with powdered sugar and serve.

Vanilla Cream Custard with Caramel Sauce
Crema di Vaniglia con Caramello
SERVES 6

Customers always ask for the recipe for our crema di vaniglia and then are amazed at how easy it is to make. It's a perfect dessert for a dinner party, elegant and rich, yet both the custard and the caramel sauce can be made the day before.

For the Custard

6 large egg yolks

⅓ cup granulated sugar

1 teaspoon vanilla extract

2 cups heavy cream

¼ cup milk

For the Caramel Sauce

1 cup sugar

1 teaspoon white wine

⅓ cup water

¼ cup heavy cream

½ teaspoon butter

∾ *The custard:* Preheat the oven to 350°.

∾ Whisk together the egg yolks, sugar, and vanilla in a large bowl, blending the ingredients well. Gradually whisk into the egg mixture first the cream and then the milk. Divide the mixture between six ¾-cup custard cups or soufflé dishes.

∾ Place the custard cups in a roasting or baking pan. Add enough hot water to the pan to come halfway up the sides of the custard cups. Cover the pan with aluminum foil and pierce the foil with the pointed tip of a knife in several places. Bake until the center of the custard moves only slightly when the cups are shaken, about 45 minutes (but begin checking after 30 minutes). Remove the custards from the water and set them on a counter to cool. Cover and chill for at least 2 hours or overnight.

∾ *The caramel sauce:* Place the sugar, wine, and water in a medium, heavy-bottomed saucepan over a medium flame. Without bringing the water to a boil, stir the mixture until the sugar dissolves completely. Increase the heat and boil, without stirring, until the mixture colors a deep amber, brushing down the sides of the pan with a wet pastry brush and swirling the pan occasionally.

∾ Remove the saucepan from the heat and stir in the cream (the mixture will bubble vigorously). When the mixture is well incorporated, beat in the butter then return the sauce to a medium flame and stir until any bits of hard caramel melts. Cool to warm before spooning over custards if you will be using the sauce immediately. Otherwise, cool, then refrigerate until needed, rewarming the sauce over a low heat and stirring until it liquifies once again (you may add a bit of water if the sauce is too thick).

Ricotta Cheesecake with Strawberry Compote

Torta di Ricotta con Composta di Fragole

SERVES 8

One of the things people seem to like best about cheesecakes is their tan and crumbly crust. We make our creamy, rich cheesecakes in individual molds—which means more crust for everyone. They are beautiful as is or with fresh strawberry compote over the top.

Note: We like the flavor of the cheesecakes best at room temperature the day they are made. They will keep well for a couple of days in the refrigerator but must be unmolded before refrigerating or else served inside the ramekins. (If you intend the latter, coat the entire inside of the ramekins with butter and cookie crumbs and do not line the bottoms with parchment paper.)

For the Cheesecake

Butter for greasing ramekins

1 cup zweiback or graham cracker crumbs

12 ounces cream cheese,
    at room temperature

6 ounces fresh ricotta cheese

1 cup granulated sugar

1 tablespoon cornstarch

½ teaspoon vanilla extract

Pinch of salt

3 eggs

1 egg yolk

2 tablespoons whole milk

¼ cup heavy cream

8 ceramic ramekins, 3½ to 4½ inches in diameter
Parchment paper

For the Compote

1 pound fresh strawberries, stemmed, halved, and coarsely chopped
Juice of 1 lemon
2 tablespoons granulated sugar
⅓ cup sweet white wine such as muscat or white zinfandel

∽ *The cheesecake:* Preheat oven to 325°.

∽ Butter the sides of the ramekins and coat with cookie crumbs. Cut out 8 circles of parchment paper the same size as the bottom of the inside of the ramekins, then place 1 parchment circle on the bottom of each ramekin (this allows the individual cheesecakes to slip out of the molds easily once cooled).

∽ Place the cream cheese in a medium mixing bowl and blend with a rubber spatula until smooth and creamy. Add the ricotta and blend well. Stir in the sugar, cornstarch, vanilla, and salt, blending well with a wooden spoon. Scrape down the sides of the bowl.

∽ Beat the eggs and 1 yolk until they are pale and fluffy (1 to 2 minutes), then slowly fold them into the cheese mixture.

∽ Using a whisk or hand mixer at low speed blend in the milk and cream.

∽ Pour 5 to 6 ounces of batter into each mold. Set the molds in a baking pan filled with 1 inch of water and bake until the edges of the individual molds have set but the center still jiggles slightly (40 to 50 minutes). Don't worry if your cheesecakes rise and crack in the center while cooking, they will settle flat as they cool.

∽ Cool the cheesecakes on wire racks. To unmold, run a knife carefully along the inside of the ramekin, turn it upside down on the center of an individual dessert plate and tap gently on the bottom.

∽ *The compote:* Mix all the ingredients together in a bowl. Let sit for 1 hour. Spoon over the top of the individual cheesecakes just before serving.

FEEDING THE BAMBINI

My son Julien's first trip to our local emergency room in Los Angeles was to have a fish bone extracted from his tiny gullet. The staff doctor wanted to know what kind of fish we had been eating. I told him. "What two-year-old eats striped sea bass for dinner?" he asked me, incredulously. "One whose father is Italian," I answered. It's as simple at that. Among Italians, there's just not a huge distinction between what the grown-ups eat and what their kids do—except that, when it comes to *il mangiare,* the kids come first.

For example, at the barbecues of my childhood, if we didn't all have hamburgers, then the adults had steaks and *we* had hamburgers. In Italy, you'll more likely see the adults having steaks while the kids sit down to tender, expensive fillets. At my house, and at the house of every child I grew up with, when my parents ate fish, we had fish sticks, unless we all had fillet of sole. Italian mothers simply tell the fishmonger that they're buying for *i bambini* to be assured the freshest most palatable fish he has to offer.

Italian children are without a doubt the most coddled on the planet. They are bundled up, cuddled, cared for, and above all else fed with a zeal that borders on, but runs just shy of, the obsessive. I have been politely scolded by every preschool teacher my children ever had for sending them to school *mezzi nudi* ("half naked"). All to no avail. After so many years in California, we were never quite able to convince ourselves of the necessity of wool undershirts, hats, gloves, and mufflers for the fifteen-second walk from the car to the overheated classroom. My children vindicated themselves by getting fewer colds than their well-bundled classmates.

Thankfully, where I failed to earn respect in the clothing-the-offspring department, my Italian friends, neighbors, and even in-laws regarded the way I fed little Julien and Michela with a more approving and benevolent eye. No doubt they had expected the poor darlings to be living on a combination of peanut butter and jelly sandwiches, Jell-O, and TV dinners.

In reality, I had no choice but to start them out eating Italian-style from the very beginning. Easygoing as my dear husband is, there was no way that he was going to let his progeny be fed their meals out of tiny glass Gerber jars. And so I cooked up *minestre* with fresh garden vegetables, I ground up juicy roast chicken with my little hand mill, and more or less fed my babies *all' Italiana.*

The initial results were fantastic. My firstborn is like a poster boy for healthy eating. He has an amazing natural inclination toward the things that the "experts" have declared "good for you." And though he assiduously avoided any small boned fish for years after his trip to the emergency room, he is an astonishingly adventurous eater by American standards—happily passing up the opportunity for a pizza if he can have a steaming bowl of spaghetti and clams and a plate of fried calamari (spiderlike tentacles and all) instead. Smugly, I patted myself on the back and told anyone who would listen that if they only took the time to offer the right foods, their children would grow up indifferent to the lure of Coca-Cola and the almighty McDonald's.

Three years after Julien, Michela came along. My lesson in humility. She heads like a junk-food guided missile toward the sorts of things that would be written in bright red under the FOODS TO BE AVOIDED section of those lists nutritionists are always waving around. One of her favorite foods is butter. She'd just as soon eat it straight out of the fridge with a spoon than dilute its flavor by spreading it on bread. On more than one occasion, we've discovered her hidden behind the couch methodically making her way through a pile of wrapped candies. She's the type of child who is always trying to "save" the vegetable soup for last, in the hopes that you'll forget she's supposed to eat it. In short, she thoroughly destroyed the myth, *my* myth, about how easy it is to get a child to eat well.

It's *not* always easy. And it's going to be more or less difficult depending on the natural inclinations of your own headstrong child. But no doubt you already know this—in your heart of hearts, I'm sure you also know that it's worth the extra effort to help your children learn how to eat well. I'm not talking about forcing "fine" food on them—foie gras, smelly cheeses, and all that. I'm talking about the simple, fresh flavors found in nature. A ripe peach, a wedge of fennel dipped in new olive oil, freshly baked bread.

For what it's worth, here are some things that have worked at our house in our ongoing attempt to instill some decent eating habits and sense of adventure in our *bambini.*

- *Let your children in on what goes on in your kitchen.* What mother hasn't watched her child forsake a room full of "toys" for the graters, peelers, whisks, and measuring cups of the kitchen? Kitchens are amazing places. Things happen there—they are chopped, beaten, whisked, heated, baked, combined, and transformed daily before your very eyes. Children actually find this all very interesting if you choose to include them in the "fun."

- *Let them help in the preparations.* Once I sent my father outside with Julien and Michela to shuck peas and peel carrots for a vegetable soup. They sat on a low stone wall in the spring sunshine, talking, shucking, peeling, and, it turns out, eating—roughly a handful of peas for every two handfuls shucked, and one out of four carrots. There's no question that having your children help out is neither an exercise in efficiency nor neatness. *However,* they'll be ever so much more likely to try something they've had a hand in creating. Besides, they'll have fun—and so, probably, will you.

- *Let them invent something.* The kitchen is your ongoing science experiment. It is a place to create and invent. Try telling your kids that you're making soup, or an omelette, or a cake—and ask them what they think you should put in it.

- *Let them plan an (occasional) menu.* Let each of your children have a chance to plan a menu one night for dinner. Give them some parameters that vaguely jibe with what you know they like (e.g., some kind of pasta, some kind of salad, and dessert). Then watch how their interest is sparked when they are allowed to use their voice and make some of the choices that are usually left to the grown-ups.

- *Plant a garden.* Vegetables, fruits, berries, herbs—plant whatever you have the time or inclination for. Then send your children out to the garden with your "shopping list." It may take a while, but before you know it, they'll be filling your order perfectly.

- *Green Eggs and Ham.* Make a rule that, within reason (you can exempt things like frogs' legs, snails, and headcheese), all things must be *tasted* at least once before being rejected.

- *Make it easier on yourself.* Keep good, healthy things around the house. Save weekends or other "special occasions" for whatever treats you'd rather your kids not eat every day.
- *Give your children some credit.* Most kids will forgo "fast food," "junk food," and all those other "nonfoods" that threaten to take over our culinary lives in favor of "real food." Just give them the chance.

Cinnamon Apple Tarts
Torta di Mele
SERVES 6

Nothing makes a kitchen more inviting than the smell of apples and cinnamon baking in the oven. Tart green apples and only a hint of crust make this a light, though warming dessert.

6 tablespoons melted butter, plus additional melted butter for greasing tart molds
¾ cup quick-cooking polenta meal
2 eggs
1½ cups granulated sugar
⅔ cup all-purpose flour
½ cup milk
½ teaspoon ground cinnamon
9 medium green apples, peeled, cored, quartered, then sliced to a ¼-inch thickness

Six 3½- to 4-inch tart molds or ovenproof ramekins.

↪ Preheat oven to 350°.
↪ Brush each tart mold with melted butter, then coat with polenta.

- In a medium mixing bowl, beat the eggs until foamy, then beat in the sugar. Slowly add the flour, milk, cinnamon, and melted butter, stirring until the mixture forms a smooth batter.
- Toss the sliced apples into the batter and mix them lightly until they are well coated.
- Distribute the batter-coated apples among the tart molds, then pour the remaining batter over the top until the molds are almost full.
- Bake until the surface of the tarts is golden and a toothpick inserted in the center comes out dry (about 1 hour).
- Serve the tarts in their ramekins, warm or at room temperature.

Mascarpone Custard with Amaretto Cookies and Mixed Berries

Crema al Mascarpone con Amaretti e Frutti di Bosco

SERVES 4

Antonio tells me that this dessert was inspired by the age-old recipe for *sbattutino* (literally, "little beaten thing"), which is said to be the typical northern Italian pick-me-up following an afternoon roll in the hay. Your sweetheart whips fresh farm eggs, sugar, coffee, and a dash of Marsala until they are smooth and silky—the ambrosial combination is meant to leave you simultaneously bright-eyed and relaxed. Cooked over a double boiler, as it is here, the *sbattutino* transforms into a wonderfully creamy custard known as "zabaione."

1 cup brewed espresso coffee
4 egg yolks
½ cup sugar
3 tablespoons dessert Marsala
24 amaretto cookies

1 cup mascarpone cheese

1 cup mixed fresh berries, such as blueberries, strawberries, raspberries, and/or currants

4 ramekins, about 3½ inches in diameter

ᕤ Brew 1 measuring cup full of espresso coffee. Let cool.

ᕤ Bring 3 inches of water to a gentle simmer in a medium saucepan. In the meantime, beat the egg yolks with the sugar in a large stainless steel bowl until they thicken slightly and lighten in color (about 2 minutes).

ᕤ Set the bowl over the simmering water. Gradually whisk in the Marsala, and gently heat the mixture, whisking constantly until it at least triples in volume and its texture becomes light and creamy and is thick enough to mound on a spoon (6 to 9 minutes). Take care not to let the water heat above a very gentle simmer or the mixture will become dense and sticky. Remove the bowl from the pan and continue whisking for another minute. Set aside.

ᕤ Soak the amaretto cookies in the coffee for about 30 seconds, then drain them onto paper towels. Line the bottom of each ramekin with the amaretti, using any broken or crumbled cookies to fill in any spaces.

ᕤ Place the mascarpone in a medium mixing bowl and blend with a rubber spatula until smooth and creamy. Fold in the egg and Marsala custard and blend until smooth. Spoon the mixture into the ramekins.

ᕤ Refrigerate for 2 hours.

ᕤ Garnish with the mixed berries and serve.

Concord Grape Pudding
Sugoli al Fragolino
SERVES 8

Every so often, Antonio proudly presents us with an unmarked case of *fragolino,* a wonderfully fragrant dessert wine made from *uva fragola,* a variety of Concord grape that tastes of tiny woodland strawberries. It is illegal to produce *fragolino* commercially—the wine carries traces of methanol, a potentially toxic form of alcohol (when ingested in amounts much greater than even the most ardent wine lover would ever imbibe). Last year, we planted an arbor of *uva fragola* in the hopes of making our own *fragolino* one day. The vines themselves are beautiful, yielding heavy clusters of midnight blue grapes covered with a fine silvery powder—not enough for making wine (yet), but perfect for eating out of hand or using to make this unusual and delicious burgundy-hued pudding.

5 pounds Concord grapes, to make 6 cups grape juice
⅔ cup flour
⅔ cup sugar

↝ Wash the grapes well, then squeeze each grape gently to slip it out of its thick, tart skin into a large mixing bowl. Kids love doing this (if you mind staining your fingers purple, wear gloves for this task). Pile the grape skins to one side, then squeeze them well to extract any additional juice. Pour the pulp of the grapes into a food processor and pulse blend lightly to break up the grapes without grinding the seeds. Pass the juice through a strainer, separating out and then discarding the seeds. Measure out 6 cups of juice (drink the rest).

↝ Set aside 1 cup of juice and pour the remaining 5 cups into a saucepan. Simmer the juice over a low flame until the liquid reduces to about 4 cups (this will take around 15 to 20 minutes) and intensifies in flavor.

↝ In the meantime, transfer the remaining cup of juice to a small mixing bowl, and slowly sprinkle in the flour, whisking continuously so that no lumps form.

Sprinkle the sugar into the reduced and simmering juice, stirring continuously for 1 minute. Remove the pot from the flame and use a wire whisk to slowly incorporate the flour and raw juice mixture. When the ingredients are well blended, return the pot to the stove and continue stirring with a wooden spoon for 5 minutes while the mixture thickens and bubbles.

Pour the pudding into cups or stemmed glasses, cool, then refrigerate. Serve with homemade cookies.

Humble (Apple and Potato) Pie
Torta di Mele e Patate
SERVES 6

The Veneto is a place of contrasts. While the cities, especially Venice, have a rich and opulent culinary history, the surrounding countryside was desperately poor for centuries. Despite the fact that such basics like flour were often in short supply, the ever-resourceful *contadina* managed to devise an array of flavorful dishes with whatever she had on hand. This pie is a perfect example—the ubiquitous apple and potato combine to make a moist and hearty midwinter dessert.

1½ pounds baking potatoes

2 medium baking apples, peeled, cored, and thinly sliced

Juice of 1 lemon

½ cup almonds, coarsely ground

¾ cup sugar

Zest of ½ lemon

1 teaspoon vanilla extract

Pinch of salt

5 eggs

2 tablespoons butter, melted

⅓ cup raisins

Butter for greasing baking pan

Yellow cornmeal for dusting

- Preheat oven to 425°.

- Boil the unpeeled potatoes until a toothpick inserts easily into their centers. Set them aside to cool.

- Soak the apple slices in a bowl with 3 cups of water and the lemon juice to prevent them from turning brown.

- Peel the potatoes, then pass them through a ricer or mash with a fork. Use a wooden spoon to combine the potatoes, almonds, sugar, lemon zest, vanilla, and salt in a medium mixing bowl. Incorporate the eggs one at a time, then add the melted butter, followed by the apples and raisins.

- Butter a 9-inch round springform pan. Add a handful of cornmeal to the pan and swish it around until the butter is amply covered. Pour the batter into the pan and cook for 30 to 40 minutes, or until a toothpick inserted into the center comes out clean.

- Serve warm or at room temperature.

Torta Nicolotta
Torta Nicolotta
ONE 10-INCH ROUND CAKE

This cake, really more of a bread pudding, originated centuries ago in one of Venice's poorest neighborhoods, San Nicolò dei Mendigoli (Saint Nicholas of the Mendicants). It is made from day-old bread soaked in milk and laced with raisins, nuts, and fennel seed. The moist, dense dessert is perfect for a cold winter afternoon with a pot of tea or rich hot chocolate.

1 pound crustless day-old bread, cubed
4 cups whole milk
1 cup shelled pistachios, unsalted

½ cup Marsala

2 teaspoons fennel seed

1 cup white flour

1 cup sugar

1 cup golden raisins

1 teaspoon vanilla

Grated zest of 1 orange

3 eggs, beaten

Butter for greasing pan

Cornmeal for dusting

∽ Preheat oven to 375°.

∽ In a large mixing bowl, soak the bread in the milk until the mixture forms a thick paste (about 30 minutes). Drain off any excess milk.

∽ In the meantime, soak the pistachios in the Marsala for 30 minutes, then drain the Marsala into a small cup and chop the nuts finely. Add the fennel seed to the Marsala and set aside.

∽ Incorporate the flour into the bread and milk mixture then use a wooden spoon to blend in the sugar, raisins, vanilla, orange zest, pistachios, fennel seed, and Marsala. Incorporate the eggs into the batter one at a time and mix well to combine all the ingredients.

∽ Butter a 10-inch round springform pan and dust with cornmeal. Pour the batter into the pan and bake for 1 hour. The top will be browned like a bread loaf and the inside very dense and moist.

Cornmeal and Winter Squash Cake
Pinza di Zucca

ONE 10-INCH CAKE

This simple, rustic cake is another northern Italian standard. Like so many "classic" recipes, it seems to have as many variations as cooks. *Pinza* is almost always made with some combination of cornmeal and white flour, although Antonio prefers the moist texture that comes from cooking the polenta separately before adding it to the batter. *Pinza* is usually served for *merenda,* as an afternoon snack, rather than after a meal as a formal dessert. Our version, loaded with dried and fresh fruit, as well as winter squash, makes this a guilt-free treat for both adults and children.

2 to 3 pounds kabocha or butternut squash (to yield 2½ cups pureed squash)
½ cup golden raisins
½ cup white wine
5 tablespoons butter, plus butter for greasing the pan
2 cups fast-cooking polenta, plus polenta for dusting the pan
1 teaspoon fennel seed
1 cup all-purpose flour
1 cup plus 3 tablespoons granulated sugar
½ cup coarsely chopped dried figs
½ cup coarsely chopped dried cherries
½ cup coarsely chopped apricots
2 red apples, peeled, cored, quartered, and sliced
Pinch of salt

Preheat oven to 350°.

Cut the squash into 1-inch slices, remove the seeds and strings and bake in a shallow baking dish, covered with aluminum foil until tender. When a fork easily pierces the skin they are ready (1 to 1½ hours). Peel off the skin, allow the squash to cool slightly, then pass through a potato ricer or puree.

∾ Soak the raisins in the wine for 30 minutes, then drain well and set aside.

∾ In the meantime, butter a 10-inch springform cake pan and dust with polenta meal.

∾ Place the butter and 4 cups of water in a pot and bring to a low boil. Pour the polenta into the water in a thin stream, stirring continuously with a wire whisk. When the mixture begins to thicken, stir with a spoon, cooking the polenta for a total of 5 minutes over a low flame.

∾ Transfer the cooked polenta to a large mixing bowl, stir in the fennel seed, then incorporate first the cooked squash, then the flour, sugar, dried fruit, apples, and salt.

∾ Pour the batter into the pan and bake for about 40 minutes or until a toothpick inserted in the center comes out clean.

Apple Fritters
Frìtole de Pomi
SERVES 6

Frìtole are synonymous with Venice—especially during Carnevale, when the narrow streets are filled with costumed revelers, and the cafés and pastry shops with fritters of every persuasion. When we tested this recipe at Ca'Brea, both Jean-Louis and Antonio seemed to be overcome by a combination of nostalgia and gluttony—the golden fritters were barely out of the oil and sprinkled with confectioners' sugar before disappearing from the plate. In no time, the entire kitchen and dining room staff were lingering around like school kids hoping for an afternoon treat—we obliged, of course.

3 cups all-purpose flour
½ cup sugar
3 eggs

1 cup milk

2 teaspoons vanilla

1 cake fresh yeast (.06 ounces) or 1 envelope dry yeast

2 apples, peeled, cored, quartered, and sliced

¾ cup golden raisins

Grated zest of 1 lemon

Grated zest of 1 orange

Abundant sunflower or canola oil for frying

Powdered sugar for dusting the fritters

~ Combine the flour and sugar in a large mixing bowl. Make a well in the center and break the eggs into it, then beat them lightly with a fork. Add the milk, vanilla, and yeast to the center of the well and then stir the liquid slowly in a circular motion incorporating the dry ingredients from the sides of the well. When the mixture becomes too stiff to stir, sprinkle in the sliced apples, raisins, and citrus zest and work the dough with your hands until the ingredients are well incorporated.

~ Knead the dough for a couple of minutes, then roll it into a ball and place it in a lightly floured mixing bowl, covered with plastic wrap. Leave the dough to rise in a warm spot in the kitchen for 2 hours.

~ When the dough has finished rising, heat about 1 quart of oil in a 6- to 8-inch saucepan. When the oil is very hot but not smoking (a drop of batter will sizzle on contact with the oil), add a heaping soupspoon of the fritter mixture at a time to the oil, working in batches of approximately 6 frìtole at a time. The fritters will swell as they fry and should be turned over at least once during their cooking. When they are evenly golden, lift them carefully out of the oil with a slotted metal spoon and blot between several layers of paper towels.

~ Sprinkle the fritters with powdered sugar and serve.

Lemon-Scented Venetian Sugar Cookies
Bussolai
ABOUT 40 COOKIES

These biscotti are the cookies of Antonio's childhood—and of anyone growing up in or around Venice. Made from the simplest ingredients—flour, sugar, butter, eggs, vanilla, and lemon—they are perfect for dipping into sweet wine, coffee, tea, or hot chocolate. Shape them into an *S* form if you intend to dip them. Otherwise, shape the dough into 4-inch thick strips, then press the ends of each strip together to form small, hollow circles. *Bussolai* store very well in an airtight container.

1 pound all-purpose flour
1 cup sugar
6 egg yolks
½ cup butter, room temperature
2 teaspoons vanilla extract
Grated zest of 1 lemon

Parchment paper

∽ Preheat oven to 400°.
∽ Combine the flour and sugar together in a large mixing bowl. Make a well in the center. Add in egg yolks, swirling them around the center of the well so they pick up the flour and sugar from the sides. Add the butter, vanilla, and lemon zest and begin to work the mixture with your hands until it forms a stiff dough, similar to the dough for a piecrust. Continue working the dough until it is soft and malleable.
∽ Cover 1 or more baking sheets with parchment paper. Shape the dough into *S*-shaped or hoop-shaped cookies and bake until lightly golden (about 15 minutes).
∽ Cool on wire racks.

Venetian Cornmeal Cookies with Dried Cherries
Zaleti con le Ciliege
MAKES ABOUT 50 COOKIES

Zaleti—"little yellow things" . . . cookies, to be exact. Soft and sweet, but not overly so. The cornmeal used in the dough adds both their characteristic pale yellow color as well as a slightly grainy texture. Every Venetian family seems to have their own recipe for these delicious cookies. Traditionally, *zaleti* include raisins, but at Ca' Brea we like the slightly tart edge that comes by making them with dried cherries. Like *bussolai,* these oval-shaped cookies are also wonderful for dipping.

2 cups dried cherries
½ cup *vin santo*
¼ teaspoon vanilla extract
1 cup plus 1 tablespoon butter
1 cup plus 2 tablespoons sugar
½ teaspoon salt
5 eggs
3 cups all-purpose flour, plus additional as needed
2 cups yellow cornmeal

Parchment paper

∽ Preheat the oven to 350°.
∽ Soak the cherries in a small bowl with the *vin santo* and vanilla for 20 minutes. Drain well.
∽ In the meantime, use a wooden spoon to cream together the butter, sugar, and salt, then beat in the eggs one at a time. When the mixture has become creamy and smooth, be-

gin to slowly incorporate the white flour and cornmeal, stirring until the batter is light and uniform. Stir in the cherries and mix well to combine.

∽ Cover one or more baking sheets with parchment paper, then use a soupspoon to scoop up the batter. Flour your hands lightly, then shape the dough into small ovals about 2½ inches long and slightly tapered at each end.

∽ Bake for 12 to 15 minutes or until golden at the edges.

∽ Cool on wire racks.

Lady's Kisses
Baci di Dama
MAKES ABOUT 40 COOKIES

These delicious little cookies get their name from their shape—two small round cookies sandwiched together between a thin coating of melted chocolate. When viewed from the side, these sweets look just like the full lips of a woman puckering up for a kiss.

1 cup blanched whole almonds

1½ cups all-purpose flour

¼ cup unsweetened cocoa

1 cup sugar

¾ cup butter, at room temperature

1 tablespoon Grand Marnier

2 ounces dark or bittersweet chocolate

Parchment paper

∽ Preheat the oven to 375°.

∽ Pulse grind the almonds in a food processor until they form a rough, grainy powder.

Sift together the flour and cocoa, then stir in the sugar and almonds and mix well. Incorporate the butter into the dry ingredients until thoroughly combined.

Roll the dough into ¾-inch balls, taking care to keep their size as uniform as possible.

Bake on one or more cookie sheets covered with parchment paper for 12 to 15 minutes, taking care that the bottoms do not burn.

When the cookies have cooled, chop the chocolate into rough pieces, add the Grand Marnier, and melt over a double boiler, stirring regularly.

To make the *baci,* use the tip of a butter knife to dab a bit of melted chocolate on the flat bottom of a cookie. Cover the flat edge with another cookie and gently press the edges together. Continue as described with the remaining cookies.

Whole Wheat Walnut Cookies
Biscotti Integrali alle Noci
ABOUT 40 COOKIES

The combination of whole wheat flour and nuts gives these cookies a lovely crumbly texture. The dough is rolled out and cut with a cookie cutter. At Ca' Brea, we cut them into 2-inch diamonds, but you can cut them into any shape that strikes your fancy.

1 cup chopped walnuts

1¼ cups whole wheat flour

Pinch of salt

¾ cup butter, warmed to room temperature

⅔ cup granulated sugar

3 egg yolks

All-purpose flour for dusting work space

⌒ Preheat oven to 350°.

⌒ Grind the walnuts in a food processor until they form a coarse powder. In a medium mixing bowl, whisk together the flour, walnuts, and salt.

⌒ In a separate bowl, cream the butter, then use a wooden spoon to gradually add in first the sugar, then the egg yolks. Stir until the ingredients are blended thoroughly.

⌒ Gradually stir the flour mixture into the butter mixture. When the dough becomes too stiff to stir with a spoon, roll it into a ball and work the ingredients together the way you would a piecrust.

⌒ Lightly dust flat work surface with flour and then use a rolling pin to roll the dough out to a ½-inch thickness. Cut the dough using 2- or 3-inch cutters. Use a spatula to transfer the unbaked cookies onto a lightly greased cookie sheet and bake, 1 sheet at a time, in the middle rack of the oven until the cookies are a light golden brown (15 to 20 minutes). Turn the sheet once during baking so that the cookies will brown evenly.

Nut Brittle
Croccante
MAKES 1½ POUNDS

Every town and city in Italy has a patron saint to watch over and protect it. Once a year, the town celebrates its particular saint by throwing a huge party in its honor. Shops, schools, and businesses are closed, processions fill the streets, fireworks light up the night sky, and traveling vendors set up stands selling anything from roasted chickens and sausages to chocolates, nougats, and crunchy, sweet brittle made with roasted nuts. In Tuscany, brittle is usually made with almonds, while in the Veneto, it is often made with hazelnuts and even offered at the end of a meal with a glass of sweet wine.

Careful: Never touch hot, liquid sugar—it will stick to your skin and give you one of the worst possible kitchen burns.

1 pound unsalted almonds, hazelnuts, or pecans
Vegetable oil for greasing
3½ cups sugar

Parchment paper

∽ Preheat the oven to 400°. Spread the nuts on a baking sheet and roast until lightly toasted, turning occasionally (7 to 8 minutes).

∽ Lightly oil a marble slab or other flat, heat-resistant work surface, or oil and refrigerate a baking sheet to chill it.

∽ Place the sugar in a heavy-bottomed saucepan over a medium flame. Heat for 1 minute, shaking the sugar in the pan occasionally, then add 2 tablespoons of water to the center of the pan. Gently stir until the sugar dissolves, then cook the syrupy mixture until it turns a warm copper color (about 10 minutes), swirling the liquid without stirring.

∽ Quickly stir in the roasted nuts with a lightly oiled wooden spoon, evenly coating the nuts in the syrup. Pour the mixture onto the marble slab or baking sheet, using an oiled metal spatula to spread the mixture to a ½-inch thickness. (Clean the saucepan by filling it with hot water and bringing to a boil, then pouring out the water and washing as usual.)

∽ Allow the brittle to cool for about 3 minutes, then oil a sharp knife and cut the brittle into small squares or rectangles. Wrap up like candies in small pieces of parchment paper twisted at each end or store between layers of wax paper in an airtight container.

ONE LAST WORD

There are lots of things I wouldn't ask an Italian how to do. I wouldn't ask him how to govern a country, and I certainly wouldn't ask him how to drive. But I would ask him how to eat—and how to do almost every task associated with the art of eating, from marketing, to cooking, to sitting down at the table with friends. No culture has been as adept at squeezing so much fun and sensual pleasure from one of life's most basic and essential needs. It is an approach worth copying. We hope you do.

Buon appetito!

Index

Monkfish (*cont.*)

in grilled polenta and seafood, 209–11

Mozzarella

eggplant rolled with Parmesan and, 70–71

smoked, whole wheat pasta with olive pesto and, 110

Mushroom(s)

cornmeal crepes filled with ragù or, 217

fresh, arugula, and Parmesan salad, 56

lasagna with bell peppers, eggplant, zucchini, and, 121–22

lemony, sautéed scallops with, 230–31

mixed, pasta soufflé with, 149–52

pork medallions with peppers and, 261–62

sautéed, with parsley and garlic, 281

savory rice layered with eggplant, ragù, and, 167–68

Mushroom(s), wild, 22–24

bruschetta, 24–25

and goat cheese filling for soffiatini, 45

homemade chicken ravioloni with chanterelles, 145–47

mixed forest, pan-roasted chicken with, 241–42

tagliatelle with shrimp and, 133–34

and winter squash soup, 191–92

see also porcini

Mussels

in grilled polenta and seafood, 209–11

and potatoes, Venetian-style, 234–35

in Venetian fish soup, 193–94

in Venetian seafood salad, 80–81

Mustard

flattened chicken marinated in herbs, vinegar, and, 238–39

whole grain, rack of lamb with walnuts and, 273–74

Nut brittle, 322–23

Octopus with Swiss chard and braised onions, 232–33

Olive(s)

black, pan-roasted lamb loin with, 272

braised monkfish with lemon peel and, 220–21

breaded green, stuffed with sausage, 18–19

in focaccia dough, 38

lemony black, 16

pan-roasted chicken with sweet peppers, capers, and, 245–46

paste, bruschetta with herbed, 25

pesto, whole wheat pasta with smoked mozzarella and, 110

spicy green, 15

Olive oil, 7–9

Onion(s)

braised, 292

braised, octopus with Swiss chard and, 232–33

confit, 92

confit, chicken and duck dumplings with, 90–91

topping for focaccia, 39–40

Orange, fennel, and pecorino salad, 55

Oregano and plum tomatoes topping for focaccia, 39

Ossobuco with polenta fritters, 251–53

Venetian, Venetian-style
cornmeal cookies with dried cherries,
319–20
fish soup, 193–94
mussels and potatoes, 234–35
seafood salad, 80–81
sugar cookies, lemon-scented, 318–19
Swiss chard, 291
Vinaigrette
balsamic, butter-braised chicken livers
with fresh spinach in, 61–62
in mixed baby lettuces, 49–50
Vinegar
flattened chicken marinated in herbs, mustard, and, 238–39
herbed, 50
rinsing chicken in, 236
see also balsamic vinegar, vinaigrette

Walnut(s)
cookies, whole wheat, 321–22
and Gorgonzola cheese topping for crespelle, 43
homemade potato tortelloni with mixed
cheeses and, 141–42

rack of lamb with whole grain mustard
and, 273–74
Whitebait, fried baby, 83
White bean soup with pasta and shrimp,
190–91
Whole wheat pasta with olive pesto and
smoked mozzarella, 110
Whole wheat walnut cookies, 321–22
Wine, 10–11, 114–16
port, in polenta fritters with berries and
Grand Marnier, 298–99
spiced red, winter pears poached in, 296
white, fresh clams poached in tomatoes,
garlic and, 81–82
see also Prosecco

Zucchini
eggplant, and goat cheese ravioli in thyme
butter, 142–44
fresh, potage of, 180–81
lasagna with bell peppers, eggplant, mushrooms, and, 121–22
and zucchìni blossoms, fried, 75–76